Building Hybrid Clouds with Azure Stack

Implementing on-premises Azure infrastructure

Markus Klein
Susan Roesner

BIRMINGHAM - MUMBAI

Building Hybrid Clouds with Azure Stack

First published: August 2017

Production reference: 1230817

Published by Packt Publishing Ltd.
Livery Place
35 Livery Street
Birmingham
B3 2PB, UK.

ISBN 978-1-78646-629-7

www.packtpub.com

Credits

Authors
Markus Klein
Susan Roesner

Reviewer
Mag. Stefan Denninger

Commissioning Editor
Kartikey Pandey

Acquisition Editor
Rahul Nair

Content Development Editor
Sweeny Dias

Technical Editor
Vishal Kamal Mewada

Copy Editors
Stuti Shrivastava
Madhusudan Uchil

Project Coordinator
Virginia Dias

Proofreader
Safis Editing

Indexer
Rekha Nair

Graphics
Kirk D'Penha

Production Coordinator
Aparna Bhagat

About the Authors

Markus Klein has been working as a senior IT architect at Orange Networks GmbH on Microsoft technology for about 20 years now (and specifically with Microsoft Cloud technology for the last 15 years), starting with System Center, Service Provider Foundation, KATAL, Azure Pack, Azure, and now Azure Stack. In 2011, he founded the Microsoft Cloud community (building clouds community) and has been recognized as an MVP in cloud and datacenter management for the sixth year in a row. He speaks at Microsoft conferences (starting in 2002 at TechEd Germany) and is a regular speaker at conferences in Europe and abroad. His Twitter handle is `@Dr_AzureStack`.

Thank you for all the support from the Microsoft Product Group of Azure Stack and all the people who somehow helped make this book possible. I do not want to add specific names to thank because I might forget someone, which is not my intention.

Many thanks to my family for giving me the chance to spend time writing this book and providing you with this information that was, in my opinion, missing in the market.

Susan Roesner is a cloud architect with expertise in a wide range of technologies and industries (public and private), including Fortune 500 organizations. Since 2009, she has been working in Microsoft virtualization and Microsoft System Center technology, IT management consulting, focusing on cloud solutions for on-premise enterprise customers as well as hosting provider in addition to compliance aspects.

Before joining Bytes at Work GmbH in 2015, she worked as an IT architect consultant, in the financial sector, and in compliance/IT security, working on projects such as SOX and ISMS implementations, on compliance audits (internal and external), and compliance policy/process creation.

www.PacktPub.com

For support files and downloads related to your book, please visit www.PacktPub.com.

Did you know that Packt offers eBook versions of every book published, with PDF and ePub files available? You can upgrade to the eBook version at www.PacktPub.com, and as a print book customer, you are entitled to a discount on the eBook copy. Get in touch with us at service@packtpub.com for more details.

At www.PacktPub.com, you can also read a collection of free technical articles, sign up for a range of free newsletters and receive exclusive discounts and offers on Packt books and eBooks.

https://www.packtpub.com/mapt

Get the most in-demand software skills with Mapt. Mapt gives you full access to all Packt books and video courses, as well as industry-leading tools to help you plan your personal development and advance your career.

Why subscribe?

- Fully searchable across every book published by Packt
- Copy and paste, print, and bookmark content
- On demand and accessible via a web browser

About the Reviewer

Mag. Stefan Denninger is a senior cloud architect with a 20 years' experience in running IT. In the last few years, he has focused on Hybrid Cloud Solutions because these are the solutions that are most complex and where there is maximum variety.

This is the field where he feels comfortable. As he started with networking staff like configuring Cisco Routers and later with MS Biztalk Server bringing Business Processes to modern environments, the bandwidth is perfect for Hybrid Solutions.

The latest projects were all based on Microsoft Azure and local Environments such as Azure Pack or even now on Azure Stack.

His Twitter handle is `@stefandenninger`.

Customer Feedback

Thanks for purchasing this Packt book. At Packt, quality is at the heart of our editorial process. To help us improve, please leave us an honest review on this book's Amazon page at `https://www.amazon.com/dp/1786466295`.

If you'd like to join our team of regular reviewers, you can e-mail us at `customerreviews@packtpub.com`. We award our regular reviewers with free eBooks and videos in exchange for their valuable feedback. Help us be relentless in improving our products!

Table of Contents

Preface

Welcome to this book. Azure Stack is one of the most important and interesting products of Microsoft today and is the future as it brings Azure and Azure technologies to your data center if you are either an enterprise or service provider. You can use the same methodology, processes, and concepts that you have already developed for public Azure and reuse them in your Azure Stack data center. As Azure Stack comes as an integrated system, there is not much implementation time; you will just have to add the hardware to your data center and connect it to your network, and you can start adding your services to it right now. As the magic technology of Azure and Azure Stack relies on Azure Resource Manager, there is no need to think differently; you would just have to think the same as with Azure, and you will be successful.

This book gives you the basics to start with Azure Stack, develop your own services, and provide them as offers to your internal or external customers.

You can send us feedback at `http://www.azurestack.rocks/author-feedback`.

What this book covers

`Chapter 1`, *The Microsoft Azure Stack Architecture*, gives you a detailed overview of the technology and design aspects that Microsoft is relying on with Azure Stack. In addition, you will see how Azure Stack can help you in your network environment to solve issues you are currently struggling with as you could not move them to public Azure.

`Chapter 2`, *Planning the Deployment of Microsoft Azure Stack for Private Clouds*, talks about how you need to be well prepared when planning to implement Azure Stack. Therefore, we will discuss infrastructure designs and you will learn how to add Azure Stack to your data center without running into most of the issues you could run into. You will need to plan in advance, and we will help you in doing that.

`Chapter 3`, *Deploying Microsoft Azure Stack*, covers how Azure Stack is available as the so-called Azure Stack Development Toolkit and Azure Stack Multi-Node Deployment. You will learn how to prepare and install Azure Stack Deployment Toolkit for your Proof of Concept and what to know before you order a preconfigured production deployment. It is also good to know the way your hardware OEM will be used to set up your environment.

Chapter 4, *Understanding Storage and Network*, gives you a technical overview of the Azure Stack components. You will learn how they interact in between. Understanding this gives you a good chance to understand what is going on internally with Azure Stack.

Chapter 5, *Provisioning Virtual Machines*, discusses how once Azure Stack is up and running, you will need to know how to implement Infrastructure as a Service. This chapter will show you how to do that properly.

Chapter 6, *Creating a Private Cloud Solution*, covers how once you start with IaaS, you will set up your private cloud with Azure Stack. We will show you the good practices of doing this.

Chapter 7, *Understanding Automation in Microsoft Azure Stack*, ascertains that the goal of cloud means providing IT services on an industrial level. This means we need to do away from manual tasks and use automation. This chapter will talk about Automation with Azure Stack.

Chapter 8, *Creating PaaS Services in Microsoft Azure Stack*, mentions that the goal of Azure Stack is not just to lift and shift your virtual machine to the cloud. You will have to move to Platform as a Service. In this chapter, we will discuss the PaaS Services that come with Azure Stack as general availability.

Chapter 9, *Managing and Administering Private Clouds with Microsoft Azure Stack*, covers running cloud services and how they are somehow different in comparison to on-premise installations. This chapter will discuss the concept of shared responsibility.

Chapter 10, *Integrating Public Cloud Services with Microsoft Azure Stack*, discusses how Azure Stack can win the race of technology when integrating Azure services into Azure Stack using a hybrid cloud model.

Chapter 11, *Creating a Hybrid Cloud Solution*, gives you an overview of what to do next when Azure Stack is up and running and how to succeed with Azure Stack-adding container features.

Chapter 12, *Infrastructure as Code – Azure Functions and Other Future Scenarios*, discusses the Code as a Service feature with Azure Stack—so called functions and give an idea of what may come with Azure Stack Agile updates in the future, what makes sense, and what does not.

What you need for this book

Learning Azure Stack means knowing how Azure works beforehand. This is the main requirement for this book. In addition, our website, http://www.azurestack.rocks, will give you more and deeper information if you want to dive deeper into specific services.

Who this book is for

The book is for administrators and architects who are planning to implement or administer a hybrid cloud infrastructure using Microsoft Cloud Technology. This book is ideal for those who are looking forward to implementing and running a hybrid cloud infrastructure with PaaS, SaaS, and IaaS services.

Conventions

In this book, you will find a number of text styles that distinguish between different kinds of information. Here are some examples of these styles and an explanation of their meaning. Code words in text, database table names, folder names, filenames, file extensions, pathnames, dummy URLs, user input, and Twitter handles are shown as follows: "The VHD gets uploaded and the manifest.json file gets created."

A block of code is set as follows:

```
{
    "$schema": http://schema.management.azure.com/schemas/2015-01-01/
    deploymentTeplate.json#,
    "contentVersion": "",
    "parameters": { },
    "variables": { },
    "resources": [ ],
    "outputs": { }
}
```

When we wish to draw your attention to a particular part of a code block, the relevant lines or items are set in bold:

```
{
    "$schema": http://schema.management.azure.com/schemas/2015-01-01/
    deploymentTeplate.json#,
    "contentVersion": "",
    "parameters": { },
    "variables": { },
    "resources": [ ],
```

```
    "outputs": { }
}
```

Any command-line input or output is written as follows:

```
RegisterWithAzure.ps1 -azureDirectory YourDirectory
-azureSubscriptionId YourGUID -azureSubscriptionOwner YourAccountName
```

New terms and **important words** are shown in bold. Words that you see on the screen, for example, in menus or dialog boxes, appear in the text like this: "Finally, it is here in the **Physical Nodes** tab, that defines the IP addresses, hostnames, and so on."

Warnings or important notes appear like this.

Tips and tricks appear like this.

Reader feedback

Feedback from our readers is always welcome. Let us know what you think about this book-what you liked or disliked. Reader feedback is important for us as it helps us develop titles that you will really get the most out of. To send us general feedback, simply e-mail feedback@packtpub.com, and mention the book's title in the subject of your message. If there is a topic that you have expertise in and you are interested in either writing or contributing to a book, see our author guide at www.packtpub.com/authors.

Customer support

Now that you are the proud owner of a Packt book, we have a number of things to help you to get the most from your purchase.

Downloading the example code

You can download the example code files for this book from your account at
`http://www.packtpub.com`. If you purchased this book elsewhere, you can visit
`http://www.packtpub.com/support` and register to have the files e-mailed directly to you.
You can download the code files by following these steps:

1. Log in or register to our website using your e-mail address and password.
2. Hover the mouse pointer on the **SUPPORT** tab at the top.
3. Click on **Code Downloads & Errata**.
4. Enter the name of the book in the **Search** box.
5. Select the book for which you're looking to download the code files.
6. Choose from the drop-down menu where you purchased this book from.
7. Click on **Code Download**.

Once the file is downloaded, please make sure that you unzip or extract the folder using the latest version of:

- WinRAR / 7-Zip for Windows
- Zipeg / iZip / UnRarX for Mac
- 7-Zip / PeaZip for Linux

The code bundle for the book is also hosted on GitHub at
`https://github.com/PacktPublishing/Building-Hybrid-Clouds-with-Azure-Stack`. We
also have other code bundles from our rich catalog of books and videos available at
`https://github.com/PacktPublishing/`. Check them out!

Errata

Although we have taken every care to ensure the accuracy of our content, mistakes do
happen. If you find a mistake in one of our books-maybe a mistake in the text or the code-
we would be grateful if you could report this to us. By doing so, you can save other readers
from frustration and help us improve subsequent versions of this book. If you find any
errata, please report them by visiting `http://www.packtpub.com/submit-errata`, selecting
your book, clicking on the **Errata Submission Form** link, and entering the details of your
errata. Once your errata are verified, your submission will be accepted and the errata will
be uploaded to our website or added to any list of existing errata under the Errata section of
that title. To view the previously submitted errata, go to
`https://www.packtpub.com/books/content/support` and enter the name of the book in the
search field. The required information will appear under the **Errata** section.

Piracy

Piracy of copyrighted material on the Internet is an ongoing problem across all media. At Packt, we take the protection of our copyright and licenses very seriously. If you come across any illegal copies of our works in any form on the Internet, please provide us with the location address or website name immediately so that we can pursue a remedy. Please contact us at copyright@packtpub.com with a link to the suspected pirated material. We appreciate your help in protecting our authors and our ability to bring you valuable content.

Questions

If you have a problem with any aspect of this book, you can contact us at questions@packtpub.com, and we will do our best to address the problem.

1
The Microsoft Azure Stack Architecture

This book will help you plan, build, run, and develop your own Azure-based datacenter running Azure Stack technology. The goal is that the technology in your datacenter will be 100 percent consistent using Azure, which provides flexibility and elasticity to your IT infrastructure.

We will learn about:

- Cloud basics
- The Microsoft Azure Stack
- Core management services
- Using Azure Stack
- Migrating services to Azure Stack

Cloud as the new IT infrastructure

Regarding the technical requirements of today's IT, the cloud is always a part of the general IT strategy. It does not depend upon the region in which the company is working in, nor does it depend upon the part of the economy; 99.9 percent of all companies have cloud technology already in their environment.

The good question for a lot of CIOs in general is: "To what extent do we allow cloud services, and what does that mean to our infrastructure?". So, it's a matter of compliance, allowance, and willingness.

The top 10 most important questions for a CIO to prepare for the cloud are as follows:

- Are we allowed to save our data in the cloud?
- What classification of data can be saved in the cloud?
- How flexible are we regarding the cloud?
- Do we have the knowledge to work with cloud technology?
- How does our current IT setup and infrastructure fit into the cloud's requirements?
- Is our current infrastructure already prepared for the cloud?
- Are we already working with a cloud-ready infrastructure?
- Is our internet bandwidth good enough?
- What does the cloud mean to my employees?
- Which technology should we choose?

Cloud terminology

The definition of the term **cloud** is not simple, but we need to differentiate between the following:

- **Private cloud**: This is a highly dynamic IT infrastructure based on a virtualization technology that is **flexible** and **scalable**. The resources are saved in a privately owned datacenter either in your company, or a service provider of your choice.
- **Public cloud**: This is a **shared** offering of IT infrastructure services that are provided via the internet.
- **Hybrid cloud**: This is a mixture of a private and public cloud. Depending on the compliance or other security regulations, the services that could be run in a public datacenter are already deployed there, but the services that need to be stored inside the company are running there. The goal is to run these services on the same technology to provide the agility, flexibility, and scalability to move services between public and private datacenters.

In general, there are some big players within the cloud market (for example, Amazon Web Services, Google, Azure, and even Alibaba). If a company is quite Microsoft-minded from the infrastructure point of view, they should have a look at the Microsoft Azure datacenters. Microsoft started in 2008 with their first datacenter, and today, they invest a billion dollars every month in Azure.

As of today, there are about 34 official datacenters around the world that form Microsoft Azure, besides the ones that Microsoft does not talk about (for example, US Government Azure). There are some dedicated datacenters, such as the German Azure cloud, that do not have connectivity to Azure worldwide. Due to compliance requirements, these frontiers need to exist, but the technology of each Azure datacenter is the same although the services offered may vary.

The following map gives an overview of the locations (so-called **regions**) in Azure as of today and provides an idea of which ones will be coming soon:

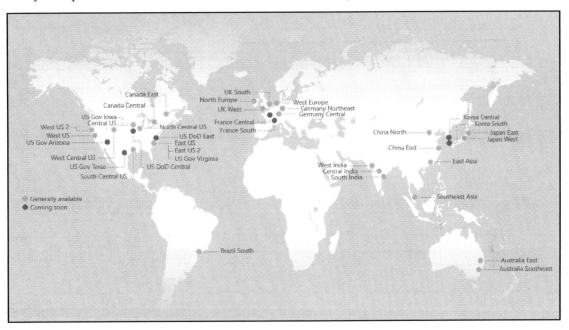

The Microsoft cloud story

When Microsoft started their public cloud, they decided that there must be a private cloud stack too, especially, to prepare their infrastructure to run in Azure sometime in the future.

The first private cloud solution was the **System Center** suite, with **System Center Orchestrator** and **Service Provider Foundation** (**SPF**) and **Service Manager** as the self-service portal solution. Later on, Microsoft launched the Windows Azure Pack for Windows Server. Today, Windows Azure Pack is available as a product focused on the private cloud and provides a self-service portal (the well-known *old* Azure portal, code name *red dog frontend*), and it uses the System Center suite as its underlying technology:

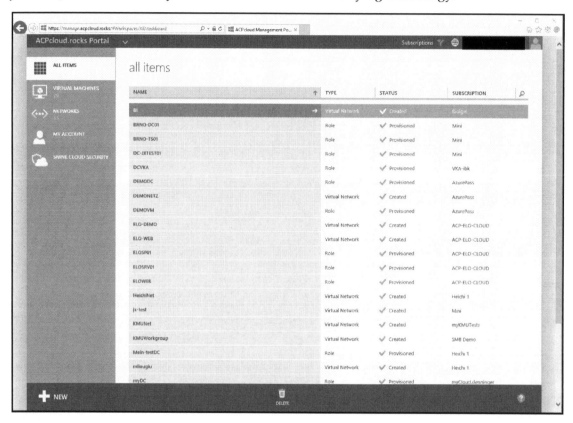

Microsoft Azure Stack

In May 2015, Microsoft formally announced a new solution that brings Azure to your datacenter. This solution was named **Microsoft Azure Stack**. To put it in one sentence: Azure Stack is the same technology with the same APIs and portal as public Azure, but you could run it in your datacenter or in that of your service providers. With Azure Stack, System Center is completely gone because everything is the way it is in Azure now, and in Azure, there is no System Center at all. This is what the primary focus of this book is.

The following diagram gives a current overview of the technical design of Azure Stack compared with Azure:

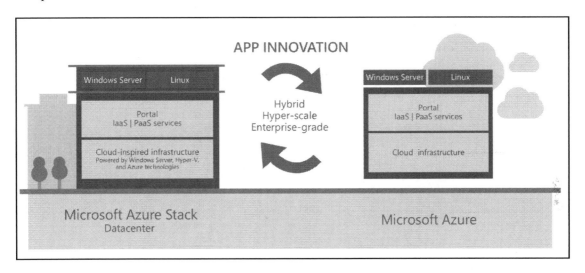

The one and only difference between **Microsoft Azure Stack** and **Microsoft Azure** is the **Cloud infrastructure**. In Azure, there are thousands of servers that are part of the solution; with Azure Stack, the number is slightly smaller. That's why there is the **Cloud-inspired infrastructure** based on **Windows Server, Hyper-V,** and **Azure technologies** as the underlying technology stack. There is no System Center product in this stack anymore. This does not mean that it cannot be there (for example, SCOM for on-premise monitoring), but Azure Stack itself provides all functionality with the solution itself.

For stability and functionality, Microsoft decided to provide Azure Stack as a so-called *integrated system,* so it will come to your door with the hardware stack included. The customer buys Azure Stack as a complete technology stack. At the **general availability (GA)** stage, the hardware OEMs are HPE, Dell EMC, and Lenovo. In addition to this, there will be a one-host development toolkit available for download that could be run as a proof of concept solution on every type of hardware, as soon as it meets the hardware requirements.

Technical design

Looking at the technical design a bit more in depth, there are some components that we need to dive deeper into:

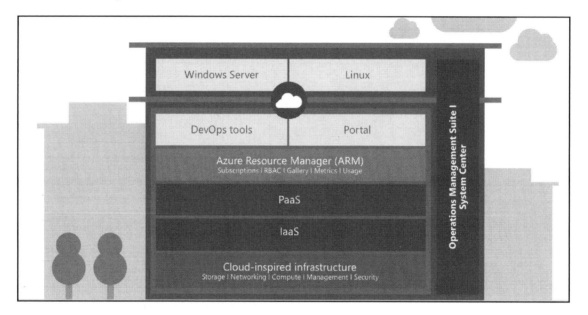

The general basis of Azure Stack is Windows Server 2016 technology, which builds the cloud-inspired infrastructure:

- **Storage Spaces Direct (S2D)**
- **VxLAN**
- **Nano Server**
- **Azure Resource Manager (ARM)**

Storage Spaces Direct

Storage Spaces and **Scale-Out File Server** were technologies that came with Windows Server 2012. The lack of stability in the initial versions and the issues with the underlying hardware was a bad phase. The general concept was a shared storage setup using JBODs controlled from Windows Server 2012 **Storage Spaces** servers, and a magic **Scale-Out File Server** cluster that acted as the single point of contact for storage:

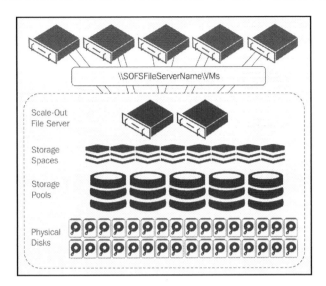

With Windows Server 2016, the design is quite different and the concept relies on a shared-nothing model, even with local attached storage:

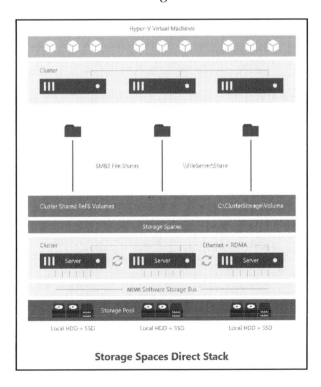

This is the storage design Azure Stack has come up with as one of its main pillars.

VxLAN networking technology

With Windows Server 2012, Microsoft introduced **Software-defined Networking** (SDN) and the NVGRE technology. Hyper-V Network Virtualization supports **Network Virtualization using Generic Routing Encapsulation** (NVGRE) as the mechanism to virtualize IP addresses. In NVGRE, the virtual machine's packet is encapsulated inside another packet:

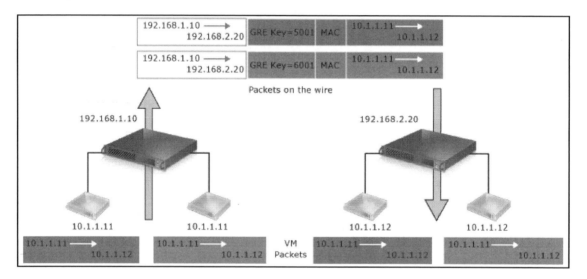

VxLAN comes as the new SDNv2 protocol; it is RFC compliant and is supported by most network hardware vendors by default. The **Virtual eXtensible Local Area Network** (**VxLAN**) RFC 7348 protocol has been widely adopted in the marketplace, with support from vendors such as Cisco, Brocade, Arista, Dell, and HP. The VxLAN protocol uses UDP as the transport:

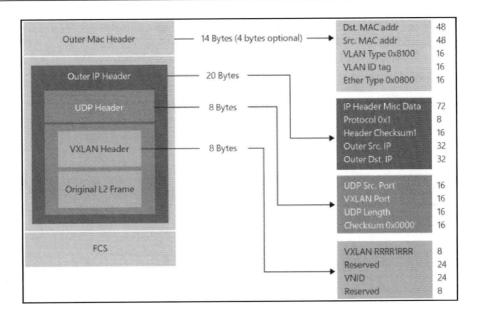

Nano Server

Nano Server offers a minimal-footprint, headless version of Windows Server 2016. It completely excludes the graphical user interface, which means that it is quite small, headless, and easy to handle regarding updates and security fixes, but it doesn't provide the GUI expected by customers of Windows Server.

Azure Resource Manager

The *magical* Azure Resource Manager is a 1-1 bit share with ARM from Azure, so it has the same update frequency and features that are available in Azure, too.

ARM is a consistent management layer that saves resources, dependencies, inputs, and outputs as an idempotent deployment as a JSON file called an **ARM template**. This template defines the tastes of a deployment, whether be it VMs, databases, websites, or anything else. The goal is that once a template is designed, it can be run on each Azure-based cloud platform, including Azure Stack. ARM provides cloud consistency with the finest granularity, and the only difference between the clouds is the region the template is being deployed to and the corresponding REST endpoints.

ARM not only provides a template for a logical combination of resources within Azure, it also manages subscriptions and **role-based access control (RBAC)** and defines the gallery, metric, and usage data, too. This means quite simply, that everything that needs to be done with Azure resources should be done with ARM.

Not only does Azure Resource Manager design one virtual machine, it is responsible for setting up one to a bunch of resources that fit together for a specific service. Even ARM templates can be nested; this means they can depend on each other.

When working with ARM, you should know the following vocabulary:

- **Resource**: A resource is a manageable item available in Azure.
- **Resource group**: A resource group is the container of resources that fit together within a service.
- **Resource provider**: A resource provider is a service that can be consumed within Azure.
- **Resource manager template**: A resource manager template is the definition of a specific service.
- **Declarative syntax**: Declarative syntax means that the template does not define the way to set up a resource; it just defines how the result and the resource itself have the feature to set up and configure itself to fulfill the syntax. To create your own ARM templates, you need to fulfill the following minimum requirements:
  - A test editor of your choice
  - Visual Studio Community edition
  - Azure SDK

Visual Studio Community edition is available for free from the internet. After setting these things up, you could start it, and define your own templates:

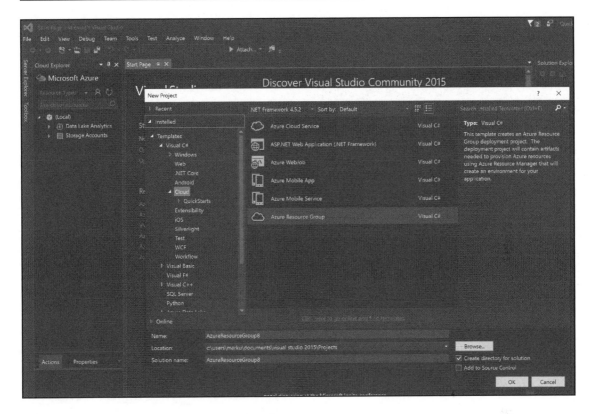

Setting up a simple blank template looks like this:

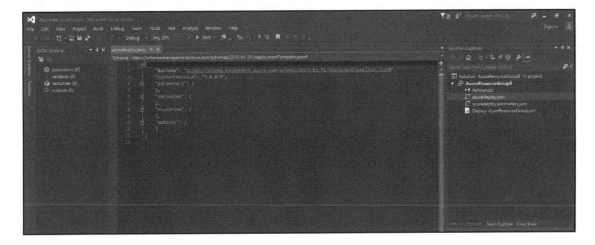

There are different ways to get a template that you can work on and modify it to fit your needs:

- Visual Studio templates
- Quick-start templates on GitHub
- Azure ARM templates

You could export the ARM template directly from Azure portal if the resource has been deployed:

After clicking on **View template**, the following opens up:

For further reading on ARM basics, the *Getting started with Azure Resource Manager* document is a good place to begin: http://aka.ms/GettingStartedWithARM.

PowerShell desired state configuration

In the previous section, we talked about ARM and ARM templates that define resources, but they are unable to design the way a VM looks inside, specify which software needs to be installed, and how the deployment should be done. This is why we need to have a look at VM extensions. VM extensions define what should be done after ARM deployment has finished. In general, the extension could be anything that's a script. The best practice is to use PowerShell and it's add-on called **Desired State Configuration (DSC)**.

DSC defines quite similarly to ARM, how the software needs to be installed and configured. The great concept is, that it also monitors whether the desired state of a virtual machine is changing (for example, because an administrator uninstalls or re-configures a machine). If it does, it makes sure within minutes whether the original state will be fulfilled again and rolls back the actions to the desired state:

```
Configuration SharePoint {

  Node WebService {

      #Install the IIS Role
      WindowsFeature IIS {
          Ensure = "Present"
          Name = "Web-Server"
      }

      #Install ASP.NET 4.5
      WindowsFeature ASP {
          Ensure = "Present"
          Name = "Web-Asp-Net45"
      }

  }
}
```

Azure Stack VMs

When Azure Stack is deployed, the following VMs are brought up on the Hyper-V hosts:

3c4bc311-14cc-43f8-8dc8-...	Running	0 %	3584 MB	12.13.13.11	8.0
AzS-ACS01	Running	0 %	8192 MB	40.07:57:43	8.0
AzS-ADFS01	Running	0 %	1584 MB	40.07:55:03	8.0
AzS-BGPNAT01	Running	0 %	1244 MB	40.08:22:31	8.0
AzS-CA01	Running	0 %	818 MB	40.07:54:32	8.0
AzS-DC01	Running	0 %	4096 MB	40.09:10:09	8.0
AzS-ERCS01	Running	0 %	2048 MB	40.08:00:42	8.0
AzS-Gwy01	Running	0 %	2048 MB	40.06:45:09	8.0
AzS-NC01	Running	0 %	4096 MB	40.08:02:10	8.0
AzS-SLB01	Running	0 %	2048 MB	40.08:01:24	8.0
AzS-Sql01	Running	0 %	4096 MB	40.06:51:13	8.0
AzS-WAS01	Running	0 %	4096 MB	40.07:57:34	8.0
AzS-WASP01	Running	0 %	8192 MB	40.07:56:56	8.0
AzS-Xrp01	Running	0 %	8192 MB	12.13:20:17	8.0

As of GA, Azure Stack consists of 13 VMs that all have their functions to make Azure Stack work. All of them are Core server instances configured with static resources (up to 8 GB of RAM and 4 vCPUs each). For the multi node environments most of these VMs are redundant and load balanced using the **Software Load Balancer** (**SLB**).

A resource provider adds features and functionality to the Azure Stack using a predefined structure, API set, design, and VM.

AzS-ACS01

The ACS01 VM is hosting the Azure Stack storage provider service. It is responsible for one of the most important resource providers. As the underlying storage technology is Storage Spaces Direct, this VM manages it.

If a tenant creates a new resource, it adds the storage account to a resource group. The storage account then manages the different storage services types on the physical host, such as BLOB, page, table, SOFS, ReFS cluster shared volumes, virtual disks, and Storage Spaces Direct. In addition, the storage account is the point to set up security, too. It's possible to add temporary (token based) and long-term (key based) storage.

When it comes to the roles for storage management, Azure Stack provides the following three levels:

- Storage Tenant Administrator (consumer of storage services).
- Storage Developer (developer of cloud-storage-based apps).
- Storage Service Provider (provides storage services for tenants on a shared infrastructure and can be divided into two separate roles):
  - Storage Fabric Administrator (responsible for fabric storage lifecycle)
  - Storage Service Administrator (responsible for cloud storage lifecycle)

The Azure consistent storage can be managed with:

- REST APIs
- PowerShell commandlets
- A modern UI
- Other tools (scripts and third-party tools)

Storage always needs to be a part of the tenant offer. It's one of the necessary pillars to providing resources within the Azure Stack.

AzS-ADFS01

The ADFS01 VM provides the technical basis for **Active Directory Federation Services (ADFS or AD FS)**, which provides one authentication and authorization model for Azure Stack. Specifically, if a deployment does not rely on Azure AD, there needs to be a feature to authenticate and authorize users from other Active Directory domains.

This VM is the most important one in disconnected scenarios, because it is the ADFS target for internal Active Directory domains connected for identity providers services.

AzS-SQL01

The SQL01 VM provides complete SQL services for Azure Stack. A lot of services need to store data (for example, offers, tenant plans, and ARM templates), and this is the place where it is stored. Compared to other products in the past (such as **Windows Azure Pack (WAP)**), there is no high load on this service because, it stores only internal data for infrastructure roles.

AzS-BGPNAT01

The BGPNAT01 VM provides NAT and VPN access based on the BGP routing protocol, which is the default for Azure, too. This VM does not exist in multi node deployments and is replaced by the TOR switch (**TOR** stands for **Top of the Rack**). As a tenant is able to deploy a VPN device in its Azure Stack-based cloud, and connect it to another on or off premises networking environment, all traffic goes through this VM. Compared to other designs, this VM is at the top of the rack switch and requires the following features:

- **Border Gateway Protocol** (**BGP**): This is the internet protocol for connecting autonomous systems and allows communication.
- **Data Center Bridging** (**DCB**): This is a technology for the Ethernet LAN communication protocol, especially for datacenter environments, for example, for clustering and SAN. It consists of the following subsets:
    - **Enhanced Transmission Selection** (**ETS**): This provides a framework for assigning bandwidth priorities to frames.
    - **Priority Flow Control** (**PFC**): This provides a link-level flow-control technology for each frame priority.
    - **Switch Independent Teaming** (**SIT**): This is a teaming mode launched with Windows Server 2012. The teaming configuration will work with any Ethernet switch, even non-intelligent switches, because the operating system is responsible for the overall technology.

AzS-CA01

CA01 runs the certificate authority services for deploying and controlling certificates for authentication within Azure Stack. As all communication is secured using certificates, this service is mandatory and needs to work properly. Each certificate will be refactored once every 30 days, completely in the Azure Stack management environment.

MAS-DC01

As the complete Azure Stack environment runs in a dedicated Active Directory domain, this VM is the source for all Azure Pack internal authentications and authorizations. As there is no other domain controller available, it's responsible for **Flexible Single Master Operation (FSMO)** roles and global cataloging, too. It provides the Microsoft Graph resource provider which is a REST endpoint to Active Directory. Finally, it is the VM running the DHCP and DNS services for the Azure Stack environment.

AzS-ERCS01

In case of an issue with Azure Stack itself (so called **break the cloud scenario**) it may be suitable to receive support from Microsoft. Therefore, there is the **MAS-ERCS01** VM which provides the possibility to connect to an Azure Stack deployment using **Just Enough Administration (JEA)** and **Just in Time Administration (JIT)** externally.

AzS-Gwy01

The `MAS-Gwy01` VM is responsible for site-to-site VPN connections of tenant networks in order to provide in-between network connectivity. It is one of the most important VMs for tenant connectivity.

AzS-NC01

`NC01` is responsible for the network controller services. The network controller works based on the **SDN** capabilities of Windows Server 2016. It is the central control plane for all networking stuff and provides network fault tolerance, and it's the magic key to *bringing your own address space* for IP addressing (VxLAN and NVGRE technology is supported, but VxLAN is the prioritized one).

Azure Stack uses virtual IP addressing for the following services:

- Azure Resource Manager
- Portal-UI (where it's admin or tenant)
- Storage
- ADFS and Graph API
- Key vault
- Site-to-site endpoints

The network controller (or network resource provider) makes sure that all communication goes its predefined way and is aware of security, priority, high availability, and flexibility.

In addition, it is responsible for all VMs that are part of the networking stack of Azure Stack:

- `AzS-BGPNAT01`
- `AzS-Gwy01`
- `AzS-SLB01`
- `AzS-Xrp01`

AzS-SLB01

`SLB01` is the VM responsible for all load balancing. With the former product, Azure Pack, there was no real load balancer available as Windows load balancing always had its issues with network devices at the tenant side. Therefore, the only solution for this was adding a third-party load balancer.

With Microsoft Azure, a software load balancer was always present, and `SLB01` is again the same one running in public Azure. It has just been moved to Azure Stack. It is responsible for tenant load balancing but also provides high availability for Azure Stack infrastructure services. As expected, providing the SLB to Azure Stack cloud instances means deploying the corresponding ARM template. The underlying technology is load balancing based on hashes. By default, a **5-tuple hash** is used, and it contains the following:

- Source IP
- Source port
- Destination IP
- Destination port
- Protocol type

The stickiness is only provided within one transport session, and packages of TCP or UDP sessions will always be transferred to the same instance beyond the load balancer. The following chart shows an overview of the hash-based traffic's contribution:

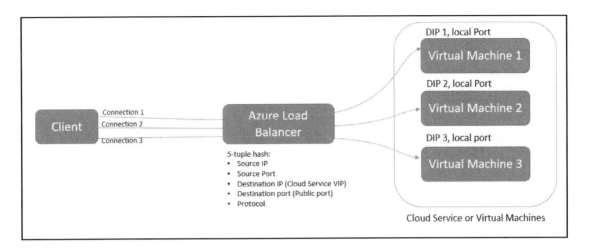

AzS-WASP01

The WASP01 is responsible for the Azure Stack tenant portal and running the Azure Resource Manager services for it.

AzS-WAS01

The VM named WAS01 runs the portal and your Azure Resource Manager instance. It is responsible for running the Azure Stack administrative portal, as you know already from Azure (codenamed **Ibiza**). In addition, your Azure Resource Manager instance is running on this VM.

ARM is your instance responsible for the design of the services provided in your Azure Stack instance. ARM will make sure that the resources will be deployed the way you design your templates and that they will be running the same throughout their lifecycle.

AzS-XRP01

The XRP01 VM is responsible for the core resource provider: compute, storage, and networks. It holds the registration of these providers and knows how they interact with each other; therefore, it can be called **the heart of Azure Stack**, too.

Services summary

As you have seen, these VMs provide the management environment of Azure Stack, and they are all available only in one instance. But we all know that scalability means deploying more instances of each service, and as we already have a built-in software load balancer, the product itself is designed for scale. Another way to scale is to implement another Azure Stack integrated system in your environment and provide a place familiar to Azure users. Indeed, there are two ways to scale. A good question is what scale unit will we need: if we need more performance, a scale with more VMs providing the same services is a good choice. The other option is to scale with a second region, which provides geo-redundancy.

(Re)starting an Azure Stack environment

As the Azure Stack integrated system is a set of VMs, we need to talk about what to do when restarting the entire environment. By default, each VM is set to go into saved mode when the environment is being shut down. In general, this should not be a problem because when the environment is restarting, the VMs should recover from the saved mode, too. If there are any delays with the VMs starting, the environment may run into issues and since a complete restart is not always a good idea, the following boot order is the *best practice*. Between each of these, there should be a delay of 60 seconds. The AD domain controller itself should reboot with the host machine:

- `AzS-BGPNAT01`
- `AzS-NC01`
- `AzS-SLB01`
- `AzS-Gwy01`
- `AzS-SQL01`
- `AzS-ADFS01`
- `AzS-CA01`
- `AzS-ACS01`
- `AzS-WAS01`
- `AzS-WASP01`
- `AzS-Xrp01`
- `AzS-ERCS01`

The shutdown sequence is the other way round.

If you want to make it easy for yourself, I would prefer to set up a PowerShell script for shutting down or restarting the VMs. Thanks to Daniel Neumann (TSP Microsoft Germany), there is a good script available on his blog at `http://www.danielstechblog.info/shutdown-and-startup-order-for-t he-microsoft-azure-stack-tp2-vms/`.

Resource providers

The main concept of the Azure Stack extensibility feature is that a web service is called a **resource provider**. This concept makes the product itself quite easy to maintain and extend:

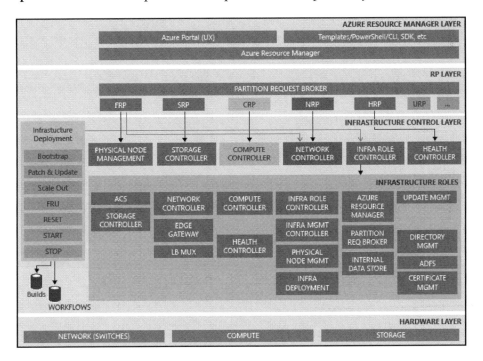

Regarding the logical design of Azure Stack shown in the preceding diagram, there are the following resource providers in the product today. The three main ones are as follows:

- **Storage Resource Provider (SRP)**
- **Compute Resource Provider (CRP)**
- **Network Resource Provider (NRP)**

We need to differentiate between them and the following additional resource providers:

- **Fabric Resource Provider (FRP)**
- **Health Resource Provider (HRP)**
- **Update Resource Provider (URP)**

Finally, we have the third-party resource providers. To make sure that each third-party resource provider acts as intended, there is a REST API and a certification for it with Azure Stack by Microsoft.

Azure Stack's core management services

By default, Azure Stack provides some core management services that everybody already knows from Azure. They are as follows:

- The authorization management service
- Subscriptions, Plans, and Offers
- Gallery
- Events
- Monitoring
- Usage

The authorization management service

Azure Stack authorization leverages the Azure authorization management service. For general availability, there are three different authentication designs. There's a good chance there's an authentication design available that works for most companies.

The Azure authorization management service works based on **Azure Active Directory (Azure AD)**, which is a multi-tenant, cloud-based identity-management service.

This means that each Azure Stack environment needs to have proper internet connectivity; otherwise, no authentication is possible. This makes life quite easy, but service providers or hosters (and even some medium and larger companies) especially do not allow communications from their internal infrastructure-management environment to the internet (public Azure) for authentication. This security requirement makes the creation of a **Proof of Concept (POC)** not as easy as before.

Starting with **TP3** there is support for Active Directory Federation Services. This service provides **single sign-on (SSO)** and secure remote access for web applications hosted on premises. In addition, it ensures that authentication is possible even if the connection to Azure AD is not available for a certain amount of time.

Subscriptions, Plans, and Offers

Another concept you may already know from Azure and even from Azure Pack is the concept of subscriptions, plans, and offers. This makes it quite easy for administrators to provide access to cloud services:

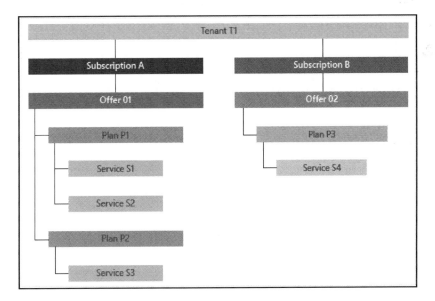

Plan

A Plan is a product that is described by predefined services from Azure Stack, for example, the **Infrastructure as a Service Plan** or **Website Plan**. Best practice is for the quality of this service to be included in the plan, too. This means we could define bronze, silver, gold, or platinum level services. This means, for example, that we have different storage IOPS from slow to high-end storage sitting on SSD drives.

Offer

An offer is a set of plans or a piece of one with a price on it. So it can be best described as a product itself.

Subscription

A subscription puts it altogether, which means that a dedicated user is given access to the cloud service with a username and password, which is linked to an offer that has predefined plans that are part of it. A Subscription could be set up by logging into the portal and creating a new subscription. This new Subscription then has to be linked to an offer by an administrator with the appropriate permissions.

Gallery

A gallery is the Azure Marketplace that is offered per subscription, which means it defines the virtual machines, web apps, websites, or other services that are part of the subscription. It defines which resources (ARM templates) will be available for deployments.

Events

The event service is an essential service for Azure Stack and provides information about a deployment-whether it is running properly or whether there are issues. So in general, it is a kind of event log of an Azure Stack resource. Like all Azure Stack services it has its own API, so you may collect data in another way than the portal (using PowerShell or other programming languages).

Monitoring

If a resource is up and running in Azure Stack, this is where the monitoring service opts in and provides general vital information. This is not the option to disable all your monitoring features for your environments. Your monitoring solutions provide an overall status of the resource itself and all services that are being provided by that service (for example, a VM providing email or database services). It is more than worth it to have it up and running too. The monitoring features of Azure Stack itself will be described later in this book.

Usage

Finally, everybody needs to make money and be profitable with a cloud solution. This is why we need a billing model. The basis for a billing model in general is the usage data that provides information about how long which resource is running and being used. This data is saved in SQL and builds the basis for your billing. The best way to report usage data is **PowerBI**. PowerBI is a SQL big data solution by Azure that gives you a nice overview of data. The billing possibilities will be described later in this book too:

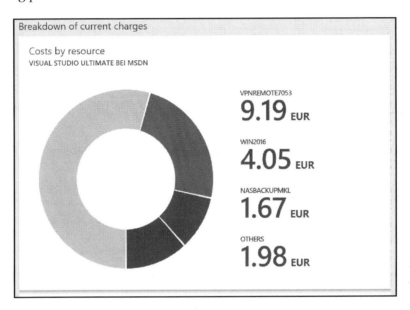

In addition to the possibilities of rich reporting, this data can be exported to CSV and reused in the customer's billing tool for charging its customers on a more or less easy and half-automated way.

If you need more features and functionality, there are third-party resource providers available to provide a more comprehensive but easy-to-use usage reporting feature that could fit better with customer needs, but this also means investing money and resources in these resource providers, because in general, you need a dedicated server to provide the business logic of this tool.

Using Azure Stack

Azure Stack provides the same features for connectivity as Azure itself, so we have the following:

- Azure Stack Portal
- PowerShell commandlets
- Azure CLI
- API

Depending on what you need, you should use one or more of them to work with Azure Stack.

Azure Stack Portal

The most general way to use Azure Stack is the Portal. This is the UI and it provides more than 95 percent of all features, including RBAC. Depending on whether you are an administrator or a generic user, you will have different features available in the portal, but you always use the same portal.

The portal looks like this after a new installation:

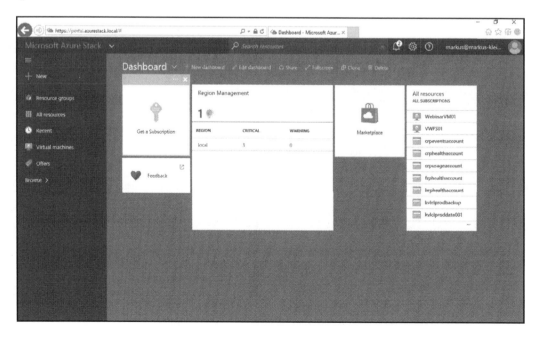

As you can see, the portal looks almost exactly like Azure's and provides the same usability. It's quite easy and intuitive to use from the end user's perspective. You don't need to train your users in general, they could just start with the same experience they hopefully already have from Azure.

PowerShell commandlets

The second way to communicate with Azure Stack is PowerShell. With the wide range of PowerShell **commandlets** (**cmdlets**), everything is possible. From the administration point of view, it is always the better choice to use PowerShell, because it is **reusable** and **redoable**, and each script is a documentation itself.

The steps to enable PowerShell are as follows:

1. Enter the following command to check for installed PowerShell modules:

   ```
   Get-PSRepository
   ```

2. Install the `AzureRM` module:

```
Install-PackageProvider -Name NuGet -MinimumVersion 2.8.5.201
-Force
```

3. Verify the installation status:

```
Get-Command -Module AzureRM.AzureStackAdmin
```

4. Now you can start over with `AzureRM` PowerShell commands. Connecting to Azure Stack using PowerShell should look like this:

```
$AADUserName='YourAADAccount@Yourdomain'
$AADPassword='YourAADPassword'|ConvertTo-SecureString -Force
-AsPlainText
$AADCredential=New-Object PSCredential($AADUserName,$AADPassword)
$AADTenantID = "YourAADDomain"
Add-AzureRmEnvironment -Name "Azure Stack" `
-ActiveDirectoryEndpoint
("https://login.windows.net/$AADTenantID/") `
-ActiveDirectoryServiceEndpointResourceId
"https://azurestack.local-api/" `
-ResourceManagerEndpoint ("https://api.azurestack.local/") `
-GalleryEndpoint ("https://gallery.azurestack.local:30016/") `
-GraphEndpoint "https://graph.windows.net/"
$env = Get-AzureRmEnvironment 'Azure Stack'
Add-AzureRmAccount -Environment $env -Credential $AADCredential
- Verbose
Get-AzureRmSubscription -SubscriptionName "youroffer" |
Select-AzureRmSubscription
Get-AzureRmResource
```

Simple, isn't it?

Application programming interface

The third option to connect to and work with Azure Stack is the API, which is again the same with Azure Stack as with Azure.

Instructions to install the Azure **Software Development Kit (SDK)** can be found at `https://azure.microsoft.com/en-us/downloads/`.

The next step is the big choice: which SDK platform should be used. The following ones are available:

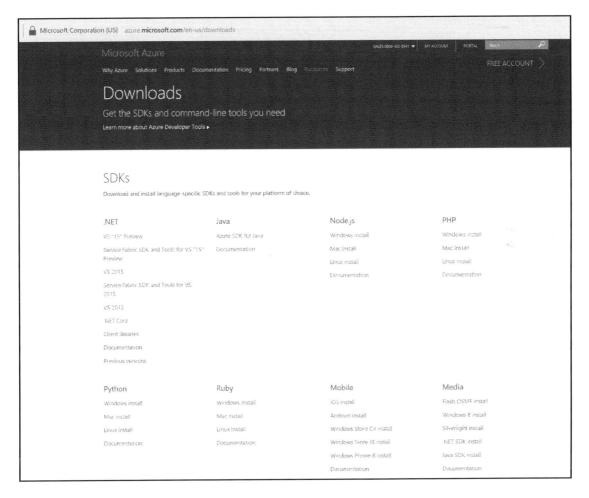

From development perspective, nearly everything is possible. In general, the most popular tool is Microsoft Visual Studio, and the developing language, .NET.

Coding for Azure Stack is always a development project. In general, you do not use it for daily tasks. You should use it for integrating Azure Stack into existing web shops or other solutions. In general, it's always a *make or buy* decision.

Custom portal for Azure Stack

Creating your own custom portal always means a huge investment and an ongoing process of supporting each update being installed on Azure Stack itself. Each service you would like to offer to your customers with the custom solution needs to be developed. This means that the developers need to understand the API, the way Azure Stack works, and how to code against this solution. From real-world project experiences, I know a custom portal is possible using the APIs, but the question should be more like, whether it is worth it, taking into account the amount of money that needs to be spent in the form of development hours and manpower.

Azure Stack CLI

Finally, the Azure Stack command-line interface is a toolset that can be installed on Azure Stack. It is available for Windows, Mac, and Linux.

The download locations are as follows:
Windows: http://aka.ms/azstack-windows-cli
Mac: http://aka.ms/azstack-mac-cli
Linux: http://aka.ms/azstack-linux-cli

Tools for Azure Stack

As Azure Stack is a solution in a box, the first question when talking about tools for Azure Stack is "where do I have to install them to be supported?". The answer, MAS-CON01, because it is the management VM. A wide variety of tools are provided that help with the administration of Azure Stack.

- **Visual Studio**: Visual Studio, including the Azure SDK, is a must have for creating and modifying ARM templates. You can download it from https://www.visualstudio.com.

- **AzCopy**: AzCopy is a command-line utility for copying data to and from Azure BLOB, file, and table storage with optimal performance. You can copy data from one object to another within or between storage accounts. As Azure Stack behaves in the same way, you can just use the same EXE for running it against itself.
- **Azure storage emulator**: The Microsoft Azure storage emulator provides a local environment that emulates the Azure storage services for development purposes. This tool is suitable for testing an application against storage services locally without connecting to Azure or Azure Stack.
- **Azure storage explorer**: If you need a solution to connect to and browse for Azure storage, it is available for various OSes:
    - **Windows**:
      `https://go.microsoft.com/fwlink/?LinkId=698844&clcid=0x409`
    - **Mac**:
      `https://go.microsoft.com/fwlink/?LinkId=698845&clcid=0x409`
    - **Linux**:
      `https://go.microsoft.com/fwlink/?LinkId=722417&clcid=0x409`

Migrating services to Azure Stack

If you are running virtual machines today, you're already using a cloud-based technology, although we do not call it cloud today. Basically, this is the idea of a private cloud. If you are running Azure Pack today, you are quite near Azure Stack from the processes point of view but not the technology part. There is a solution called **connectors** for Azure Pack that lets you have one portal UI for both cloud solutions. This means that the customer can manage everything out of the Azure Stack Portal, although services run in Azure Pack as a legacy solution.

Basically, there is no real migration path within Azure Stack. But the way to solve this is quite easy, because you could use every tool that you can use to migrate services to Azure.

Azure Website Migration Assistant

The Azure Website Migration Assistant will provide a high-level readiness assessment for existing websites. This report outlines sites that are ready to move and elements that may need changes, and it highlights unsupported features. If everything is prepared properly, the tool creates any website and the associated database automatically and synchronizes the content.

You can learn more about it at
`https://azure.microsoft.com/en-us/downloads/migration-assistant/`:

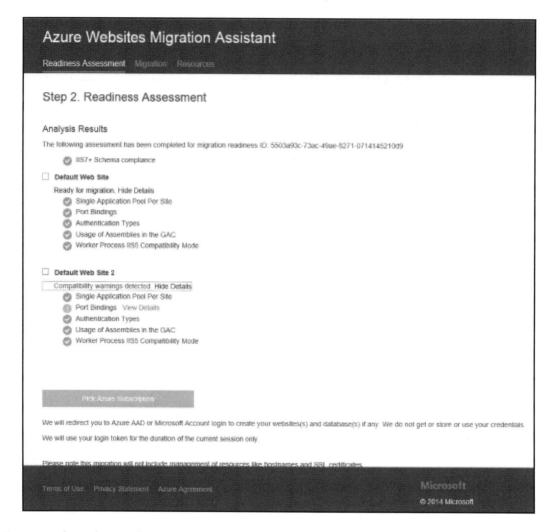

For virtual machines, there are two tools available:

- **Virtual Machines Readiness Assessment**
- **Virtual Machines Optimization Assessment**

Virtual Machines Readiness Assessment

The **Virtual Machines Readiness Assessment** tool will automatically inspect your environment and provide you with a checklist and detailed report on steps for migrating the environment to the cloud.

 The download location is `https://azure.microsoft.com/en-us/downloads/vm-readiness-assessment/`.

If you run the tool, you will get an output like this:

Virtual Machines Optimization Assessment

The Virtual Machines Optimization Assessment tool will at first start with a questionnaire and ask several questions about your deployment. Then, it will create an automated data collection and analysis of your Azure VMs. It generates a custom report with ten prioritized recommendations across six focus areas. These areas are security and compliance, performance and scalability, and availability and business continuity.

 The download location is
https://azure.microsoft.com/en-us/downloads/vm-optimization-asse
ssment/.

Summary

Azure Stack provides a real Azure experience in your datacenter. The UI, administrative tools, and even third-party solutions should work properly. The design of Azure Stack is a very small instance of Azure with some technical design modifications, especially regarding the compute, storage, and network resource providers. These modifications give you a means to start small, think big, and deploy large when migrating services directly to public Azure some time in the future, if needed.

The most important tool for planning, describing, defining, and deploying Azure Stack services is Azure Resource Manager, just like in Azure. This provides you with a way to create your services just once, but deploy them many times. From the business perspective, this means you have better TCO and lower administrative costs.

Azure Stack itself will be available as an integrated system (for production use). The minimum number of hosts is four and the maximum is 20 for version 1. For the development toolkit or setting up lab environments, there is a single host deployment available based on very basic hardware requirements. For general availability, the hardware OEMs are Dell EMC, HPE, and Lenovo; Cisco and other OEMs will follow soon.

Setting up Azure Stack is a straightforward solution using PowerShell. The deployment is divided into two main phases: the data collection section and the deployment section. Both sections steps can be easily resumed if they run into any issues. There is no deployment interruption at all.

In the following chapter, you will learn how to plan the deployment of Azure Stack and what you should think about before starting.

2
Planning the Deployment of Microsoft Azure Stack for Private Clouds

In this chapter, we will learn how to plan the implementation of Azure Stack. To make sure that your deployment of Azure Stack will succeed, you should prefer to plan the project itself somehow. The following topics are subplans I always create before setting things up; this will make sure that you don't forget important points:

- Solution design
- Sizing Azure Stack
- Authentication in Azure Stack
- Securing Azure Stack
- Compliance with Azure Stack
- Preparing the deployment
- Monitoring Azure Stack
- Business continuity
- Billing with Azure Stack
- Common design scenarios

Solution design

Before starting to plan Azure Stack, an important requirement needs to be defined, and you, as the administrator or the person responsible for the project, should ask yourself the following question:

What is my *cloud offering* with Azure Stack? If we set up Azure Stack, it'll be there, but no services will be available if you do not define them beforehand. To be more clear, it is even important to know the offerings before starting the planning phase. A lot of the aspects of an offering change the deployment itself a little; for example, if you do not plan to offer **Database as a Service (DBaaS)**, why should you plan for the SQL resource provider (SQL bridging resource provider)? Therefore, the most important thing is to define your offerings before starting with the deployment. A lot of people fear writing hundreds of pages before planning the first steps which may take days. From my experiences, this is completely different: the goal is to have one document per offering, with a two-page maximum. This will then be the basis for implementation as a service in Azure Stack using **Scrum** sprints.

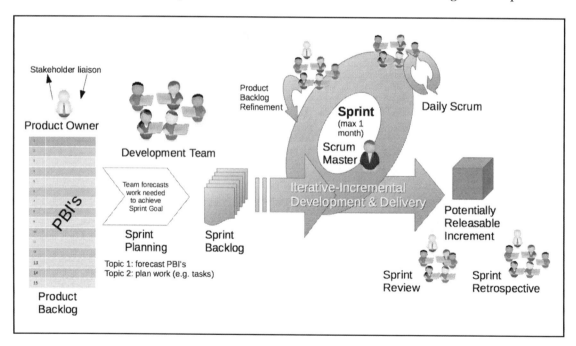

Basically, Scrum is a project-management model for agile software development, but it is easy to transfer it to other projects, too. Based on the solution's design documents, each offering can be set up as a Scrum sprint and can be implemented that way. The goal is to make sure everybody does their best to fulfill their daily tasks without major interferences or collisions. With other project-management solutions, the huge issue for the project's team members is, in general, that there is no time for their daily tasks, and they will have to work overtime to make the project work properly.

Scrum tries to be as flexible and agile, so each project member can decide how much of their working time they are able to spend on the project that week. This will be decided at the beginning of the weekly sprint plans.

The following questions should be answered per cloud offering:

- What is the offering description for your customer?
- What components does the offering consist of (for example, compute, storage, and network)?
- Which other offerings are required to deploy this service?
- For which customers are you planning to offer the service?
- Do we need an RBAC within the offering? If yes, how do we need to set it up?
- What's the process to order it?
- What are the inputs and the outputs of the offering?
- What optional services could be added to the offering from a customer's perspective?
- Do we need a specific compliance for the offering?
- How much does it cost and, based on which item, do we charge it (for example, per user, per device, per hour, or per server)?

 The better your solution design, the more detailed the deployment can be planned and the better we are planning for scale in the future! The maximum number of offerings you should start with should not be more than three to five basic offerings, and later on, when the service is up and running, you should introduce more and more services on a regular basis.

Most customers start with the following offerings as version 1 and later on keep adding additional services:

- Virtual machines (for Windows Server 2016 and 2012 R2 only)
- SQL Database as a Service (with Microsoft SQL Server only)
- Born-in-the-cloud web apps
- Cloud Foundry

Virtual machines

Basically called **Infrastructure as a Service**, a virtual machine is nothing more than transferring your existing physical server to the cloud. The existing one could be either a physical server or already a virtual one. The best scenario would be to be already on Hyper-V so that there is no real migration to the cloud and it is only a transfer. If the server is a physical one, you need to think about how to migrate it to the cloud infrastructure. The best thing would be to start with a completely new virtual machine and migrate your existing workloads to this new VM. This can be done in general using a smooth migration in coexistence, maybe, with the move to a new release of the technology (Microsoft Exchange, SharePoint, file services, and so on). From my experience, this is actually the best thing to start with cloud technology as a customer if you have not yet started.

SQL Database as a Service

SQL database services (no matter whether it is Microsoft SQL or MySQL) is one of the easiest services to consume from the cloud infrastructure. Often, it is called **SQL as a Service** too. From a technical point of view, this means ordering a database that is running in the cloud infrastructure on a highly available SQL Server environment (depending on the loads your cloud provider is offering). To make it easy, this means your database(s) will run and be managed in the cloud infrastructure, and from the customer side, you will only get a connection point to this database (for example, using ODBC connection strings).

Born-in-the-cloud web apps

In the past, there was an additional offering called **Website as a Service**, which provided websites and web services running on an IIS stack on cloud technology. Today, this feature is called **web apps** or even **born-in-the-cloud** apps. So what is this? Is it only a name change or a complete technology change? As you already know, the most common answer as a consultant is "it depends," and so it is here too. If you are only running a website (for example, on IIS using a CMS such as Joomla or WordPress), it is nearly only a name change from your point of view. But from the technology point of view, a web app is a service that is being provided using Azure Stack technology as a PaaS solution, but underneath, it is nothing more than one or even more VMs that are being managed by Azure Stack. And so what is a *cloud-born app*? It's a web app that doesn't use technology called **client/server**. It is a web app running on whatever device (workstation, notebook, tablet, or even mobile device) is connecting to an underlying web service (running on cloud technology or even in the cloud) that in general stores all data to a SQL database.

Cloud Foundry

Cloud Foundry is an open source solution that provides a multi-cloud application platform. It was established by the Cloud Foundry Foundation and was originally developed by VMware. Later on, it moved to Pivotal Software, which is a joint venture by General Electric, VMware, and EMC. Since 2015, there is a commercial release of Cloud Foundry and a non-profit one. Today, the most interesting reason for running Cloud Foundry in your environment is that it supports all development and testing stages when developing software solutions. Cloud Foundry runs on a set of virtual machines using the Linux operating system stack and has its own management language called **BOSH**, which spins up resources such as containers, storage, compute, and networking in an isolated, secure, and resilient way. Even load balancing is included by default. Azure Stack supports Cloud Foundry (non profit release), too with the same ARM template that is running with Azure; and you even can manage and control these resources from within the Azure Stack.

Of course, there is a lot more that you can implement in Azure Stack and provide offerings based on, but you should always keep in mind to start small and plan big. So within different releases after version 1 was launched, you could add different services, but if you would do it for version 1, I expect that you would fail because of a lack of administrative resources.

Mesosphere Enterprise Server (DC/OS)

DC/OS is an Apache Server based solution that provides the abstraction of data center resources with stateless application support. As a solution running on different cloud platforms it performs the feature to move an application from A to B without any interruption. This mean in general, that even if an application is not cloud aware designed, other solutions will break the app because, if IaaS VMs flip over from one host to another. DC/OS provides the functionality that the application does not recognize the flipping and makes sure the application will run.

Sizing Azure Stack

Now that all offerings have been defined, we can go one step ahead: the sizing of the environment.

As you know already, Azure Stack is not just a software solution; it will be delivered as an **integrated system**. This means that it consists of hardware and the appropriate software on top. There are numerous reasons for that. If you go directly with the Public Cloud Azure offering, you do not have to care about the underlying hardware. As Azure Stack is nothing more than bringing Azure to your data center, this is simply the same. For general availability, we will have the following OEMs that offer Azure Stack:

- Dell EMC
- HP Enterprise
- Lenovo
- After GA, additional hardware vendors (like Cisco and others) will soon join. Their offerings nearly look the same; only some minor things such as disk size will be different.

This integrated system is, to be honest, a hyper-converged system, which means that Hyper-V nodes and storage nodes are the same physical hardware. It does not have dedicated hardware for each layer.

In addition, for **Proof of Concept (PoC)**, there is a software-only release available that is running all components but will be delivered as a one-node solution. This means that all features are available, but you are lacking performance, stability, and high-availability tests within your PoC. In addition, no updates are published for the PoC release; you always need to redeploy Azure Stack if new bits are published.

The smallest footprint of Azure Stack in production is a four-node setup, which includes the **top-of-the-rack (ToR)** switches and maybe the aggregate switch. If you are later scaling resources, you will have to order another rack and add it to your Azure Stack. If the first rack is missing an aggregate switch, this needs to be added too. One thing you need to have in mind is that the portal and Azure Resource Manager will always be in your first rack for version 1. This means that you will need to take special care of your first rack, because if you lose it, your complete Azure Stack management is gone. For this, I would prefer you have a working and tested backup and restore process in place to make sure that if something happens with the first rack, you would be able to restore it as priority number one.

Why do we have this special design? Maybe you know that the initial versions of Azure had the same setup and it changed later. So with Azure Stack, we could expect the same in future releases.

A good question is what your hardware OEM will need to set up your Azure Stack deployment as expected. There is a deployment collection Excel file that you will get from the hardware vendor you have chosen. All information in this document needs to be collected, and then, it will be the basis for the deployment.

So we need to prepare all these details within our planning of the design. Let's start first with the sizing of the solution. The following questionnaire will help you get an answer for the design:

- How many end customers are you planning today and within the next 5 years that will be onboard to the solution? What kind of customers are you offering your services to, keeping in mind you have a buffer of 30-50% for unexpected growth?
- How many resources do your offerings require per service implementation? Think about a gold, silver, and bronze offering for performance, and keep in mind to have a buffer too if, unexpected load will run in these 30-50% services.
- Are you willing to offer highly available solutions to the end customer's (fault domains)? If so, how many and in which different fire locations would you like to place the stacks? Which service will be highly available? What does that mean to the connectivity? Do we need **quality of service (QoS)**? Think about offering different solutions as non-HA or HA ones.
- How many regions are you planning? (For GA, only one region is planned, later on, additional ones will be possible, too.)
- Are you planning to offer your services on a national or international market? This will give you an idea of the compliance regulations you will need to map.

- What's your monitoring concept for the solution? Do we need to add Azure Stack to an existing monitoring service (such as Nagios, System Center Operations Manager, and Operations Management Suite)? What does this mean to the existing load? How should we connect this, as an installation of an agent is not possible because the system is locked down?
- That backup solution needs to be added, so what does this mean to your resources? Do you need to add a certain percentage of resources for the placement of the backup?

A lot of Azure Stack customers would ask whether they would need to run the complete project with the hardware OEM. This is really not the case as the consulting company you are currently working with might have a deeper knowledge of Azure Stack than the hardware supplier. The consulting company can help you prepare your Azure Stack project and decide which hardware OEM would be the one you want to go with. They could even help you fill in the Excel sheet. Later, when the hardware is up and running, your consulting company could help you prepare the offerings with Azure Stack and even create the ARM templates with or for you.

The best thing would be to have a workshop to define a basic concept of Azure Stack in your data center. During this, the answers to the previous questions should be the basis of the discussion. After having answered these questions (including the sizing ones), we can now go on and describe the big picture of your Azure Stack deployment.

After deciding how many hosts the footprint would go live for a start, the next question is always based on regions. For version 1, we could only set up one region; if we need more, there are two basic options to go with:

- Make sure your second data center is well connected and you have all management in your primary data center.
- Set up a different Azure Stack installation in your second data center and deploy all ARM templates and the portal again without any connection to the primary one.

For future releases, we can expect to have connectivity and single points of deployment of more than one region.

Authentication in Azure Stack

Authentication is one of the most important topics if you plan to implement Azure Stack. As it comes without any direct connection to your data center's infrastructure, you'll need to decide how to connect it to your preferred authentication mechanism.

For Azure Stack, the basic authentication service is **MS-Graph**. This service is being used with Azure and Office 365, too. Basically, it is a REST service to an internal directory service and it builds the basis of authenticating all virtual machines and services within the Azure Stack itself.

Regarding user authentication for customers, there are two choices:

- **Azure Active Directory (Azure AD)**
- **Active Directory Federation Services (ADFS)**

Azure Active Directory for Azure Stack

If your Azure Stack environment is able to connect to the internet directly, Azure AD is the preferred authentication mechanism. This means Azure Stack will directly interoperate with Azure AD for user authentication. The appropriate authentication token will be provided from Azure AD and passed to Azure Stack using the internet. With this user ID, Azure Stack decides all permissions based on the defined RBAC model and provides access to the corresponding services.

Azure AD is a cloud-based authentication service with 99.9% SLA. It provides a token-based authentication model and can be extended with multi-factor authentication services. Depending on the network security in the infrastructure where Azure Stack has been placed, this authentication provider may or may not be available.

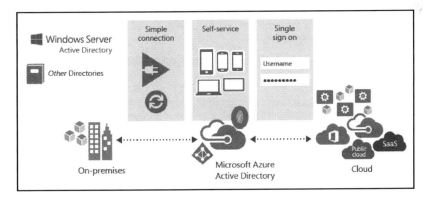

Choosing Azure AD as the authentication solution, you could connect different Azure AD services to your Azure Stack. There is no need to have *1:1* connectivity. So Azure AD as the authentication solution gives you a way to have *1:N* connectivity, and support as many Azure Ads as you need.

This may be the best solution for you if you are a service provider, or even acting as one although you are not a real one.

If Azure Stack live in a highly secure environment, choosing this authentication provider may not be possible. This means that you would need a completely disconnected scenario.

Active Directory Federation Services for Azure Stack

The second authentication option, ADFS, is the default option for disconnected scenarios. ADFS interoperates with your existing Active Directory, and therefore, authentication with existing accounts is possible.

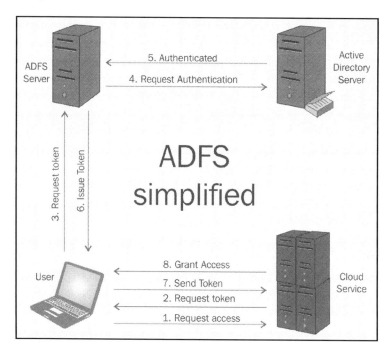

In the set of virtual machines running within your Azure Stack setup, a dedicated ADFS VM will be needed. If you are using ADFS within your Azure Stack implementation, you are bound to *one ADFS trust*. This means there is no chance of connecting your customer's Active Directory to your cloud service using ADFS directly. If you need it, you will have to set up an ADFS trust to a domain service in between, which then directly connects to your Azure Stack environment using another ADFS hop.

Choosing the authentication provider

The choice between both identity management solutions is quite simple: ask yourself whether you want a connected or disconnected scenario; if you want a disconnected one, you should be fine by accepting that there is only one ADFS connection that can be implemented. Azure AD is the more flexible one, but needs internet connectivity, ADFS does not need internet connectivity but supports a higher infrastructure security level.

Securing Azure Stack

If you are planning to implement Azure Stack in your infrastructure, you should make sure you have a security concept for it. If your customers will run their company's workloads in your environment, you will have to show them that your environment is secure. Therefore, we need to take care of some important points that should be part of your security concept for Azure Stack.

Secure by default

As Azure Stack is delivered as an integrated system, it will be *secure by default*, which means every VM has integrated hardening by default. And even though everything is a VM of either Windows Server 2016 Full Server Edition or Core Server Edition, you are unable to install anything on the VMs themselves. This means that no antivirus or backup solution can be installed as you can only use the Microsoft integrated solutions (Windows Defender and InMage) with it. The ways to deal with this are described in a later chapter.

Certificates

As the Azure Stack portal is the customer-facing portion of your environment besides the API, one of the most important things is to run proper HTTPS certificates with your Azure Stack environment. This states that no self-signed certificates should be in place that produce error messages when accessing the environment.

As each service running with Azure Stack is a REST-based web service, the easiest way is to order and implement a wildcard certificate from a well-known trust center (for example, Verisign and eTrust).

Otherwise, the different **subject alternate names** (**SAN**) would drive costs higher than expected. The choice of the proper trust center depends upon your customers: if you are running Azure Stack in a German data center, you should maybe think of a German trust center to work with. This would provide more security in the mind of your customers to run their services from within your data center.

Testing/staging environment

In most companies, a testing/staging environment might be normal, but in others, it is not the case. This is why I decided to talk about it.

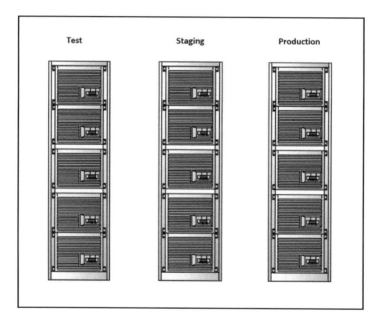

Your production Azure Stack is running your customer's production workloads. This means that testing new offerings with it may not be a good idea. With regard to Azure Stack integrated systems, does this mean that I need to buy another integrated system for testing/staging? The short answer is no, because the costs would be way too high, I am afraid. But this is where the single-node deployment comes in, because does it really matter how performant your testing/staging environment is? No! So for testing and staging, I would expect to have a single-node deployment. Testing would mean that your internal administrators are testing new offerings themselves; staging means that you would provide the new services to some customers knowing not to put productive workloads on it.

Role-based access control

If we talk about default security with Azure Stack, you will get an operator role with Azure Stack defaults and a user role. These roles are predefined. In preparation for the Azure Stack to go-live, you need to prepare a **role-based access control (RBAC)** design. This means you need to prepare a setup of permissions that your tenants would really need and define it within Azure Stack using the portal or the API. You need to create a subset of roles that exist and the *good practice* is to define them as follows:

- Tenant administrator
- Tenant operator
- Tenant user
- Tenant read-only helpdesk user (optional)

The following method is intended to set up a user in the Azure Stack portal:

1. Log on to the portal.
2. Create a new account in Active Directory.
3. Set the appropriate user role.
4. Generate a temporary password.
5. Transfer authentication information to the user.

Setting up a new user using PowerShell would be done as follows:

```
# Connect to AAD
$AADCred = get-credential
# Add a new tenant account
connect-msolservice -credential $AADCred
$NewUser = new-msoluser -DisplayName "Tenant1 Admin"
-UserPrincipalName <username>@<domainname.tld>
-Password <password> Add-MsolRoleMember
-RoleName "Tenant Administrator" -RoleMemberType User
-RoleMemberObjectId $NewUser.ObjectId
```

 To keep things easy, think big, but think easy! A hierarchy of user roles and permissions does not make it easy for the support team to help your tenants!

As you have seen, setting up user accounts and user roles is quite easy, and to have a documented way of how you did it, I would suggest running PowerShell commands when setting things up and saving the scripts as documentation.

Key Vault

When implementing Azure Stack, I would suggest you keep things as secure as it could be. This doesn't mean only the implementation itself should be secure. If you are providing IaaS, you should set up the Key Vault service. By default, all VMs are generation 1 Hyper-V machines; no shielded VMs (using virtual TPM keys) are possible, and therefore, only disc encryption is available. I may be repeating myself, but just like there are no shielded VMs in Azure, we have the same in Azure Stack.

In general, Key Vault needs to be enabled per subscription. To check whether everything is properly configured, you could run the following PowerShell command:

```
Get-AzureRmResourceProvider -ProviderNamespace Microsoft.KeyVault
| ft -AutoSize
```

The output should look as follows:

```
ProviderNamespace RegistrationState ResourceTypes Locations
Microsoft.KeyVault Registered {operations} {local}
Microsoft.KeyVault Registered {vaults} {local}
Microsoft.KeyVault Registered {vaults/secrets} {local}
```

If this is not the case, you will see `Unregistered`. To register the Key Vault feature, you will need to run the following command:

```
Register-AzureRmResourceProvider -ProviderNamespace Microsoft.KeyVault
```

Then everything should be fine.

> To enable Key Vault, the following URL will help you with all that's needed:
>
>
>
> `https://docs.microsoft.com/en-us/azure/azure-stack/azure-stack-kv-intro`.
>
> You have the option to deploy VMs using passwords or certificates. I would prefer using certificates because passwords are usually more insecure than certificates!

Azure Stack syndication with Azure Marketplace

In general, for each resource that you would like to offer to your tenants, you could set up your own ARM template and deploy it to your tenants. This is a little complex, but you can make sure everything is configured to a 100%, just like you want it.

To make life easier, Azure Stack will provide an Azure Stack **syndication** with Azure Marketplace. This means that you can select and completely deploy an Azure offering to your Azure Stack data center and run it directly in your environment.

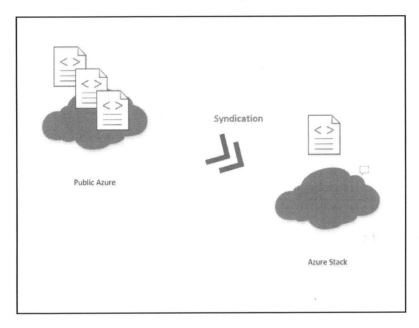

Compliance with Azure Stack

Whether you are a service provider or an internal IT provider for an enterprise, today's IT needs to fulfill compliance requirements.

Depending on which market you are working in, there are different compliance models, such as the following:

- ISO/IEC 27001
- PCI-DSS
- HIPAA

- SoX
- BSI
- Secure data center level 1-3

If you have to fulfill a specific compliance requirement with your Azure Stack implementation, you should check in advance which one you will need. This depends upon the industry, location, customers, and lots more.

The following decision chart should help you plan your compliance:

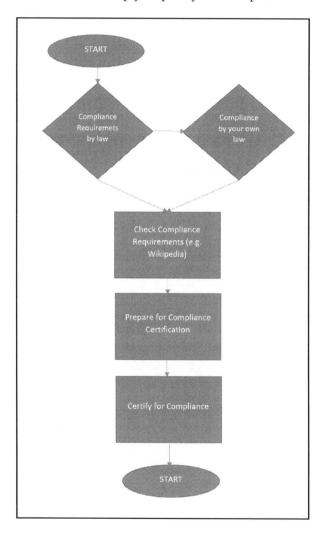

The different versions of compliance may be important, but I would not plan too much compliance at once because otherwise, you might get lost fulfilling compliance regulations. You can find more here:

https://en.wikipedia.org/wiki/Data_center.

Preparing the deployment

As the deployment of Azure Stack consists of more than implementing a new software solution, you need to prepare some more steps to make the project work as expected.

Most of the work really starts after you have chosen the hardware OEM for Azure Stack (remember HPE, Dell-EMC, or Lenovo). Your hardware vendor will send you a list for finalizing all details for the pre-deployment before delivering the system to your customer. This is a lot of work, but to be honest, there is more.

The minimum footprint of Azure Stack is half a rack of servers (four hosts, to be more specific). This means you would have to prepare the space for it in your data center, with all the details, such as:

- Redundant power supply
- Connection to your existing UPS
- Connection to your existing cooling system
- Connection to your data center backbone (border switches) with a minimum of two ports
- Integration with you data center's security requirements

Regarding connectivity, the requirements depend upon the design you have chosen (Azure AD as authentication or the disconnected scenario with ADFS in place). As Azure Stack comes fully independent with your existing IT infrastructure, the prerequisites are small.

The most important questions for the preparation of the deployment are as follows:

- Could you provide the required internet access (mandatory for AAD)?
- Do you have an existing ADFS infrastructure (if you have chosen the disconnected scenario)? If not, you need to prepare your infrastructure with the ADFS implementation (https://technet.microsoft.com/en-us/library/dn486820(v=ws.11).aspx).

- Which firewall rules need to be prepared?
- Do you need to recertify your data center within the Azure Stack implementation?
- How would you give the hardware OEM access to your data center for setting up Azure Stack and connecting it with your existing environment?
- Are there further regulations you need to think about beforehand?

Furthermore, the details you will need to prepare are quite more complex:

- Which IPv4 range should Azure Stack run in?
- What's the location name for Azure Stack (`local` by default)?
- Are there any naming conventions that need to be fulfilled for servers (for example, computer naming conventions)?
- What is the initial password for your operational Azure Stack user?
- Do you need to fulfill password security requirements (maximum password length and age)?
- If you are using AAD: What's the AAD domain you need to connect Azure Stack to?
- If you are using ADFS: What is the context you would need to connect Azure Stack to?
- What are the details of the ADFS servers? Are they Windows 2012 R2 or higher (lower versions are not fully tested and supported)?
- Do you need to define different SLAs from your existing ones?
- Do you need to fulfill further requirements that are not on the list already?

After discussing all these topics, you need to make a time schedule for the implementation. This means that we need to plan the following details:

- Planned generic data center preparations completed (around 4 weeks before the delivery of the Azure Stack integrated system).
- Servers for the testing and/or staging environment up and running in an existing rack environment.
- Firewall configuration done and tested.
- Required accounts and passwords set up and available.
- If you are using the disconnected scenario: ADFS up and running and testing done for ADFS connection being in general possible.
- Don't forget that you may need space in your data center for future enhancements!

From a consultant perspective, all the previously mentioned topics need to be placed in a project plan; then, you could easily decide whether the delays delay the complete project, or they can be compensated with other tasks because they can be run in parallel.

If you planned your Azure Stack deployment this way, it is quite certain that the project will succeed with respect to time and money. This is the generic basis for all further steps (for example, setting up your tenant services and ARM templates).

Monitoring Azure Stack

Monitoring management (often called **event management**) is a generic part of running your data center based on an industry standard. If your IT solution is based on predefined SLAs, you'll need to know whether there are any issues with some services your offering is based on before your customers know. This means that you need a proactive monitoring solution. The only thing you need to have in mind is that you are unable to install any agents on your Azure Stack integrated system, because they are secured by default. So we need to plan agentless monitoring methods.

As with Microsoft, there are two different products that may help you:

- System Center Operations Manager (the corresponding Management Pack is already available)
- Microsoft Operation Management Suite (the solution is still in work and will be released after GA, but as Azure Stack is running on premise in your data center, you could just use the SCOM MP and let then SCOM sync everything to OMS in the Azure cloud).

But do you run some of these monitoring solutions already? Or do you monitor your servers using a Nagios derivate? If so, you will already have a community plugin available (https://exchange.nagios.org/directory/Plugins/Cloud/Monitoring-AzureStack-Alerts/details).

You could just install and use it with your existing Nagios implementation, and as it does not require agents, it is a solution you could start with now and get your own experience in your data center (for example, with the single-host PoC version of Azure Stack).

Event management is a basic toolset and provides you with a way to implement workarounds and/or changes in your environment in a documented and useful manner.

Business continuity with Azure Stack

Besides how to set up, run, configure, optimize, and monitor your data center solution, one of the most important things is to make sure that you will have a business continuity concept, even if you run into trouble with your management solution.

 With Azure Stack, we need to have in mind some special concepts that we have to consider with our business continuity plan:

- You cannot install anything directly on the Azure Stack VMs.
- Azure Stack portal and Azure Stack ARM live only in the first rack.

 As you may have your central backup solution, you need to make sure that it fits into the plan for backing up (and restoring) your Azure Stack integrated system.

Azure Stack backup concept

The basic concept of Azure Stack is that you cannot install anything on Azure Stack virtual machines as it would break the supportability from Microsoft. The basic concept of Microsoft is that each VM has an integrated InMage Scout agent.

 InMage was acquired by Microsoft in 2014. It provides a consistent backup using a block-level, change-tracking solution and therefore makes sure that you always have a consistent backup of your VM in another storage location.

With Azure Stack, this storage location is positioned outside the Azure Stack hosts, depending on the hardware vendor on another server. This storage can be integrated into the backup solution of your choice.

Location of ARM and portal in Azure Stack

As the basic concept of the first version of Azure Stack is basically a copy of Azure, **Azure Resource Manager (ARM)** and portal lives only on the first rack (with which you started using Azure Stack). As of today, *no* redundancy model is available, which means losing the first rack because of a disaster would mean that all the VMs of your tenants would still be alive, but no management solution would exist anymore.

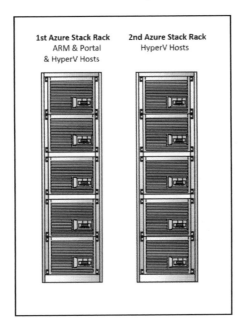

The good question of dealing with this *speciality* is: how do I protect my first Azure Stack solution, and how do I need to deal with it if there is a disaster?

Backup and restore your first Azure Stack rack

For your first rack of Azure Stack, I recommend the following concept for backing up and restoring:

The most important thing is that if there is an issue with any VM, it means a priority 1 issue with an *at once* SLA. This means the backup of the VMs that have been saved to the storage outside of Azure Stack needs to be restored in the quickest way possible. I would place them on high speed disk drives in a different fire area but near the area where the rack has been placed.

If there are any issues with the underlying hardware of your Azure Stack number-one rack, you would need the quickest SLA with the hardware vendor. Even a *cold standby* solution could be suitable.

This is the only way to make sure that the downtime of the portal and ARM is as short as possible.

Restoring Azure Stack environments (rack 2 to x)

For all other racks with tenant VMs you are running within your Azure Stack infrastructure, the high availability design is similar to Azure as the tenant itself needs to provide itself with configuring availability sets in different regions in general. Because there will only be one region possible with Azure Stack in version 1, this cannot be the solution. The provider needs to set up a backup and restore process with his customer using **Data Protection Manager** (**DPM**) or another third-party backup solution.

The most important thing is to define SLAs with your tenants that will make sure that the customer will not use their VMs and thus, give them a good balance for restoring the resources. On the other hand, there needs to be the option to react as a service provider from the manpower side.

Update management with Azure Stack

Azure Stack will receive updates for everything (firmware, drivers, and Azure Stack updates) on a regular basis (expected monthly). The process of providing this update will depend on what updates are available.

For driver and firmware updates, Azure Stack will use the well-known update procedures from hardware vendors. This updates will be provided using a dedicated server, so called Hardware LifeTime Hosts (HLH) that is not part of the Azure Stack integrated system. Azure Stack updates will be pushed to your environment from Microsoft using a dedicated update server. This server will in addition know about all the updates being provided from the hardware vendor and will inform your company's Azure Stack operator that updates are available. Each Azure Stack operator needs to define the right moment in time to push these updates to Azure Stack. This updating procedure does not mean that there will be an offline window. Azure Stack will spin up another VM with the same setup (a *1:1* copy) and apply the patches to that. Then Azure Stack will switch to this VM automatically without any downtime window.

Billing with Azure Stack

Finally, as we all need to make money with our data center solution, another important concept is how to handle the billing: *pay per use* or *pay per ordered resource*? Depending on your business model and your customer, the answer is always, "it depends."

If you are acting as a service provider with customers who want to control their costs by powering their resources on or off, the *pay per use* model is the best. If you have customers who need to plan their budget, *pay per ordered resource* is the best.

Both these models are basically possible with Azure Stack licensing itself, because you could pay for your license per use (like with Azure) or pay per *yearly buyout*, which means you could just set a price per resource, and if you order it, you will need to pay for it whether it is online or offline.

So as you can see, both solutions are fine and you could also cover the licenses for Microsoft with them.

The next question is, how we could count the used resources automatically and find the basis for sending the invoices to the customers. The basic concept of **Azure Stack** is to provide a **billing adapter** that gives you a way to export the details, transfer them to your billing solution, import them and-hopefully-automatically create and send the invoices to your customer.

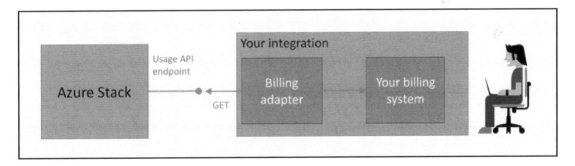

The concept is a little different compared to Azure Pack: there, we had the feature of service reporting, but it was deprecated in System Center 2016.

Basically, Azure Stack provides a REST API for collecting all details using PowerShell commands and transferring them either directly to your billing system or to PowerBI and creating some interesting reports with the data. As a service administrator, you could export all data for all subscriptions; as an individual tenant, you can only export your usage data. So even a tenant themselves, is able to get their data in depth and maybe bill their end-customers if they are not the consumer themselves.

A full list of all parameters you could get out of Azure Stack could be found at
`https://docs.microsoft.com/en-us/azure/azure-stack/azure-stack-usage-related-faq`.

The Azure Stack API is being provided directly with Azure Resource Manager, so getting this detail is quite simple by using the following command:

```
# Connect to ARM using your appropriate account
Login-AzureRmAccount
#Get all resources used per your subscription
Get-AzureRmSubscription -SubscriptionName "your subcription"
| Select-AzureRmSubscription
```

For more information regarding usage data, the following URL might help:

`https://docs.microsoft.com/en-us/azure/azure-stack/azure-stack-provider-resource-api`.

The PowerShell command `Get-UsageAggregates` gives you a more detailed way to set a start and end date, an aggregation per day or per hour, and the instance-level detail:

```
Get-UsageAggregates [-AggregationGranularity
<AggregationGranularity>] [-ContinuationToken <String>]
-ReportedEndTime <DateTime> -ReportedStartTime <DateTime>
[-ShowDetails <Boolean>] [<CommonParameters>]
```

This command will return 1,000 lines of resources per call; if you need more, set the `continuation` parameter to more than the predefined limit.

For example, the following sets a start and an end date for the usage data:

```
PS C:\>Get-UsageAggregates -ReportedStartTime "1/1/2016"
-ReportedEndTime "12/31/2016"
```

The output could then be saved to a file, and imported to Power BI, or your favorite billing solution as a basis for your invoicing.

Finally, as with Azure Pack, there are different third-party solutions available that provide a more flexible billing solution. First, we have the well-known **Cloud Cruiser** solution, which provides the following extra features:

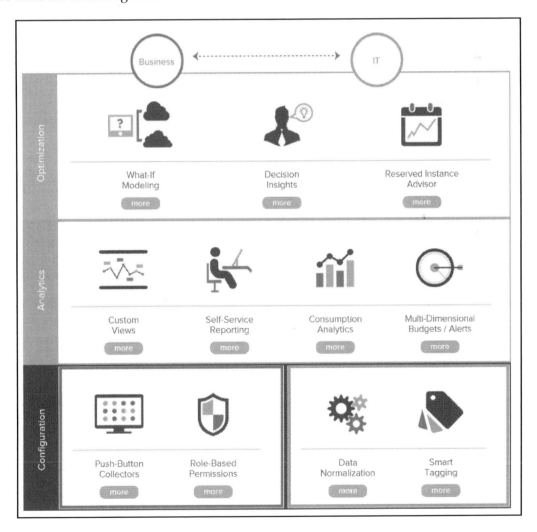

The second most well-known product is from **Cloud Assert** and is called **Azure Usage**:

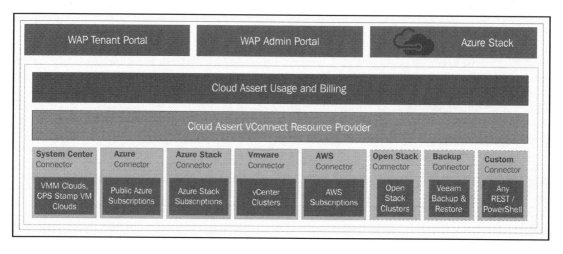

Common design scenarios

By default, there are a few different scenarios for implementing Azure Stack features with an infrastructure. Each scenario can be set up with a connection to Azure AD and as a disconnected scenario using ADFS.

Azure Stack without a preexisting infrastructure

The easiest setup is to provide a new Azure Stack infrastructure for a new data center without a preexisting infrastructure that needs to be integrated or connected. The most important question then is, whether to set up Azure Stack with or without internet connectivity for authentication.

Azure AD connectivity means that lots of different directories can be connected directly using Azure AD. So a direct connection means that all authentication tokens are provided via the internet.

ADFS-based authentication is bound to one domain, but as this will be an in-between one and all ADFS connectivity is bound to this in-between domain, this may be a little bit more complex with some more points of possible failure.

Setting up Azure Stack then means, providing the appropriate racks, power, and internet connectivity somewhere in your data center and starting to offer your services directly with Azure Stack.

Azure Stack with existing Azure Pack

If you need to deploy Azure Stack as a company already using Windows Azure Pack, there are some points you should think about to make life easier. Both solutions use different portals and technologies today; Azure Pack is based on System Center and Windows Server, while Azure Stack is Azure technology.

If you want to deploy Azure Stack and connect your tenant clouds running on Azure Pack to Azure Stack, the easiest way is to configure Azure Pack to authenticate using Azure AD or even ADFS. This means that regardless of the portal that the tenants are using, the same authentication account is being used.

The next step is to think about the implementation of the **WAP connector for Azure Stack** as this connector gives you a way to start, and stop resources within one portal, and this one is the new Azure Stack portal. You will be able to switch between clouds and connect from your Azure Stack portal to the resources running on Azure Pack (WAP). This connector will be part of your Azure Stack deployment, if you need it, but as a prerequisite, we need to run the latest update rollup package with Azure Pack to enable the web service required in Azure Pack to allow connections from Azure Stack.

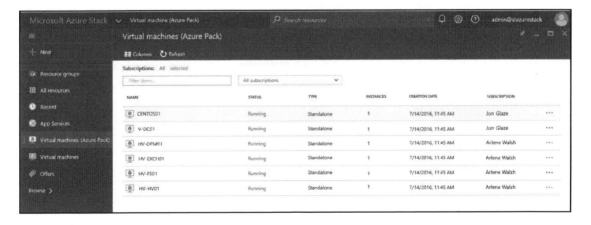

If you're thinking about migrating resources from a WAP cloud to an Azure Stack cloud, I clearly recommend planning a smooth migration of services (step by step). This means you should look with your tenant at each service (for example, SharePoint, Exchange, and CRM) and plan a transition to a new server, maybe with the chance to move to a new release of the currently running service (for example, each release of 2016). After all, resources of one cloud have been migrated to the Azure Stack cloud you could dismiss the Azure Pack cloud. If all clouds are being migrated to Azure Stack, you could completely tear down your Azure Pack implementation.

Another way to migrate services from Azure Pack to Azure Stack is using the **Azure Site Recovery** (**ASR**). So you will need to migrate the existing resources to Azure (using ASR) and then from Azure back to Azure Stack. To make this happen, there needs to be support for Azure Stack in ASR.

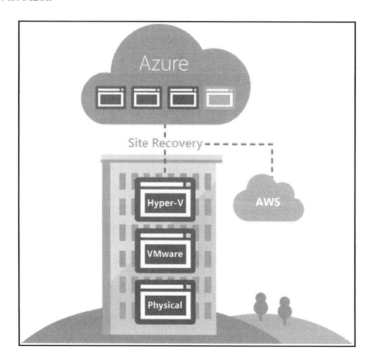

Regardless of all the previous steps, you need to decide whether you want the AAD-connected or the ADFS-disconnected scenario.

Azure Stack with existing OpenStack

If you are running with an existing OpenStack solution, I would think that 90% of you are running Cloud Foundry on OpenStack, too. This means at first, that we need to set up Cloud Foundry on Azure Stack, which will be described later in this book. Then, we need to connect resources that are currently running on OpenStack to a cloud that is already on Azure Stack. The migration should be then planned as a smooth one too, and each service should be migrated from the old to the new environment. Finally, if all services are being transferred to Azure Stack, you could again tear down your OpenStack environment, and the migration is done, too.

If you are using what solution ever today and need to migrate to Azure Stack, the method described here should also fit your migration strategy:

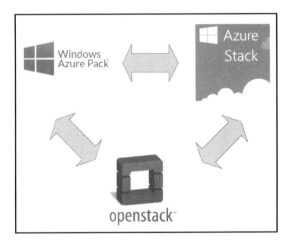

Enhancing existing Azure Stack

If you are already running Azure Stack and need to enhance it with new racks of Azure Stack Integrated System, you will need to stick to your hardware OEM because with version 1, there is no support of a mixed setup of hardware in one Azure Stack location.

In general, if you have started with the smallest footprint, you do not have an aggregate switch installed. Azure Stack is connected directly to your network infrastructure. So for the first step of the deployment, we will need a downtime to reconnect it and implement the aggregate switch. The next step will then be, to enhance the existing environment using new hosts within the Administrative portal of Azure Stack.

Summary

Azure Stack itself provides different scenarios with interoperability and migration options from Windows Azure Pack, OpenStack, or other data center management solutions. The big issue is that the goal of a great project implementing Azure Stack, just like every other project in IT, is good project planning. If you think about the basic features you will need to consider, then your project should not fail.

The main topics we covered were:

- Solution management
- Capacity planning management
- Authentication management
- Security management
- Compliance management
- Deployment management
- Configuration management
- Event management
- Business continuity management
- Billing management
- Migration management

This chapter tried to give you guidance on the implementation and tried to make sure that you will not forget important things. This will make sure your project succeeds.

In the next chapter, we will learn how to set up Azure Stack *Single Host PoC Edition*. This will make you understand how Azure Stack really works in depth.

3

Deploying Microsoft Azure Stack

Although Microsoft provides Azure Stack as an integrated solution and everything comes pre-installed, you will need to setup your development/testing environment(s). The production environment is mainly set up in the same way but has missing components like BGPNAT- and console-VM but it works the same way like the *single host PoC* does.

This is why we will need to have a chapter where we will have to talk about deployment. In detail, we will talk about:

- Disconnected versus connected scenario
- Deploying Azure Stack development toolkit
- Deploying the multi-node Azure Stack environment
- Troubleshooting Azure Stack installations
- Monitoring Azure Stack installations
- Connecting Microsoft Azure Stack
- Defining Azure role based access

Disconnected versus connected scenario

Azure Stack itself has two different ways of how it could be set up:

- Connected scenario
- Disconnected scenario

Both scenarios provide different features and are somehow valid for different customer scenarios, which will be described in detail now.

The connected scenario means that Azure Stack is directly connected to the internet and relies on the following features that are being provided by Azure:

- Azure Active Directory for authentication
- Azure Marketplace syndication (as a possible option)
- Azure billing (as a possible option)

Azure AD authentication and Marketplace syndication are nice features, because you will not have to provide an on premise solution for them. The other side is that it needs to be setup with an Azure subscription where the billing feature relies on it too. So, the customers will receive a bill for the Azure and Azure Stack based scenarios.

In regards to costs for Azure Stack, there is no further need on payments to Microsoft, because everything will be handled with the Azure subscription, or to say it in a different way. You will need to pay the same for Azure Stack that you pay for Azure in regards to software costs.

The disconnected scenario means that Azure Stack is not directly connected to the internet, so it will rely on:

- ADFS features
- Azure Stack billing API

To connect Azure Stack to an existing on premise Active Directory, **Active Directory Federation Services** (**ADFS**) is the feature to use. As ADFS means a *1:1* authentication scenario, you will need to work around with pass-through Active Directories or anything else. In addition this means that you will need to define your own processes to add Marketplace images or a billing feature as the API is being provided but no authentication feature is available. In regards of Microsoft billing, Azure Stack will be licensed and paid with a yearly subscription under the Azure radar.

Deploying Azure Stack development toolkit

Azure Stack Development Toolkit (Azure Stack single node PoC) is for testing and development purposes. It can be downloaded from `http://azure.microsoft.com/en-us/overview/azure-stack`.

After downloading the ZIP file, it needs to be extracted and will provide you the Azure-Stack VHDX (`CloudBuilder.vhdx`). This is the main basis for all Azure Stack, you will have to boot it from an existing Hyper-V environment.

The installation will be split in three main steps:

- Downloading Azure Stack tools
- Preparation for booting into the `CloudBuilder.vhdx`
- Installation Azure Stack natively within the `CloudBuilder.vhdx`

Downloading Azure Stack tools

Before starting the deployment, we will need to prepare the host. This will be done with the following PowerShell commands. It will download the necessary PowerShell scripts from GitHub:

```
# Variables
$Uri = 'https://raw.githubusercontent.com/Azure/AzureStack-
Tools/master/Deployment/'
$LocalPath = 'c:\AzureStack_SupportFiles'
# Create folder
New-Item $LocalPath -type directory
# Download files
( 'BootMenuNoKVM.ps1', 'PrepareBootFromVHD.ps1', 'Unattend.xml',
 'unattend_NoKVM.xml') | `
foreach { Invoke-WebRequest ($uri + $_) -OutFile ($LocalPath +
'\' + $_) }
```

Preparing the Azure Stack VHDX boot

The next step will be to prepare the `CloudBuilder.vhdx` to boot into it. This will be done as follows:

```
.\PrepareBootFromVHD.ps1 -CloudBuilderDiskPath C:\CloudBuilder.vhdx
-ApplyUnattend
```

Where the parameters have the following meaning:

Parameter	Required/Optional	Description
CloudBuilderDiskPath	Required	The path to the CloudBuilder.vhdx on the PoC host.
DriverPath	Optional	Lets you add additional drivers for the PoC host in the VHD.
ApplyUnattend	Optional	Specify this switch parameter to automate the configuration of the operating system. If specified, the user must provide the AdminPassword to configure the OS at boot (requires provided accompanying file unattend_NoKVM.xml). If you do not use this parameter, the generic unattend.xml file is used without further customization. You'll need KVM access to complete customization after it reboots.
AdminPassword	Optional	Only used when the ApplyUnattend parameter is set, requires a minimum of six characters.
VHDLanguage	Optional	Specifies the VHD language, defaulted to en-US.

Within the next few minutes the VHDX boot of Azure Stack will be prepared and all necessary things will be done to prepare the boot and finally boot into it.

After having successfully booted into the VHDX, the next step is now to prepare the deployment itself, which is the main task of the Azure Stack setup. This is being done with the following PowerShell script: InstallAzureStackPoC.ps1. Depending on which setup you are planning, you will need to use different parameters. And finally, when you are not relying on a DHCP Server available during the deployment, you will need to run the setup with fixed IPs and static configurations for time server and DNS.

The deployment itself is running somewhere between 2½ and 4 hours, depending on the underlying hardware:

- Setup for the Azure AD connected scenario:

    `.\InstallAzureStackPoC.ps1`

- Setup for the disconnected scenario:

    `.\InstallAzureStackPoC.ps1 –UseADFS`

Installing AzureStackPoC.ps1 optional parameters

The PowerShell script has the following parameters:

Parameter	Required/Optional	Description
InfraAzureDirectoryTenantAdminCredential	Optional	Sets the Azure Active Directory username and password. These Azure credentials must be an organizational ID.
InfraAzureDirectoryTenantName	Required	Sets the tenant directory. Use this parameter to specify a specific directory where the AAD account has permissions to manage multiple directories. Full name of an AAD tenant in the format of .onmicrosoft.com.
AdminPassword	Required	Sets the local administrator account and all other user accounts on all the virtual machines created as part of the PoC deployment. This password must match the current local administrator password on the host.
AzureEnvironment	Optional	Select the Azure environment with which you want to register this Azure Stack deployment. Options include public Azure, Azure in China, Azure in US Government.
EnvironmentDNS	Optional	A DNS server is created as part of the Azure Stack deployment. To allow computers inside the solution to resolve names outside of the stamp, provide your existing infrastructure DNS server. The in-stamp DNS server forwards unknown name resolution requests to this server.

NatIPv4Address	Required for DHCP NAT support	Sets a static IP address for the MAS-BGPNAT01 VM. Only use this parameter if the DHCP can't assign a valid IP address to access the internet.
NatIPv4DefaultGateway	Required for DHCP NAT support	Sets the default gateway used with the static IP address for the MAS-BGPNAT01 VM. Only use this parameter if the DHCP can't assign a valid IP address to access the internet.
NatIPv4Subnet	Required for DHCP NAT support	IP subnet prefix used for DHCP over NAT support. Only use this parameter if the DHCP can't assign a valid IP address to access the internet.
PublicVLan	Optional	Sets the VLAN ID. Only use this parameter if the host and the MAS-BGPNAT01 vm must configure VLAN ID to access the physical network (and internet). For example; .\InstallAzureStackPoC.ps1 -Verbose -PublicVLan 305
Rerun	Optional	Use this flag to rerun deployment. All previous input is used. Re-entering data previously provided is not supported because several unique values are generated and used for deployment.
TimeServer	Optional	Use this parameter if you need to specify a specific time server.

It is strongly advised not to use DNS names during the deployment. IP-addresses do not rely on DNS name resolution which may not work properly during some steps of the installation itself.

Basically, the deployment will run and should look similar to the following:

```
Administrator: C:\Windows\System32\WindowsPowerShell\v1.0\powershell.exe

] - 1/14/2017 11:50:52 AM
VERBOSE: Nodes to Configure: WIN-UMROSH26A85 - 1/14/2017 11:50:52 AM

Action 'Deployment'
    0% Running action plan...
    Step 0 - Phase 0 - Configure physical machine and external networking
        0% Deploy and configure physical machines, BGP and NAT
        Task Cloud - Deployment-Phase0-DeployBareMetalAndBGPAndNAT
            Running action
            Action 'Deployment-Phase0-DeployBareMetalAndBGPAndNAT'
                Running action plan...
                [oooooooooooooooooooooooooooooooooooooooooooooooooo       ]
        Step 18 - (STO) Configure Storage Cluster
            Create storage cluster, create a storage pool and file server.
            [                                                              ]
            Task Cloud\Infrastructure\Storage - Deployment
                Running interface

VERBOSE: Performing the operation "Copy File" on target "Item:
C:\Users\AzureStackAdmin\AppData\Local\Temp\ungi5ddg.qjk\StorageEndpoint.pssc Destination:
\\WIN-UMROSH26A85\C$\ProgramData\JEAConfiguration\StorageEndpoint.pssc". - 1/14/2017 11:50:52 AM
VERBOSE: Copying files Done - 1/14/2017 11:50:52 AM
VERBOSE: Configuring JEA endpoint... - 1/14/2017 11:50:52 AM
VERBOSE: Calling Register-PSSessionConfiguration for JEA endpoint StorageEndpoint... - 1/14/2017
11:50:52 AM
VERBOSE: Configuration is done for StorageEndpoint - 1/14/2017 11:52:07 AM
VERBOSE: & : END on WIN-UMROSH26A85 as AZURESTACK\AzureStackAdmin - 1/14/2017 11:52:08 AM
VERBOSE: Interface: Interface Configure completed. - 1/14/2017 11:52:08 AM
COMPLETE: Task Cloud\Fabric\JEA - Configure
VERBOSE: Task: Task completed. - 1/14/2017 11:52:08 AM
COMPLETE: Step 17 - (FBI) Configure PowerShell JEA for Storage.
VERBOSE: Step: Status of step '(FBI) Configure PowerShell JEA for Storage.' is 'Success'. -
1/14/2017 11:52:08 AM
STARTING: Step 18 - (STO) Configure Storage Cluster
VERBOSE: Step: Running step 18 - (STO) Configure Storage Cluster - 1/14/2017 11:52:08 AM
STARTING: Task Cloud\Infrastructure\Storage - Deployment
VERBOSE: Task: Running interface 'Deployment' of role 'Cloud\Infrastructure\Storage'. - 1/14/2017
11:52:08 AM
VERBOSE: Interface: Path to module: C:\CloudDeployment\Roles\Storage\Storage.psm1 - 1/14/2017
11:52:08 AM
VERBOSE: Interface: Running interface Deployment (Roles\Storage\Storage.psm1, DeployStorage) -
1/14/2017 11:52:08 AM
```

 If you are not a PowerShell guy, you will have a GUI version for the pre-deployment called `ADSK-INSTALLER.ps1` that is part of the deployment tools from GitHub.

Deploying the multi-node Azure Stack environment

As already mentioned the multi-node Azure Stack deployment works with the same bits and bytes like the development toolkit does. The huge difference is that with the multi-node environment there is a minimum of four different nodes running Azure Stack and one additional one, the so called **life cycle host**.

The deployment is split into the following phases:

- Collecting deployment details
- Preparing and finalizing the environment

Collecting deployment details

As Azure Stack will not be a piece of hardware, that a customer will install Azure Stack software on, there needs to be a standardized way to collect information that are needed for a deployment. Therefore Microsoft has prepared an MS Excel sheet with your hardware **Original Equipment Manufacturer (OEM)**. This sheet is spread into three sections and looks as follows. The first section is collecting customer environment details:

- The customer environment section:

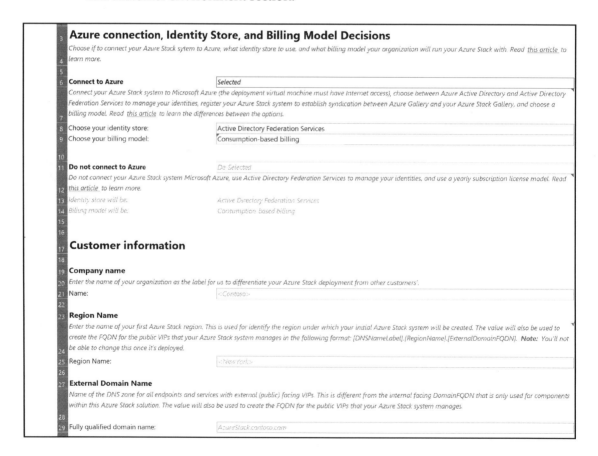

- ## The customer information section:

Private Domain Information	
A dedicated Active Directory Domain Controller will be created for Azure Stack infrastructure management as part of the Azure Stack deployment. Plan and provide the following information to customize how you want the domain to be created.	
Fully qualified domain name:	azurestock: local
Domain admin user name:	<DomainAdmin username for the to-be-created Azure Stack infrastructure AD domain>
Domain admin password:	<No need to enter here, but this will be needed at deployment time. So plan for it beforehand.>

Certificates for external end points

Sets the password for all required certificates to be imported into the Azure Stack solution for the public facing end points. Note:

1) All certificates must be placed into a specific set of folders on the DVM, after it's bootstrapped by running "InitializeAzureStackDeployment.ps1". See previous section for details on what certificate must be placed on which folder.

2) All certificate files must use the same password when they were encrypted (or exported). Using different password for different certificate is not supported.

Password for all certificates:	<No need to enter here, but this will be needed at deployment time. So plan for it beforehand.>

Azure Active Directory Information *(applicable when you select to deploy Azure Stack in a Connected mode)*

The following parameters are required to deploy Azure Stack by using Azure Active Directory (AAD) as your identity store. Infrastructure services and their principal objects will be created in that identity store. You can skip this if you deploy your Azure Stack in a "Disconnected" mode from Azure.

Infrastructure AAD directory tenant name:	<Name of the AAD directory where all app and service principal objects will be created during deployment>
Infrastructure Azure Environment:	<Select the Azure environment of the AAD directory entered above>
Infrastructure AAD tenant admin credential:	<This is the credentials for the directory tenant admin. No need to enter here, but this will be needed at deployment time. So

Naming prefix

During the deployment, a set of names will be automatically generated (the names include management virtual machine names, AD object names, etc.). Please plan to provide an alpha-numeric prefix string up to eight characters long, and it will be prepended to those environment resources for easy identification.

Naming Prefix String:	<default to "MAS">

Environment information

Time Zone

You will be asked to provide the time zone setting for the system that you're deploying. Only one time zone setting is allowed for all the computers in the Azure Stack solution.

Time Zone:	<default to the time zone on the DVM>

- ## The DNS section:

DNS Forwarder	
A DNS server will be created as part of the Azure Stack deployment. To allow computers inside of the solution to resolve names outside, provide your existing infrastructure DNS server that the built-in DNS server should forward all unknown name resolution requests to.	
Upstream DNS Servers	

Time Synchronization (Optional)

You have an option to sync the internal time server (on the AD VM inside of your Azure Stack deployment) to an external time server. Provide the external time server information (hostname or IP address) below. If not provided, by default, we'll set the default public time server to "time.windows.com".

Time Server:	<default to "time.windows.com">

The network settings tab

The next section is collecting all details regarding the network settings:

- The working mechanism of Azure network security:

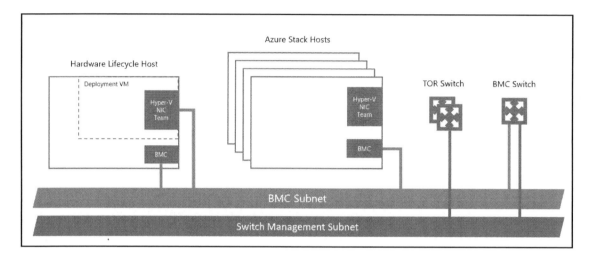

- The deploying and managing networks:

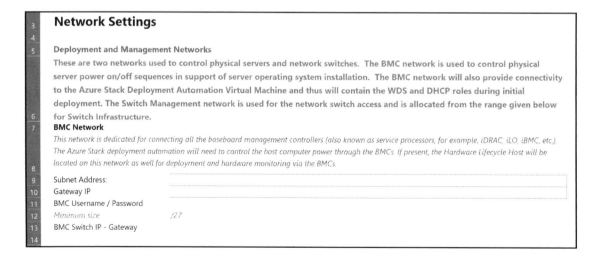

- The infrastructure and storage subnet:

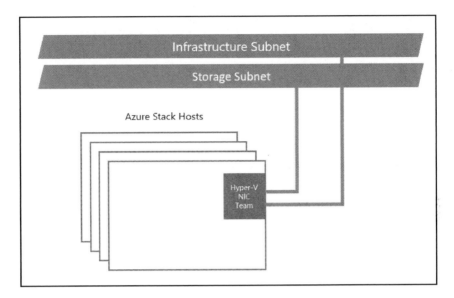

- The storage and infrastructure networks:

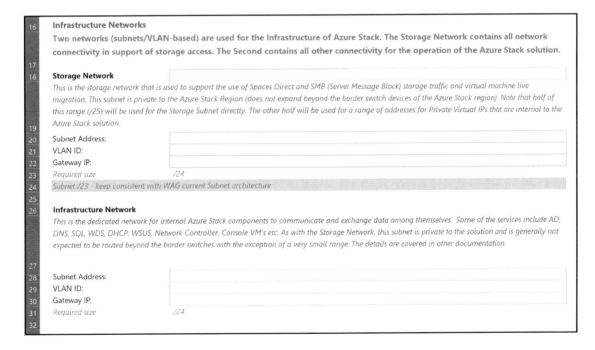

Infrastructure Networks

Two networks (subnets/VLAN-based) are used for the Infrastructure of Azure Stack. The Storage Network contains all network connectivity in support of storage access. The Second contains all other connectivity for the operation of the Azure Stack solution.

Storage Network

This is the storage network that is used to support the use of Spaces Direct and SMB (Server Message Block) storage traffic and virtual machine live migration. This subnet is private to the Azure Stack Region (does not expand beyond the border switch devices of the Azure Stack region). Note that half of this range (/25) will be used for the Storage Subnet directly. The other half will be used for a range of addresses for Private Virtual IPs that are internal to the Azure Stack solution.

Subnet Address:
VLAN ID:
Gateway IP:
Required size   /24

Subnet /23 - keep consistent with WAG current Subnet architecture

Infrastructure Network

This is the dedicated network for internal Azure Stack components to communicate and exchange data among themselves. Some of the services include AD, DNS, SQL, WDS, DHCP, WSUS, Network Controller, Console VM's etc. As with the Storage Network, this subnet is private to the solution and is generally not expected to be routed beyond the border switches with the exception of a very small range. The details are covered in other documentation.

Subnet Address:
VLAN ID:
Gateway IP:
Required size   /24

- ## The infrastructure subnet:

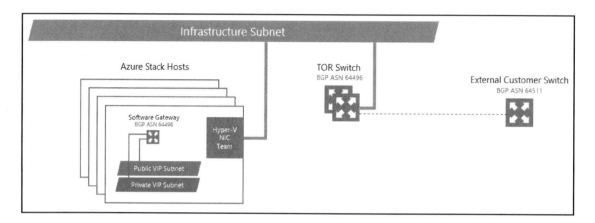

- ## The SDN managed networks:

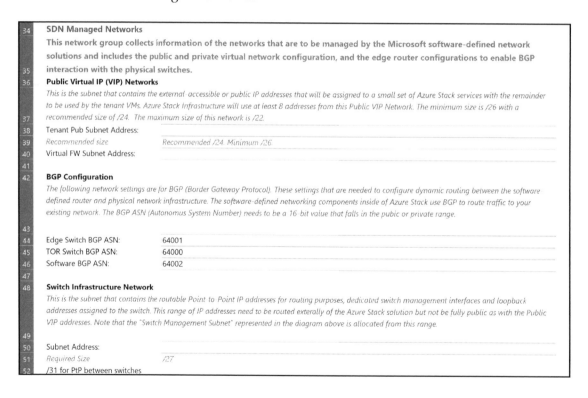

- The optional parameters:

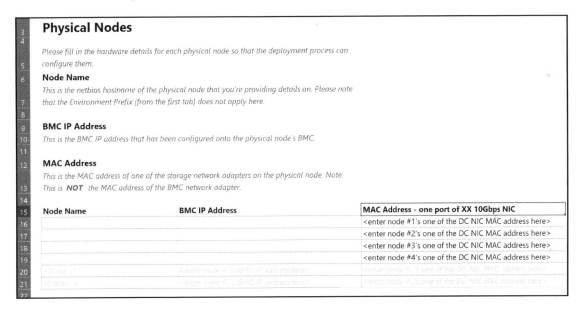

54	**Syslog Server IP Address** *(optional)*
55	*This is the IP address for the syslog server where all switch log files will be configured to send to:*
56	Syslog Server IPv4 Address

The physical nodes tab

Finally, it is here in the **Physical Nodes** tab, that defines the IP addresses, hostnames, and so on. The following screenshot shows how it looks:

Physical Nodes

Please fill in the hardware details for each physical node so that the deployment process can configure them.

Node Name

This is the netbios hostname of the physical node that you're providing details on. Please note that the Environment Prefix (from the first tab) does not apply here.

BMC IP Address

This is the BMC IP address that has been configured onto the physical node's BMC.

MAC Address

*This is the MAC address of one of the storage network adapters on the physical node. Note: This is **NOT** the MAC address of the BMC network adapter.*

Node Name	BMC IP Address	MAC Address - one port of XX 10Gbps NIC
		\<enter node #1's one of the DC NIC MAC address here\>
		\<enter node #2's one of the DC NIC MAC address here\>
		\<enter node #3's one of the DC NIC MAC address here\>
		\<enter node #4's one of the DC NIC MAC address here\>

Preparing and finalizing the environment

Based on all the previous topics discussed, the hardware OEM will start its deployment using the same bits and bytes like the deployment toolkit of Azure Stack. To make sure that no human error occurs while transferring these details to the PowerShell deployment file, it would be best to do some magic PowerShell stuff and link the deployment script directly to the previous details.

The deployment itself is being done from the **Life-Cycle-Host** (**LCH**) and it can be split into the following phases:

- Deploying the switch configuration to the switches
- Preparing the first VMs (domain controller, DNS, and so on) locally on the LCH
- Setting up the underlying **Storage Spaces Direct** (**S2D**) cluster
- Moving the already existing VMs to the cluster
- Deploying the complete set of management VMs (in a minimum of two VMs per management role and a load balancer in front of it)
- Spreading the VMs across the Azure Stack hosts

After having setup the environment, some final configurations (like registering all hosts to the physical host management solution, which depends upon the hardware OEM) are done. That's it.

On comparing the Azure Stack multi-node environment with the development toolkit one host, the following things are different (regarding the environment itself):

- BGPNAT-VM is missing because it is a set of physical switches
- Each VM exists a minimum twice in the environment
- For high availability, a load balancer sits in front of each management solution

Integrating with Microsoft Azure Stack

When you decide to go with Azure Stack, the good question is always how it interacts with or even breaks my existing network infrastructure?

By default, the answer is quite simple: No, it doesn't!

As Azure Stack is an integrated system (some others say, it is an appliance), is comes as an autonomous system with two power plugs and two network plugs. From the sizing size, it is a rack with the servers and the switches inside.

So, what do you need for it from the technical side: space for the rack, redundant power, and redundant networking. The network cables need to be connected to your switch environment. The network connectivity is based on IPv4 as Azure Stack today does not support IPv6. In addition to this, Azure Stack networking technology means running **Border Gateway Protocol** (**BGP**) from the networking side, but as this is only bound internally to the Azure Stack rack, there is no need to have BGP up and running in your own network environment.

Regarding the future development, Azure Stack may be split around more than one rack (today it is 12 servers, by the next calendar year 24 servers are expected to be supported with S2D and therefore with Azure Stack), it is not a real issue as each rack will have its dedicated aggregate switches and communication will just stay internally and not outside the Azure Stack environment.

Regarding directory services connectivity for authentication and authorization, there is no need for it anyway as Azure Stack relies on autonomous directory services (you have the choice between AAD or ADFS) too.

Troubleshooting Azure Stack installations

With this chapter, you will learn how to troubleshoot the installation of Azure Stack. As the multi-node deployment will not be deployed by yourself, this chapter is something for a consultant, who keeps running into issues. If you are running the deployment toolkit release, this is really something you will have to care about.

Technical basis for Azure Stack deployments

The technical basis, on which Azure will rely on, during the installation is as follows:

- The internet connectivity
- Availability of DNS for internet name resolution
- Availability of a reliable time server (if no internal one is available, it will try to connect to `time.windows.com`)
- DHCP services (if this is your deployment option) or availability of static IPs
- Network connectivity during the whole deployment time

As most of the requirements of the deployment will be available in 99% of each company, the issues mostly will be part of different topics.

Technical issues and their solution

Basically, Azure Stack writes a detailed log file during the installation and when going through it, you will easily see where the error occurred. This log file is located on the deployment host in the following folder: `C:\CloudDeployment\Logs`.

You will find the following log files in it for each installation named `summary.<date>-<serial no>`. This file will somewhat look like this:

As you can see the file is in XML and is quite easy to read. If there is any error, you should find the corresponding error in there too. This may look somewhat like this:

```
Deployment.2017-05-22.08-08-48.0 - Editor                                              –  ☐  ✕
Datei Bearbeiten Format Ansicht ?
-------        ---------
       --------
Restart-Machine {ComputerName=MAS-BGPNAT01, Credential=System.Management.Automation.PSCredential}
         Helper...
Install-BGPNAT  {Parameters=CloudEngine.Configurations.EceInterfaceParameters, ErrorAction=Stop,
Verbose=True} SetupB...
                {}
         BGP.ps...
<ScriptBlock>   {C:\CloudDeployment\CloudDeployment.psd1,
CloudEngine.Configurations.EceInterfaceParameters}   <No file>


at Trace-Error, C:\CloudDeployment\Common\Tracer.psm1: line 44
at Restart-Machine, C:\CloudDeployment\Common\Helpers.psm1: line 799
at Install-BGPNAT, C:\CloudDeployment\Roles\BGP\SetupBGP.psm1: line 122
at Deployment, C:\CloudDeployment\Classes\BGP\BGP.psm1: line 19
at <ScriptBlock>, <No file>: line 9
2017-05-22 08:58:15 Verbose   Step: Status of step '0.25 - (NET) Setup BGP and NAT' is 'Error'.
2017-05-22 08:58:15 Error     Action: Invocation of step 0.25 failed. Stopping invocation of action
plan.
2017-05-22 08:58:15 Verbose   Action: Status of 'Deployment-Phase0-DeployBareMetalAndBGPAndNAT' is
'Error'.
2017-05-22 08:58:15 Verbose   Task: Status of action 'Deployment-Phase0-DeployBareMetalAndBGPAndNAT'
of role 'Cloud' is 'Error'.
2017-05-22 08:58:15 Verbose   Step: Status of step '0 - Phase 0 - Configure physical machine and
external networking' is 'Error'.
2017-05-22 08:58:15 Error     Action: Invocation of step 0 failed. Stopping invocation of action plan.
```

As you can see, there is an error message in one of the last lines stating that the '0.25 - (NET) Setup BGP and NAT' is 'Error'.

In most of the cases it helps to restart the deployment using the following syntax:

```
.\installazurestackPoC.ps1 -rerun
```

This command is looking for the first error message during the deployment and which deployment step it is in. Then, it will restart the deployment starting from this step again. From the experiences in the field, there is a good chance to be successful after one or even two to three reruns. It just may be that some installation steps are not fully in synch and as the management VMs rely on each other, some minutes of waiting time may help.

If everything works fine, the final log lines in this file should somewhat look like this:

```
summary.2017-05-31.09-49-11.0.log - Notepad
File Edit Format View Help
        <Action Type="Deployment-Phase2-DeployConsoleVMs" Scope="Internal" EceErrorAction="Stop" StartTimeUtc="2017-05-31T14:56:35.2645
          <Steps>
            <Step FullStepIndex="60.221" Index="221" Name="(FBI) Setup Console VMs" Description="Installs Console server on the guest V
              <Task RolePath="Cloud\Fabric\Console" InterfaceType="Deployment" StartTimeUtc="2017-05-31T14:56:35.2958103Z" Status="Succe
            </Step>
            <Step FullStepIndex="60.222" Index="222" Name="(FBI) Setup Console VMs" Description="Move DVM Contents to the Console VM." S
              <Task RolePath="Cloud\Fabric\Console" InterfaceType="Configure" StartTimeUtc="2017-05-31T15:00:55.3869099Z" Status="Succes
            </Step>
          </Steps>
        </Action>
      </Task>
    </Step>
    <Step FullStepIndex="230" Index="230" Name="(NET) Enable SLB probes for all VIPs." Description="Enable SLB probes for all VIPs" Star
      <Task RolePath="Cloud\Fabric\SlbVips" InterfaceType="Configure" StartTimeUtc="2017-05-31T16:22:46.1150978Z" Status="Success" Retry
    </Step>
    <Step FullStepIndex="231" Index="231" Name="(NET) Validate all VIPs." Description="Validate all VIPs" StartTimeUtc="2017-05-31T16:27
      <Task RolePath="Cloud\Fabric\SlbVips" InterfaceType="Validate" StartTimeUtc="2017-05-31T16:27:22.1473447Z" Status="Success" RetryA
    </Step>
    <Step FullStepIndex="232" Index="232" Name="(NET) Validate NC and SLB." Description="Validate NC and SLB" StartTimeUtc="2017-05-31T1
      <Task RolePath="Cloud\Fabric\NC" InterfaceType="Validate" StartTimeUtc="2017-05-31T16:37:51.437121Z" Status="Success" RetryAttempt
    </Step>
    <Step FullStepIndex="240" Index="240" Name="PHASE.3 -(FBI) Migrate Configuration to ECE Service on FabricRing" Description="Migrate
      <Task RolePath="Cloud\Fabric\FabricRingServices\ECEFabricRing" InterfaceType="Migrate" StartTimeUtc="2017-05-31T16:47:20.5016426Z"
    </Step>
    <Step FullStepIndex="241" Index="241" Name="PHASE.3.1 -(FBI) Migrate Configuration to ECE Service on SeedRing" Description="Migrate
      <Task RolePath="Cloud\Fabric\SeedRingServices\ECE" InterfaceType="Migrate" StartTimeUtc="2017-05-31T16:48:06.3180792Z" Status="Suc
    </Step>
    <!-- TODO: Bug 9117469 Enable this back once Credssp issue is fixed across the roles. Keeping it enabled now to support post Deploym
         <Step Index="250" Name="Phase 3 - Cleanup settings used at deployment time" Description="Cleanup deployment-only settings">
           <Task RolePath="Cloud" InterfaceType="Configure" />
         </Step>
         -->
    <Step FullStepIndex="251" Index="251" Name="Prepare for future host reboots" Description="Set reboot policy" StartTimeUtc="2017-05-3
      <Task RolePath="Cloud\Infrastructure\POC" InterfaceType="Startup" StartTimeUtc="2017-05-31T16:48:52.180671Z" Status="Success" Retr
    </Step>
  </Steps>
</Action>
```

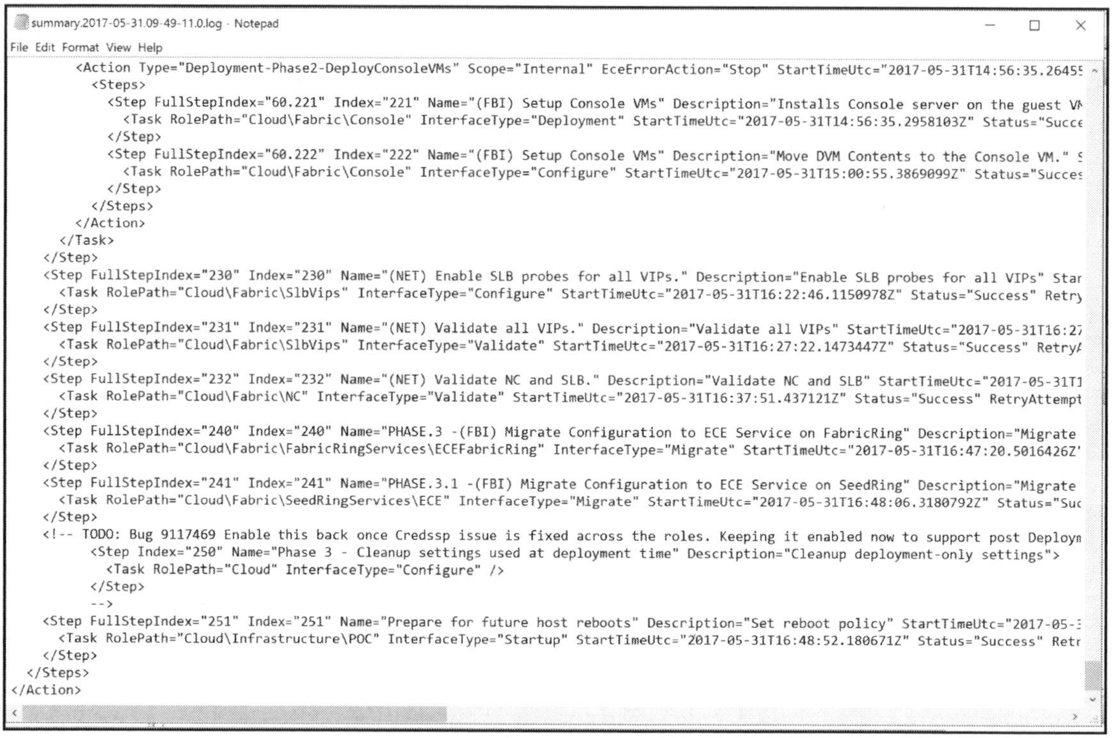

If your deployment does not work properly, or the rerun parameter fails again and again, you may need to restart completely from scratch. This means you will have to reboot the system and boot into the Hyper-V basis installation, delete the `CloudBuilder.vhdx` and copy a new one in its place. Then start the deployment. In addition to the log files examining the event logs from the Windows Event Viewer of each VM could help too.

Monitoring Azure Stack installations

Business continuity is an important thing when you are relying on Azure Stack as the main environment in your company. This means it is somehow the heart of your IT. The basis for business continuity is monitoring the management:

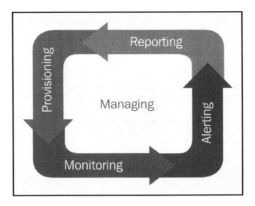

As most of you already have a monitoring tool in place, the good question is does it work to monitor my Azure Stack with it too?

The answer is if your solution does not require to install an agent on each virtual machine that needs to be monitored, you are mainly fine with it. If it would rely on a dedicated agent, the answer basically is NO. This is because you are unable to install anything on the management VMs on Azure Stack. With your customer VMs everything is fine anyway.

If your favorite monitoring solution is one of the following, you are fine anyway as they provide official support by now to monitor Azure Stack integrated systems.

Nagios plugin for Azure Stack alerts

The plugin is available for free and can be accessed here, `https://exchange.nagios.org/ directory/Plugins/Cloud/Monitoring-AzureStack-Alerts/details`.

It simply transfers all alerts from Azure Stack via API to Nagios.

System Center Operations Manager management pack

System Center Operations Manager (SCOM), is a part from System Center **Operations Management Suite (OMS)**, and works with so called **management packs**, that are more or less an XML file with all monitoring details regarding the specific product.

It can be downloaded from, `https://azure.microsoft.com/en-us/blog/management-pack-for-microsoft-azure-stack-now-available/`.

The prerequisites for the installation are:

- System Center Operations Manager 2012 R2 or 2016
- .NET Framework 4.5 installed on all SCOM management servers

You just need to import them to your SCOM management group and connect it to the Azure Stack, there is no auto discovery available. To enable monitoring, you will need to add the Azure Stack deployment to your SCOM environment. This is a *1:n* connectivity which means that one SCOM management group can monitor multiple Azure Stack environments:

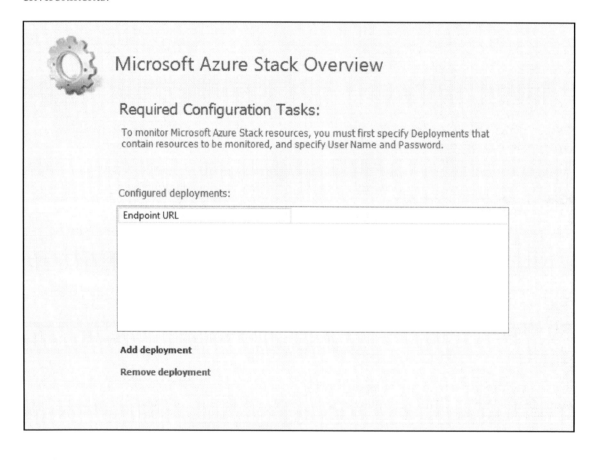

The connection is being done with a read-only administrative account in Azure Stack and registering the resource manager API **Endpoint URL**. The **Health Dashboard** allows you to view and drill into the health of multiple deployments of the Azure Stack. To successfully connect to the Azure Stack, you will need an administrative account of the appropriate Azure Stack environment:

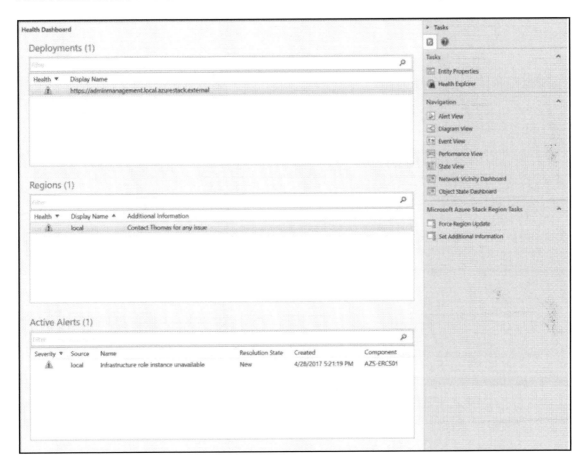

The management pack introduces a comprehensive set of views. You can find them in the `Microsoft Azure Stack` folder:

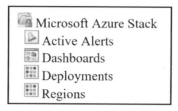

In general, you will recognize that the Azure Stack management pack and the Azure one are quite similar as the technology source for both is quite comparable (it's the cloud inspired infrastructure).

Hybrid management with Operations Management Suite

If a company is already running cloud services in Azure and it is not just only IaaS there may be a chance that OMS is already deployed, because as of today monitoring virtual machines using a monitoring tool of your choice may be possible. But when it comes to PaaS, the good question is always, how could these services be monitored as the installation of monitoring agents is impossible so does OMS.

The core functionality of OMS is provided by a set of services that run in Azure. Each service provides a specific management function, and you can combine services to achieve different management scenarios.

The OMS Suite contains the following services:

- **Log analytics**: Monitor and analyze availability and performance of resources including physical and virtual machines
- **Automation**: Automate processes and enforce configurations for physical and virtual machines
- **Backup**: Backup and restore important data
- **Site recovery**: Provide high availability for critical applications

In regards to Azure Stack, the first two features are the most important ones. For Azure Automation, there is a specific chapter in this book later on. Log analytics is the underlying basis for OMS. It collects all defined log files of a server system and provides a relationship between those details. Coming back to Azure Stack, if your Azure environment is already being monitored with OMS, why shouldn't this be possible with Azure Stack. If the goal is to monitor Azure Stack agentless. This is because there is no chance with Azure Stack to install agents on the underlying management virtual machine environment.

The solution for this could then be setting up a hybrid monitoring solution as SCOM has its management pack for Azure Stack already. There is no need to somehow join the Azure Stack domain, as it is just networking connectivity. SCOM on premise should then be connected with SCOM hybrid mode to OMS. This results in having all the Azure Stack data available within the OMS using a hybrid setup with SCOM connected to OMS.

Connecting Microsoft Azure Stack

After having deployed Azure Stack to the existing IT infrastructure, there are two more very basic things that need to be accomplished. These are:

- Enabling the Azure Marketplace syndication
- Defining Azure role based access

Enabling the Azure Marketplace syndication

Once the Azure Stack is in place, the question is always, which OS images need to be uploaded and enabled. As creating an image and later sustaining it takes a lot of time, the good practice is to rely on already existing images from Azure as they are updated from Microsoft and there is no need for further patching tasks. When discussing with customers they often state that this Microsoft image is not their CI based image. As Azure Stack provides the ability for **Desired State Configuration (DSC)** with PowerShell, that's the way to accomplish this.

The feature to enable Azure image download to Azure Stack is called **Marketplace Syndication**. This works and is supported with both scenarios for Azure Stack (connected and disconnected scenario). The requirements are:

- Own an active Azure subscription
- Have access to the internet with your Azure Stack management environment

 Remember that downloading bits from Azure will costs some money (the first 5 GBs are free of costs, each additional GB is € 0.07 max, depending on the subscription type.

To enable the syndication the following steps need to be done from one of the Azure Stack hosts:

1. Install Azure Stack PowerShell tools on your host.
2. Download and run the script from GitHub: `https://github.com/Azure/AzureStack-Tools/blob/master/Registra tion/RegisterWithAzure.ps1` with the following syntax:

```
RegisterWithAzure.ps1 -azureDirectory YourDirectory
-azureSubscriptionId YourGUID -azureSubscriptionOwner YourAccountName
```

3. Wait for the script to finish:

```
VERBOSE: Creating remote powershell session on MAS-WAS01 - 3/5/2017 11:47:02 PM
VERBOSE: Initializing remote powershell session on MAS-WAS01 with common functions. - 3/5/2017 11:47:02 PM
VERBOSE: Loading infra vm helpers (C:\CloudDeployment\Common\InfraVmHelpers.ps1) to session on MAS-WAS01 - 3/5/2017 11:47:02 PM
VERBOSE: Invoking command on remote session... - 3/5/2017 11:47:02 PM
VERBOSE: Removing remote powershell session on MAS-WAS01. - 3/5/2017 11:47:03 PM
VERBOSE: Interface: Interface Configure completed. - 3/5/2017 11:47:03 PM
COMPLETE: Task Cloud\Fabric\FabricRingServices\UsageBridge - Configure
VERBOSE: Task: Task completed. - 3/5/2017 11:47:03 PM
COMPLETE: Step 1 - Configure Usage Bridge
VERBOSE: Step: Status of step '1 - Configure Usage Bridge' is 'Success'. - 3/5/2017 11:47:03 PM
VERBOSE: Action: Action plan 'ConfigureUsageBridge' completed. - 3/5/2017 11:47:03 PM
COMPLETE: Action 'ConfigureUsageBridge'
VERBOSE: Activate-Bridge.ps1 : END on WIN-C5IKG4G47KQ as AZURESTACK\AzureStackAdmin
STEP 4: Activate Azure Stack completed
Registration complete. You may now access Marketplace Management in the Admin UI
```

4. On the Azure Stack admin portal go to **Marketplace Management**:

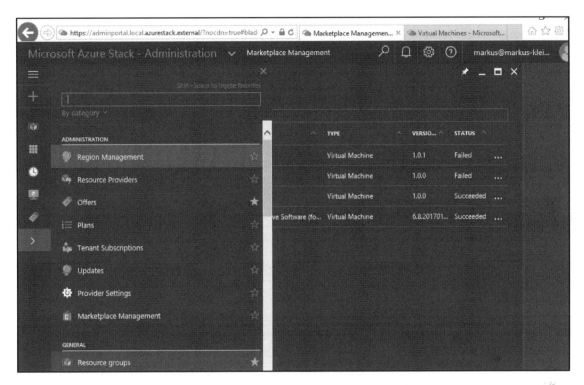

5. Select the appropriate images and wait for the download. This provides an easy way for **Marketplace Management**. If errors will occur while the syndication is being configured, there is a log file available in the Cloud Deployment Log folder too:

ActivateAzureBridge.2017-05-31.11-47-58.0	5/31/2017 11:48 AM	Text Document	4 KB
ConfigureBridgeIdentity.2017-05-31.11-45-28.0	5/31/2017 11:46 AM	Text Document	17 KB
ConfigureUsageBridge.2017-05-31.11-48-37.0	5/31/2017 11:49 AM	Text Document	4 KB
Deployment.2017-05-31.05-01-23.0	5/31/2017 5:30 AM	Text Document	563 KB
Deployment.2017-05-31.05-33-58.0	5/31/2017 9:49 AM	Text Document	6,115 KB
NewRegistrationRequest.2017-05-31.11-46-06.0	5/31/2017 11:46 AM	Text Document	3 KB

Each of these log files provide detailed information on each configuration steps. The enablement process consists of five parts:

- `NewRegistrationRequest`
- `ConfigureBridgeIdentity`
- `ActivateAzureBridge`
- `ConfigureUsageBridge` (if enabled it will bill Azure with your existing Azure subscription which is *pay as you go*)

After the syndication has been enabled all images tagged with Azure Stack by Microsoft will be available in the list. As Marketplace items are always updated, and it is an ongoing process it is a valid step to update the items on a regular basis.

Defining Azure Stack role based access

Azure Stack RBAC is a built-in Azure Stack permission service which enables fine-grained access management for Azure Stack resources. The following basic built-in roles are available with Azure Stack:

- **Owner**: Has full access to all resources including the right to delegate access to others
- **Contributor**: Can create and manage all types of Azure Stack resources but cannot grant access to others
- **Reader**: Can view existing Azure Stack resources

RBAC is used to grant specific access to resources and configurations if needed, for example, network settings, without access to other resource settings. It is possible to grant custom permissions and access to specific operations to persons and departments in charge.

Custom RBAC-roles can be set on subscription, resource group, and resource level, the role will be inherited to the child resources. Azure Stack RBAC-roles can be managed by Azure Stack ARM portal, PowerShell (the Azure Stack PowerShell cmdlets are needed) and Azure Stack management APIs.

RBAC-role management

Within Azure RBAC-role there are `Actions` and `NotActions` defined in JSON file, these properties exactly set the required permissions.

The action property specifies the allowed actions (access) on Azure resources. Whereas, the NotActions property specifies the actions (deny) that are excluded from the allowed actions. However, by defining actions, access to Azure resources is automatically allowed. The permissions are inherited to all child resources.

Build RBAC-role

The following example shows the structure of a RBAC-role based on JSON-file, the file lists: Name, Description, Actions, NotActions, and AssignableScopes (can be set to complete subscription, resource group, or specific resource). Actions and NotActions list the exact Microsoft resources with the resource provider name, where access should be allowed or denied (for example, the resource provider to write Azure virtual network resources is disabled by set Microsoft.Network/virtualNetworks/write in not-actions).

Wildcards are supported, all child settings will be selected. Example for Actions and NotActions:

```
"Actions": [
    "/*/write/",
    "/*/read/",
    ],
  "NotActions": [
    "Microsoft.Network/virtualNetworks/write",
    ],
```

Template for role is as follows:

```
{
  "Name": "<VF>-<Permission Type>",
  "IsCustom": true,
  "Description": "<Description>",
  "Actions": [
        "*",
    ],
  "NotActions": [
        "*",
    ],
  "AssignableScopes": [
      "/subscriptions/<Subscription ID>/resourceGroups/<name of RG>"
      ]
}
```

Manage RBAC by PowerShell

The JSON-file can be uploaded by PowerShell and create a new role (subscription owner is needed to upload custom RBAC-roles to Azure Stack ARM portal):

```
New-AzureRMRoleDefinition -inputfile <filepath>
```

- If role information is required, there also is a PowerShell cmdlet:

```
Get-AzureRmRoledefinition -name <Name given in JSON-file>
```

- The role permissions can be updated by refreshing the JSON-file (add the ID from `Get-AzureRmRoledefinition` to JSON file) and by adding/removing more `Actions`/`NotActions` by use of a PowerShell cmdlet:

```
Set-AzureRMRoleDefinition -inputfile <filepath>
```

- To delete RBAC-roles, the role must not have members and can be deleted by PowerShell:

```
Get-AzureRmRoledefinition -name <Name given in JSON-File>
| Remove-AzureRMRoleDefinition
```

- To add users or groups to the new RBAC-role:

```
New-AzureRmRoleAssignment
-UserPrincipalName <Username@doamin.tld>
-RoleDefinitionName <RBAC-roleName>
```

- Users and groups who are assigned to the RBAC-role can be listed:

```
Get-AzureRmRoleAssignment -ResourceGroupName <RG Name>
-RoleDefinitionName <RBAC-roleName>
```

Manage RBAC by Azure ARM portal

It is also possible to add users and groups to RBAC-role by Azure Stack ARM portal:

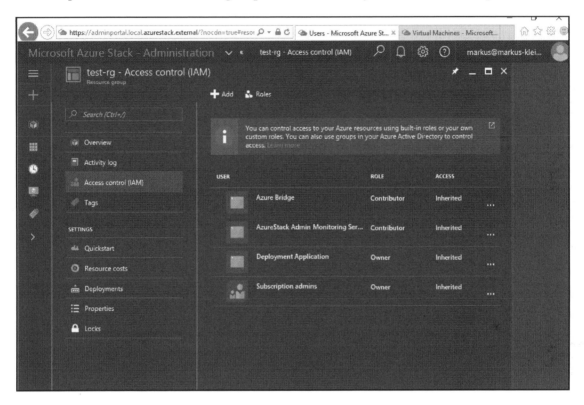

As there is an existing RBAC policy for Azure, it may fit into Azure Stack too, as Azure Stack follows the Azure design *1:1*.

Fine-grained permissions

Consider for example, two new custom RBAC-roles are needed to solve a customer's Azure authorization requirements. The network-join role is introduced to protect the core networks by disabling many resource provider permissions to deploy services and change settings, only network-join permissions are enabled. The contributor behaves like the built-in contributor, but network deployments and configurations are disabled and the existing network resources should be used.

Network-join

The network-join role permissions to deploy and configure services are disabled, it is possible to join existing networks for usage.

Following fine-grained permissions are used to protect the core network resources:

```
"Actions": [
    "/*/write/",
    "/*/read/",
    "Microsoft.Resources/deployments/*",
    "Microsoft.Resources/deployments/validate/action",
    "Microsoft.Network/routeTables/*/action",
    "Microsoft.Network/routeTables/*/write",
    "Microsoft.Network/virtualNetworks/virtualNetworkPeerings/write",
    "Microsoft.Network/virtualNetworks/peer/action",
    "Microsoft.Network/virtualNetworks/subnets/write",
    "Microsoft.network/virtualNetworks/subnets/join/action",
    ],
  "NotActions": [
    "Microsoft.Network/virtualNetworks/write",
    "Microsoft.Network/*/delete",
    "Microsoft.Network/publicIPAddresses/*/write",
    "Microsoft.Network/networkInterfaces/write",
    "Microsoft.Network/networkInterfaces/delete",
    "Microsoft.Network/networkSecurityGroups/securityRules/delete",
    "Microsoft.Network/networkSecurityGroups/securityRules/write",
    "Microsoft.Network/virtualNetworks/delete",
    "Microsoft.Network/virtualNetworks/virtualNetworkPeerings/delete",
    "Microsoft.Network/routeTables/delete",
    "Microsoft.Authorization/policyDefinitions/*/write",
    "Microsoft.Authorization/policyDefinitions/*/delete",
    "Microsoft.Authorization/policyAssignments/*/write",
    "Microsoft.Authorization/policyAssignments/*/delete",
    "Microsoft.Authorization/roleAssignments/*/write",
    "Microsoft.Authorization/roleAssignments/*/delete",
    "Microsoft.Authorization/roleDefinitions/*/write",
    "Microsoft.Authorization/roleDefinitions/*/delete",
    "Microsoft.Authorization/policyDefinitions/*/delete",
    "Microsoft.NotificationHubs/Namespaces/*/write",
    "Microsoft.NotificationHubs/Namespaces/*/delete",
    "Microsoft.EventHub/Namespaces/eventhubs/*/delete",
    "Microsoft.Authorization/locks/*/write",
    "Microsoft.Authorization/locks/*/delete",
    "Microsoft.Compute/*/write",
    "Microsoft.Compute/*/delete",
    "Microsoft.KeyVault/*/write",
    "Microsoft.KeyVault/*/delete",
```

```
"Microsoft.AppService/*/write",
"Microsoft.Storage/*/write",
"Microsoft.Storage/*/delete",
],
```

Custom-contributor

The following permissions are part of the custom role custom-contributor. The role behaves like the Azure Stack built-in contributor role. Within the custom-contributor role network deployments and configurations are disabled. In case of deploying new Azure Stack resources and services, users have to use the existing core network resources:

```
"Actions": [
    "*",
],
"NotActions": [
    "Microsoft.ClassicNetwork/*/write",
    "Microsoft.ClassicNetwork/*/delete",
    "Microsoft.Network/publicIPAddresses/*/write",
    "Microsoft.Network/virtualNetworks/delete",
    "Microsoft.Network/virtualNetworks/write",
    "Microsoft.Network/virtualNetworks/peer/action",
    "Microsoft.Network/virtualNetworks/virtualNetworkPeerings/write",
"Microsoft.Network/virtualNetworks/virtualNetworkPeerings/delete",
    "Microsoft.Authorization/*/Delete",
    "Microsoft.Authorization/*/Write",
    "Microsoft.Authorization/elevateAccess/Action",
],
```

Azure Stack RBAC as good practice provides a role based security concept when providing fine-grained permissions. As with Azure Stack this is a must, setting these roles up by default and before the Azure Stack can go live. If not done so, the worst case would be that at first everybody would have all permissions and later on it it would need to be cut down.

Summary

To summarize this chapter, there was a deep dive into the deployment steps for Azure stack while discussing all basics for the one host deployment toolkit release and the multi-node deployment. The life cycle host server which is responsible for the deployment process and later runs the hardware management solution provided from the hardware OEM. Regarding errors during the deployment, it is good to know the corresponding log files and finally rerun the deployment to solve any issues.

After the deployment is finished, there is the need to provide physical connectivity (in regards of power, cooling, and networking, each of them in a redundant way). And two major steps before starting with the first workloads are mainly important: Marketplace syndication for bringing Azure images down to Azure Stack, and implementing Azure Stack role based access control for preparing to set up the corresponding roles within a company and transfer them to Azure Stack.

In the next chapter you will learn how to provision virtual machine clouds, also called as **Infrastructure as a Service (IaaS)**.

4
Understanding Storage and Network

If we look at Azure Stack and compare it to Azure, the huge difference is that Azure Stack is based on containers with hundreds and thousands of servers running a kind of Windows Server with some kind of Hyper-V, specially designed for Azure data centers. As Azure Stack works starting with four servers and as first step moves to 12 servers, there needs to be a kind of difference in the underlying technology. Microsoft always talks of a cloud inspired infrastructure with Azure Stack. This means the technology is somehow similar to Azure, but it is only similar and not the same.

In this chapter, we will talk about the technical basis of Azure Stack as it makes it easier for you to troubleshoot an environment that you understand from the technical perspective. Azure Stack is running based on Windows Server 2016 and the Hyper-V technology.

The most important technologies we will look at are as follows:

- Windows Server 2016 Storage Spaces Direct
- Windows Server 2016 Software Defined Networks

The reason for this is simple: starting at the upper level going down, we have Azure Stack Services that rely on Azure Stack **Resource Providers (RPs)**, managed by **Azure Resource Manager (ARM)**. In general, this is the same as with Azure. Going down from ARM is when the difference begins. With Azure Stack Deployment Toolkit, we have a single server Storage Space cluster with Hyper-V VMs for the Azure Stack management services on top. If we take a look at the multi-node deployments, we will see four to 12 servers running in a single Window Server 2016 clustered environment with at least two management VMs per service with a software load balancer that is experienced by Azure public sitting in front of it. Now let's look at how it goes by taking a deep dive into it.

Windows Server 2016 Storage Spaces Direct

Azure Stack does not work with existing storage systems (based on iSCSI, fibre channel, or anything else). As of today, storage is cheap and there is no real need any more for expensive **Storage Area Networks (SAN)**.

This is the main statement that was the basis for developing Windows Server 2012 Storage Spaces and scaling out file server technology. But as you all may know, this technology is great, but in the first releases, it was not as reliable and performant as everybody promised. With Windows Server 2016, this changed completely as Microsoft decided to go with a different technology design: each Storage Spaces Direct member will have its own direct attached storage and S2D technology makes sure that the data is saved in a highly available multi-node environment. This provides a chance to fulfill the following statements:

- It is simple to configure
- It provides great performance with up to 4k random IOPS per server
- It provides fault tolerance with built-in resiliency
- It has to be resource-efficient based on **Resilient File System (ReFS)** and needs minimum CPU performance
- It has to be easy to manage with built-in monitoring and APIs
- It needs to be scalable as it works (today) with up to 16 servers and 400 drives

In general, S2D has two deployment designs:

- Converged: The storage and compute in different cluster environments
- Hyper-converged: The storage and compute in one single cluster

Azure Stack is designed based on a hyper-converged environment, which can be described as follows:

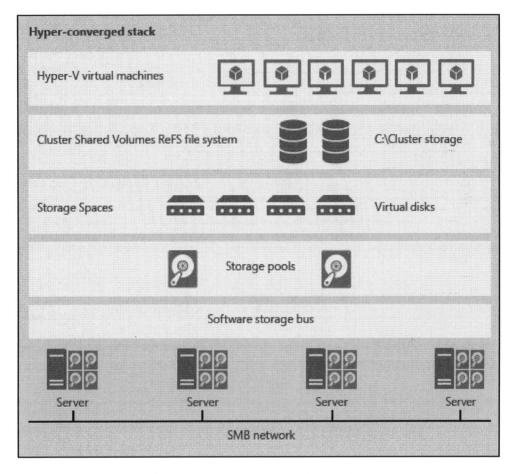

Source: https://docs.microsoft.com/en-us/windows-server/storage/storage-spaces/media/storage-spaces-direct-in-windows-server-2016/converged-full-stack.png

This works based on the following design aspects:

- The networking technology is based on SMB3, including SMB direct and SMB multichannel. This all works over the Ethernet networking technology based on RDMA (iWARP and RoCE).
- Each server has local attached storage based on NVMe, SAS, or SATA drives with at least two SSDs and four additional ones. SATA and SAS need to work behind a SAS expander or a **host bus adapter (HBA)**.
- All servers are connected to one failover cluster.
- The storage service bus creates a software-defined storage fabric.
- The storage bus layer cache makes sure that the best available server-side read/write caching is always available.
- The storage pool is automatically created by discovering all drives and adding them to the pool.
- Storage Spaces are responsible for fault tolerance using mirroring and/or erasure coding. It generally provides three-way mirroring, which means two storage copies and fail, but the data is still available.
- **ReFS** (know as **Resilient File System**) is designed for virtualization, which provides automatic correction of filesystem issues.
- **CSV** (known as **Cluster Shared Volumes**) are the namespaces provided to the servers that look like local storage.
- Finally, the **Scale-Out-File Server** provides file access remotely using the SMB3 technology over the network.

In the following overview, you can see how these components interact with each other and what a **Hyper-converged storage stack** could look like:

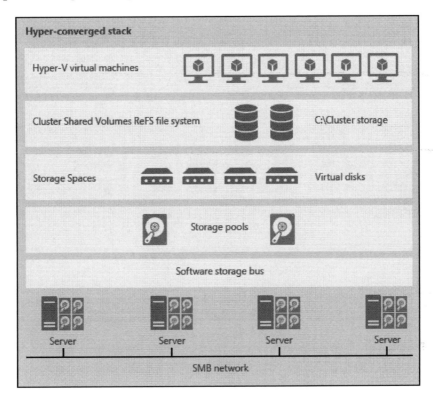

Source:
https://docs.microsoft.com/en-us/windows-server/storage/storage-spaces/media/hyper-converged-solution-using-storage-spaces-direct-in-windows-server-2016/storagespacesdirect
hyperconverged.png

 If you want to play with Windows Server 2016 Storage Space independently from Azure Stack, you will need to meet the hardware requirements described here: `https://docs.microsoft.com/en-us/` `windows-server/storage/storage-spaces/storage-spaces-direct-` `hardware-requirements.`

A generic design for Storage Spaces is a **Three-Way Mirror**, which means that all data is being saved on three different services, which provides a high level of resiliency:

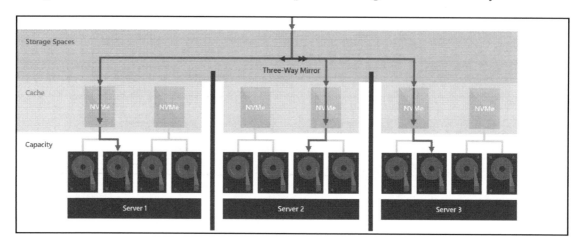

Source: https://docs.microsoft.com/en-us/windows-server/storage/storage-spaces/media/understand-the-cache/cache-server-side-architecture.png

Storage design from hardware OEMs

This is the technology design of an Azure Stack based technology. If we look at the different Azure Stack hardware designs, it looks like this for the first three hardware vendors:

- DELL EMC
- HPE
- Lenovo

DELL EMC

Dell EMC hat prepared the following sizing options for Azure Stack:

Configurations	Low Capacity	Mid Capacity	High Capacity
Processor	Model 6126 - 12 core 2.6 Ghz	Model 6130- 16 core 2.1Ghz	Model 8168 - 24 core 2.7Ghz
Memory	384 GB	576GB	768B
Cache	6 x 960/800GB SSD = ~5.7TB SAS	6x.1.6/1.92TB SSD = ~11.5TB SAS	6x1.6/1.92TB SSD= ~11.5TB SAS
Storage (HDD)	10 x 4TB = 40TB	10x8TB=80TB	10X10TB=100TB
TORs	2x Dell Networking S4048 10GbE/1x Dell Networking S3048 1GbE		
Network Adapter	Mellanox Connectx-4 Dual Port Low Profile		
Border Switch	NA		
Management Node	Dell PE R430 (16C, 64GB Mem, OS+ Data 2 x 800/960GB 2.5" MU SSD)		

Source:
https://azurestackeaiblob.blob.core.windows.net/content-file/Dell%20EMC%20data%20sheet%20-%20Dell%20EMC%20cloud%20for%20Microsoft%20Azure%20Stack.pdf?sv
=2015-12-11&sr=b&sig=ww2ResQsXIXpQXzFI2xnwuhNlFLkhrf7nLX0EVsUZ24%3D&st=2017-08-17T20%3A48%3A45Z&se=2017-08-18T20%3A53%3A45Z&sp=r

HPE

For HPE the options vary most, so there is quite a bunch of configuration possibilities available, as you can see in the following table:

Technical specifications

Microsoft Azure Stack	Hybrid Cloud platform software for Azure consistent, software-defined Infrastructure-as-a-Service (IaaS) and Platform-as-a-Service (PaaS)
Compute nodes	(4) HPE DL380 Gen9 12LFF CTO Servers each with: • (2) HPE DL380 Gen9 E5-26xxv4 processors • (8, 12, 16, or 24) HPE 32 GB 2Rx4 PC4-2400T-R • (4) HPE 1.2 TB 6G SATA WI-2 LFF SCC SSD • (10) HPE 6 TB 6G SATA 7.2K 3.5in 512e SC HDD • (1) HPE Ethernet 10 Gb 2P 546FLR-SFP+ Adapter • (1) HPE H240ar Smart HBA • (1) HPE H240 Smart HBA • (1) HPE TPM Module 2.0 Kit • (1) HPE OneView w/iLO Advanced	Servers can be configured with a matching pair of: • HPE DL380 Gen9 E5-2699v4 GHz 2.2 (22 cores) • HPE DL380 Gen9 E5-2698v4 GHz 2.2 (20 cores) • HPE DL380 Gen9 E5-2695v4 GHz 2.1 x (18 cores) • HPE DL380 Gen9 E5-2683v4 GHz 2.1 x (16 cores) • HPE DL380 Gen9 E5-2660v4 GHz 2.0 (14 cores) • HPE DL380 Gen9 E5-2650v4 GHz 2.2 (12 cores) Memory choices are 256 GB, 384 GB, 512 GB, 640 GB and 768 GB
Hardware lifecycle host	(1) HPE DL360 Gen9 8SFF CTO Server (2) HPE DL360 Gen9 E5-2620v4 Kit (4) HPE 16 GB 2Rx4 PC4-2400T-R Kit (4) HPE 600 GB 12G SAS 10K 2.5in SC ENT HDD	(1) HPE Ethernet 10 Gb 2P 546FLR-SFP+ Adapter (1) HPE TPM Module 2.0 Kit (1) HPE OneView w/iLO Advanced (1) Microsoft Windows Server® 2016
Switches	(2) HPE 5900AF 48XG 4QSFP+ Switch (Workload) (1) HPE 5900AF 48G 4XG 2QSFP+ Switch (Management)	
Environment	HPE 642 1075 mm or 1200 mm Shock Intelligent Rack with PDUs, cabling, hardware kits, and options	
Factory Build/Install	Factory build and services for Azure Stack including basic install and connection to customer network	
Support and Financial Services	HPE Global Support HPE Networks Support HPE Proactive Care Advanced Service HPE Foundation Care for Azure	HPE Datacenter Care for Azure (Specialist Advice, Hybrid Support, Operations Support Services) HPE Datacenter Flexible Capacity (Access to scalable resources hosted in your own data center with pay-per-use² monthly service fees)
Professional Services options	HPE Microsoft Azure Advisory Workshop and POC HPE Professional Services for Azure hybrid cloud (networking, security, workload migration, hybrid identity, backup, and site recovery)	
Add-on HPE hybrid IT solutions	HPE Operations Bridge (Analytics-driven, autonomous operations management across Azure Stack, Azure, and traditional IT)	

Source:
https://azurestackeaiblob.blob.core.windows.net/content-file/HPE%20data%20sheet%20for%20customers%20-%20HPE%20ProLiant%20for%20Microsoft%20Azure%20Stack.
pdf?sv=2015-12-11&sr=b&sig=Kc6vdPNlzS7s5xwFYLuvhJgC0zoiTAEOi7mdf4%2BUsq4%3D&st=2017-08-17T20%3A48%3A45Z&se=2017-08-18T20%3A53%3A45Z&sp=
r

Lenovo

Finally, Lenovo decided to go with some so called **T-shirt sizes** with Azure Stack options:

	Entry SXM4200	Enterprise Starter SXM4200	Enterprise Full SXM6200
Rack	9565-RCC (25U)	9565-RCD (42U)	9565-RCE (42U)
Compute Nodes	• 4-8x x3650 M5 • 2x Intel® Xeon® E5-2680, 2683 or 2690 v4 CPUs • 256GB or 512GB memory per node	• 4-12x x3650 M5 • 2x Intel Xeon E5-2680, 2683 or 2690 v4 CPUs • 256GB or 512GB memory per node	• 12x x3650 M5 • 2x Intel Xeon E5-2680, 2683 or 2690 v4 CPUs • 256GB or 512GB memory per node
Management Node	1x x3550 M5; 2-socket Xeon E5-2620 v4 CPUs; 64GB memory		
Hyperconverged Storage	• 10x 4TB Capacity Tier (40TB raw) + 4x 800GB SSD Cache Tier • Or, 10x 6TB Capacity Tier (60TB raw) + 4x 1.6GB SSD Cache Tier		
Network	• 1x 1Gbps Lenovo RackSwitch G8052 (management) • 2x 10Gbps Lenovo RackSwitch G8272 (compute/storage traffic) • Mellanox ConnectX-4 Dual Port 10/25GbE Network Controller		
Integrated Solution Software	• Azure Stack technologies, including Microsoft Windows Server 2016, Hyper-V, Storage Spaces Direct (S2D); Lenovo XClarity		

Source:
https://azurestackeaiblob.blob.core.windows.net/content-file/Lenovo%20solution%20brief%20-%20Lenovo%20ThinkAgile%20SX%20for%20Microsoft%20Azure%20Stack.pdf
?sv=2015-12-11&sr=b&sig=unnEH%2BBAL2cb6UW6UPkmkudRlaA%2FkJEF0NiTA%2BQI%2BR0%3D&st=2017-08-17T20%3A48%3A45Z&se=2017-08-18T20%3A53%3A45Z&sp=r

Additional hardware OEMs will follow (Cisco and Huawei have already been announced) and need to be added in the future. They may also come with different hardware technologies, but the future will show what their design looks like. As of today, from the details mentioned here, you will recognize all work with nearly the same hardware (and even networking) design. We will look into networking a little bit later.

Troubleshooting Storage Spaces Direct

As Azure Stack is a fully integrated system and you really do not have to know all details of what is going on in the system in depth (as you will buy some kind of support as a service with the solution), it is always good to know some basic technology monitoring and troubleshooting steps in order to help the support team better when working on issues. For a dedicated look on Storage Spaces, I expect you to have a look at different experts who've published books on it.

Windows Server 2016 itself provides some basic monitoring tools for Storage Spaces Direct for the following:

- Replica
- Quality of Service
- Storage Spaces health service (latency, throughput, IOPS, and failover clustering issues)

Monitoring replica and QoS are not that difficult and are being serviced with default performance and monitoring tools such as Performance Monitor.

The Storage Spaces health service is dedicated to the new storage technology running by default, providing you with online details on the health behavior of your storage environment. It provides a PowerShell API and the basics for integration with common monitoring tools (such as OMS, SCOM, or Nagios) and even Power BI, which can help you provide simple but powerful snapshots of the service health.

A basic PowerShell command is `Get-ClusterResource`, which will help see all cluster resources and their status:

On an Azure Stack development toolkit, the outlook is as follows, and in the first lines, you will see the resources `Scale-Out File Server`, `Storage QoS Resource` and the `SU1FileServer` that should all have the status `Online`.

Health services continuously monitors the error messages on the S2D cluster and knows the following segments of issues:

- Severity (low, high, critical)
- Possible error
- Troubleshooting recommendation
- Location and position
- Hardware component and description

It collects issues for the following components:

- Cluster hardware (for example, temperature, nodes, and network issues)
- Storage hardware (for example, disks and fans)
- Software Stack S2D (for example, low capacity)
- Storage QoS (for example, policy issues)
- Storage Replica (for example, RPO issues, replication, and synchronization)
- Health service (for example, HDD quarantine and automation issues)

Let's run the command illustrated here and check the `HealthStatus`:

```
PS C:\Windows\system32> Get-StorageSubSystem

FriendlyName                              HealthStatus OperationalStatus
------------                              ------------ -----------------
Windows Storage on WIN-1SO73MMRB84        Healthy      OK
Clustered Windows Storage on S-Cluster    Healthy      OK

PS C:\Windows\system32> _
```

As you can see in the preceding screenshot, `HealthStatus` is `OK`.

```
PS C:\Windows\system32> Get-StorageSubSystem *cluster*

FriendlyName                              HealthStatus OperationalStatus
------------                              ------------ -----------------
Clustered Windows Storage on S-Cluster Healthy         OK

PS C:\Windows\system32> Get-StorageSubSystem *cluster* | Debug-StorageSubSystem
PS C:\Windows\system32> _
```

The preceding command provides a more detailed overview if there are any issues. If the feedback is nothing (like earlier), it means there are no issues at all. The technology for this command is based on the sensors of the hardware system and the technology to present issues to the operating system is called **Storage Enclosure Service (SES)**.

In addition, the service has a real-time monitoring feature to collect the following metrics:

- Pool capacity
- Physical capacity
- Volume capacity
- IO latency
- IOPS
- IO throughput
- RAM

To get these details, the following command will help:

```
PS C:\Windows\system32> Get-StorageSubSystem *cluster* | Get-StorageHealthReport
CPUUsageAverage                 :   13.61 %
CapacityPhysicalPooledAvailable :    370 GB
CapacityPhysicalPooledTotal     :   3.64 TB
CapacityPhysicalTotal           :   3.64 TB
CapacityPhysicalUnpooled        :      0 B
CapacityVolumesAvailable        :   2.51 TB
CapacityVolumesTotal            :   3.27 TB
IOLatencyAverage                : 227.01 us
IOLatencyRead                   : 214.74 us
IOLatencyWrite                  : 300.44 us
IOPSRead                        : 451.19 /S
IOPSTotal                       : 526.55 /S
IOPSWrite                       :  75.36 /S
IOThroughputRead                : 898.84 KB/S
IOThroughputTotal               :   2.37 MB/S
IOThroughputWrite               :   1.49 MB/S
MemoryAvailable                 : 153.37 GB
MemoryTotal                     :    256 GB



ExtendedStatus :
ReturnValue    : 0
PSComputerName :


PS C:\Windows\system32> _
```

As you can see, the lab environment currently has enough resources to run the environment.

The parameter count will provide you the last x parameters the system has been collecting, so you will see the development over a specific time.

These PowerShell commands are great to get an overview (regardless of the **Azure Stack - Administration** portal) and get a more detailed pane of glass:

In the administration portal, the dashboard with the altering and resource provider panes are mostly only a first indication if something does not work as expected.

Windows Server 2016 Storage Spaces Direct synopsis

On the preceding pages, you may have noticed that Storage Spaces is a great technology to provide powerful and highly performant storage for the hyper-converged environment. You do not have to invest in expensive SAN technology to provide storage to your tenants. Locally connected storage to your servers based on SATA, SAS or SSD technology using **Storage Spaces Direct (S2D)** gives you an easy and cost-sensitive way to solve this technology challenge.

In comparison to Windows Server 2012 first releases the stability, performance and resiliency with Storage Spaces is not comparable anymore to S2D. It is quite simple to install and, more importantly, to monitor using an integrated toolset of PowerShell commands. In addition, you will be able to integrate this into your existing monitoring solutions using connectors or management packs to provide your helpdesk with one view for all the technology in your environment.

Windows Server 2016 Software Defined Networks

With Windows Server 2012, Microsoft announced a first stack to set up SDN using the network virtualization using **Generic Routing Encapsulation (GRE)** Protocol. It attempts to solve the issues in large deployments and works at the layer 2 and layer 3 networking level. The technology was developed by Microsoft, and it was a first step to go with SDN networks.

With Windows Server 2016, Microsoft switched to a better-known and industry-wide defined standard for SDN, called **Virtual Extensible LAN (VXLAN)**. It used a technology that is more or less similar to the encapsulation technology for VLANs using the networking level 4 instead of using VXLAN tunnel endpoints (VTEPs). VXLAN is a development to be standardized on an overlay encapsulation protocol with the result that it increases scalability for up to 16 million logical networks and allows layer 2 features across IP networks. It has been developed by VMware, Arista, and Cisco.

Virtual networks still require physical hardware devices and IP networks to connect servers and VMs. The packets transmitted between VMs are encapsulated within physical network IP packets to enable the overlay network.

A good sample of the design is described in the following figure:

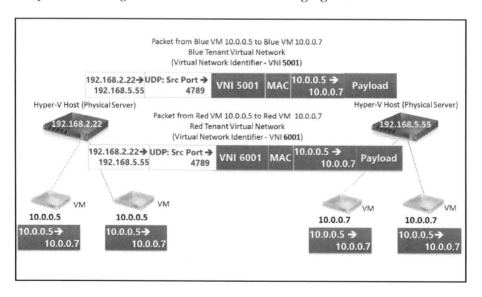

Source: https://msdnshared.blob.core.windows.net/media/2016/10/VXLANEncap.jpg

Hyper-V networking virtualization technologies

Windows Server 2016 works with two different Hyper-V networking virtualization technologies: **HNVv1** and **HNVv2**.

HNVv1 is the Windows Server 2012-based SDN technology that is being understood from Hyper-V and **System Center Virtual Machine Manager** (**SCVMM**). The configuration relies on WMI management and PowerShell to define the isolation settings and **Customer Address** (**CA**)-virtual network-to **Physical Address** (**PA**) mappings and routing. With Windows Server 2016, this version is still available, but there's no addition or new features.

HNVv2 is the new version based on Windows Server 2016 using the Azure **Virtual Filtering Platform** (**VFP**) forwarding extension in the Hyper-V Switch. This technology is fully integrated with Microsoft Azure Stack and includes the network controller in the SDN Stack. You can configure it using a **RESTful Northbound** (**NB**) API that has been added to a host agent via multiple **Southbound Interfaces** (**SBI**). The host agent defines the policy in the VFP extension of the Hyper-V switch.

In regard to networks, there is the virtual network and a virtual subnet. Each virtual network defines a boundary to isolate the traffic. In VLAN technology, this is done using a segregation IP address range and a VLAN ID or 802.1 tag. HVN with NVGRE and VXLAN uses encapsulation and creates overlay networks for the segmentation. This gives the tenants a chance to have overlapping IP subnets. The virtual network is the unique routing ID to identify the network resource in the controller. A **Uniform Resource Identifier** (**URI**) is there with an appended resource ID used to reference the virtual network.

A virtual subnet is layer 3 IP subnet for the virtual machines in the same virtual subnet. It creates a broadcast domain (similar to VLAN) and enforces the isolation using the so-called NVGRE **Tenant Network ID** (**TNI**) or VXLAN **Network Identifier** (**VNI**) field. The virtual subnet belongs to a single virtual network and it is assigned a unique **Virtual Subnet ID** (**VSID**) using the TNI or VNI key in the encapsulated packet header. The VSID must be unique in the data center and is in the range of 4096 to 2^{24-2}.

Switching and routing in HVNE

HNVv2 makes sure that there are correct layer 2 switching and layer 3 routing semantics to work as a physical switch. A VM that is connected to a HVN tries to establish a connection with another VM in the same subnet by learning its CA MAC. If the ARP of this VM is not on the table, it will send an ARP broadcast to the destination VM's IP to be returned.

The Hyper-V switch will send it to the host agent that will take a look at its database for the corresponding MAC address for the requested destination VM's IP address. If it is available, the host agent will modify the ARP response and send it back to the requesting VM. After the VM has collected all the required layer 2 header information, it sends the frame to the corresponding Hyper-V Port on V-Switch. The switch then tests this frame with the corresponding matching rules of the V-Port and applies different transformations to the frame based on these rules.

If a VM is connected to an HNV virtual network and wants to create a connection to a VM in a different virtual subnet, HNV assumes a star topology with the logic of only one IP address in the CA space to the next hop to reach all IP prefixes (the default gateway). As of today, this is a limitation to the technology as non-default routes are currently not supported.

Package encapsulation

Each virtual network adapter has two IP addresses: the **Customer Address (CA)** and the **Physical Address (PA)**.

The following diagram describes this a little bit more from a big picture perspective:

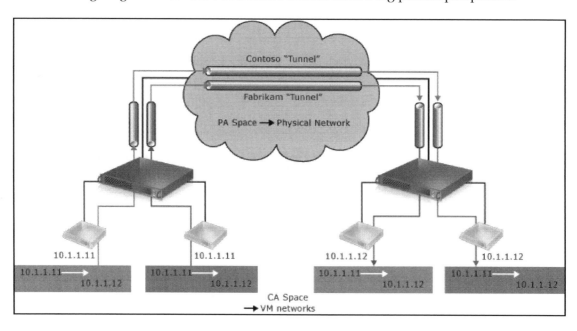

Source: https://docs.microsoft.com/en-us/windows-server/networking/media/Hyper-V-network-virtualization-technical-details-in-windows-server/vnetf2.gif

As you can see, the machines have their own CA, which is being send via a virtual network tunnel. The PA is the basic destination target, and later, the destination will find out the internal recipient of this networking package. Each CA is mapped to a physical host using the same PA. The network controller is responsible for the mapping database using the so-called MS_VTEP schema:

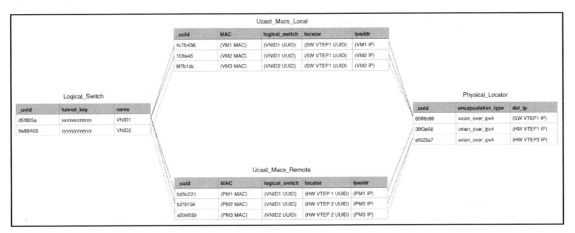

Source: https://www.relaxdiego.com/assets/images/hardware_vtep.png

NVGRE Encapsulation

To get an idea about the difference in the VXLAN technology, we will take a look at the encapsulation of NVGRE at first:

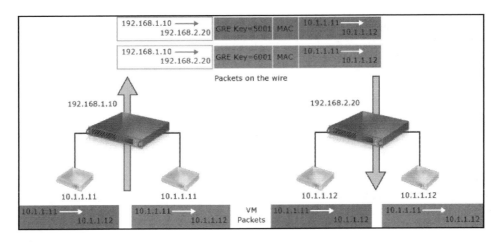

Source: https://docs.microsoft.com/en-us/windows-server/networking/media/Hyper-V-network-virtualization-technical-details-in-windows-server/vnetf3.gif

As you can see with the preceding figure, the VM's packet is encapsulated inside another IP packet. The header of this new packet has the source and destination PA IP addresses in addition to the virtual subnet ID, which is stored in the GRE header. This means that each package has the PA information and therefore, the number of IPs and MAC addresses can be reduced a lot because the number of data needed to learn by the virtual networking infrastructure is enlarged by the number of VMs. From a security perspective, the virtual subnet IDs in the packages also make it easy to correlate the packages from one tenant.

As the PA sharing for Windows Server 2012 R2 is one per VSID per Host, this encapsulation is not the best from a scaling perspective; for Windows Server 2016, it is one PA per NIC team member.

VXLAN encapsulation

The VXLAN encapsulation works as follows:

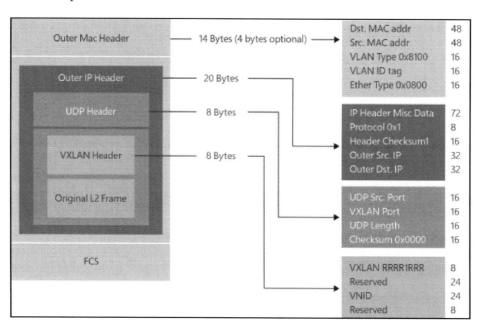

Source: https://docs.microsoft.com/en-us/windows-server/networking/media/Hyper-V-network-virtualization-technical-details-in-windows-server/vxlan-packet-header.png

The VXLAN with the RFC 7348 has increasingly become an industrial standard as most of the vendors support it out of the box. The protocol itself used UDP port 4789 as the destination port and the UDP source port is based on the hash information the the packet itself. The VXLAN header will be enhanced by a reserved 4-byte field and a 3-byte field for the **VXLAN Network Identifier** (**VNI**)-VSID-and finally another reserved 1-byte field. Finally, the VXLAN header adds the original CA L2 frame.

> RFC 7348 can be accessed using this URL: http://www.rfc-editor.org/info/rfc7348.

The hierarchy from **vSwitch** to the VPH header can be described as follows:

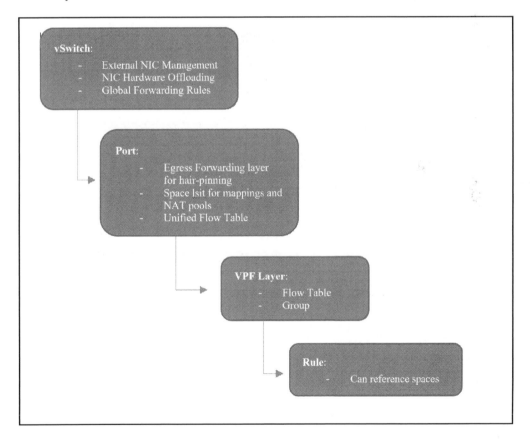

The VFP technology supports MAC forwarding for VXLAN and NVGRE capsulation as well as VLAN forwarding using MAC. It always has a so-called slow path and a fast path for traffic transmission. The first package always needs to go through each layer of rules, but later on, the flow table will have a list of actions and will process it for all unified flow entries.

Software load balancer

The software load balancer is one of the most important components of networking:

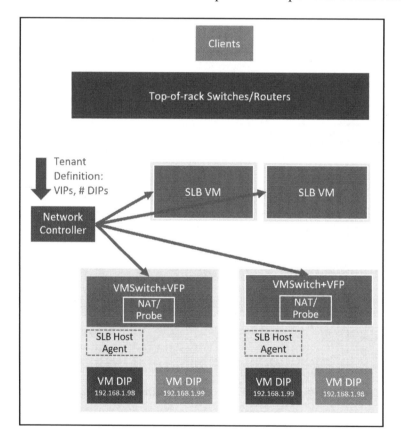

This is the communication route from the clients to the VM itself. As you can see, we have some different components that influence it:

- **Network Controller**
- **SLB VM**
- **SLB Host Agent**
- VFP in vSwitch

As all internal traffic with Azure Stack relies on the BGP protocol, we will need to take a look into it:

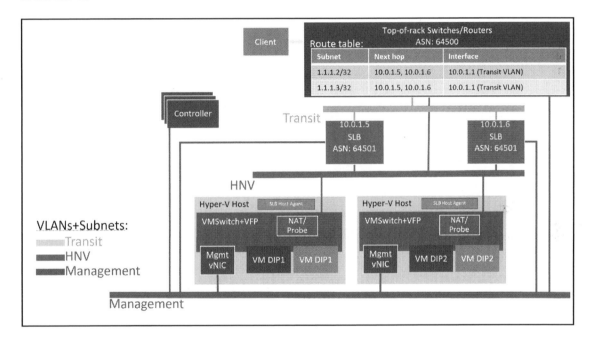

As all BGP traffic stays internally, there is no need to have BGP configured in the rest of your network.

Gateway architecture

The second important thing with Azure Stack is the gateway. We will take a look at this architecture now:

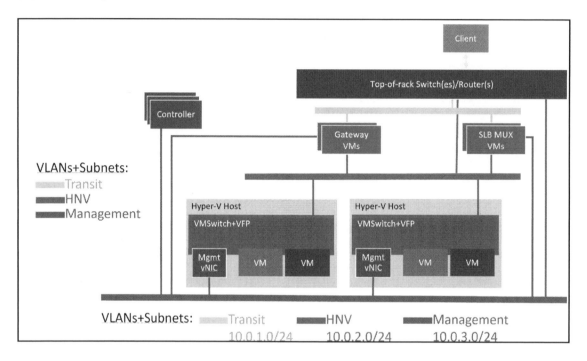

Now you have learned how the gateway and the software load balancer are working and that Azure Stack is using BGP only for internal communication. The next step is to take a look at how the internal SDN setup for communications between Windows Server 2016 Hyper-V hosts works and how they will interact:

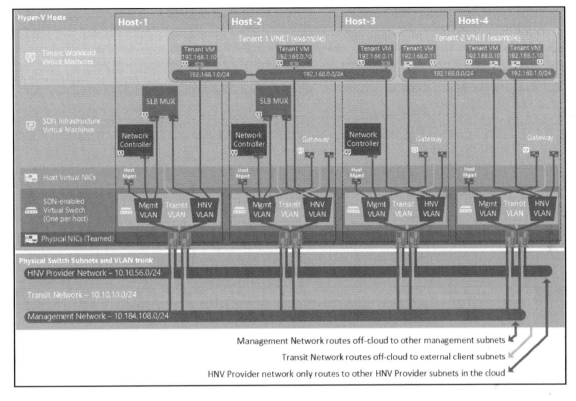

Troubleshooting SDNs

As learned earlier, Azure Stack uses SDN for networking. It provides easy management and great scalability. Again, like with Software Defined Storage earlier in this chapter, if there is anything regarding networking issues and you have to call the **Support as a Service** from your hardware vendor, it is good to know some basics. It's the same with networking.

The basic error types within SDN can be divided into the following categories:

- Missing or unsupported configuration
- Errors in policy application
- Software bugs
- External errors

As you already have seen with storage, for networking, some great PowerShell tools are the tools for troubleshooting the system.

To check the configuration state of a Hyper-V host, the following script will help:

```
Debug-NetworkControllerConfigurationState -NetworkController <FQDN or NC
IP> [-Credential <PS Credential>]

# Healthy State Example - no status reported
$cred = Get-Credential
Debug-NetworkControllerConfigurationState -NetworkController 10.127.132.211
-Credential $cred

Fetching ResourceType:       accessControlLists
Fetching ResourceType:       servers
Fetching ResourceType:       virtualNetworks
Fetching ResourceType:       networkInterfaces
Fetching ResourceType:       virtualGateways
Fetching ResourceType:       loadbalancerMuxes
Fetching ResourceType:       Gateways
```

The value for the `NetworkController` parameter can be the FQDN or IP address based on the subject name of the X.509 certificate that has been created for network controller. The credentials parameter is only required if the network controller is using the Kerberos authentication and the account has to be part of the network controller management security group.

The following error codes, messages, and actions to take are available with the preceding PowerShell commands:

Code	Message	Action
`Unknown`	Unknown error	None.
`HostUnreachable`	The host machine is not reachable	Check the management network connectivity between network controller and host.

`PAIpAddressExhausted`	The PA IP addresses are exhausted	Increase the HNV provider logical subnet's IP pool size.
`PAMacAddressExhausted`	The PA MAC addresses are exhausted	Increase the MAC pool range.
`PAAddressConfigurationFailure`	Failed to plumb PA addresses to the host	Check the management network connectivity between network controller and host.
`CertificateNotTrusted`	Certificate is not trusted	Fix the certificates used for communication with the host.
`CertificateNotAuthorized`	Certificate not authorized	Fix the certificates used for communication with the host.
`PolicyConfigurationFailureOnVfp`	Failure in configuring VFP policies	This is a runtime failure. No definite workarounds. Collect logs.

PolicyConfigurationFailure	Failure in pushing policies to the hosts due to communication failures or other errors in the NetworkController	No definite actions. This is due to failure in goal state processing in the network controller modules. Collect logs.
HostNotConnectedToController	The Host is not yet connected to the network controller	Port profile not applied on the host or the host is not reachable from the network controller. Validate that the host ID registry key matches the Instance ID of the server resource.
MultipleVfpEnabledSwitches	There are multiple Vfp enabled switches on the host	Delete one of the switches since network controller host agent supports only one vSwitch with the VFP extension enabled.

PolicyConfigurationFailure	Failed to push VNet policies for a vmnic due to certificate errors or connectivity errors	Check whether proper certificates have been deployed (certificate subject name must match FQDN of host). Also verify the host connectivity with the network controller.
PolicyConfigurationFailure	Failed to push vSwitch policies for a vmnic due to certificate errors or connectivity errors	Check whether proper certificates have been deployed (certificate subject name must match the FQDN of host). Also verify the host connectivity with the network controller.
PolicyConfigurationFailure	Failed to push Firewall policies for a vmnic due to certificate errors or connectivity errors	Check whether proper certificates have been deployed (certificate subject name must match the FQDN of host). Also verify the host connectivity with the network controller.

DistributedRouterConfigurationFailure	Failed to configure the distributed router settings on the host vNic	TCPIP stack error. May require cleaning up the PA and DR host vNICs on the server on which this error was reported.
DhcpAddressAllocationFailure	DHCP address allocation failed for a vmnic	Check whether the static IP address attribute is configured on the NIC resource.
CertificateNotTrusted CertificateNotAuthorized	Failed to connect to mux due to network or cert errors	Check the numeric code provided in the error message code: this corresponds to the Winsock error code. Certificate errors are granular (for example, cert cannot be verified, cert not authorized, and so on).

`HostUnreachable`	Mux is unhealthy (common case is BGP router disconnected)	BGP peer on the RRAS (BGP virtual machine) or **top-of-rack (ToR)** switch is unreachable or not peering successfully. Check BGP settings on both software load balancer multiplexer resource and BGP peer (ToR or RRAS virtual machine).
`HostNotConnectedToController`	SLB host agent is not connected	Check whether SLB host agent service is running. Refer to SLB host agent logs (auto running) for reasons why; in case SLBM (NC) rejected the cert presented by the host agent, the running state will show nuanced information.
`PortBlocked`	The VFP port is blocked due to lack of VNET/ACL policies	Check whether there are any other errors, which might cause the policies to be not configured.

Overloaded	Load balancer mux is overloaded	Performance issue with mux.
RoutePublicationFailure	Load balancer mux is not connected to a BGP router	Check whether the mux has connectivity with the BGP routers and that BGP peering is set up correctly.
VirtualServerUnreachable	Load balancer mux is not connected to the SLB manager	Check connectivity between SLBM and mux.
QosConfigurationFailure	Failed to configure QoS policies	See whether sufficient bandwidth is available for all VM's if QoS reservation is used.

Source: https://docs.microsoft.com/en-us/windows-server/networking/sdn/troubleshoot/troubleshoot-windows-server-2016-software-defined-networking-stack
and https://docs.microsoft.com/en-us/windows-server/networking/sdn/troubleshoot/troubleshoot-windows-server-2016-software-defined-networking-stack

Software Defined Network synopsis

You saw that there is a general technology from VXLAN that has been implemented for the networking technology that Azure Stack is based on as the cloud inspired infrastructure is working with Windows Server 2016 hosts. You learned that. VXLAN is the underlying encapsulation mechanism and there are the software load balancer and gateway, which has been adopted from Microsoft Azure and brought into Azure Stack. The troubleshooting tools available are based on Windows Server 2016. Although the integrated system stack includes support as a service from the hardware vendor you have chosen, it was great to know some basic steps to prepare a support call with the vendor if you are experiencing issues.

Now that we have experienced the underlying technologies of the cloud inspired infrastructure of Azure Stack, we are ready to go and see the environment and take a look at how a private cloud environment is possible with Azure Stack.

Summary

Now that we have experienced the underlying technologies of the cloud inspired infrastructure of Azure Stack, we are ready to go and see the environment and take a look at how a private cloud environment is possible with Azure Stack.

5
Provisioning Virtual Machines

One of the great aspects of Microsoft Azure Stack is the new Azure Resource Manager. It provides the ability to create templates for simple VMs to complex multi-VM applications running within your (local) Azure Stack environment, in a Service Provider environment, who is using Azure Resource Manager/Azure Stack, or in a Microsoft Azure location. There is a large community offering sample deployment templates for use with Azure Resource Manager. This chapter provides an overview of Azure Resource Manager templates and authoring templates to provision virtual machines. In addition we will look at offering virtual machines using the Azure Stack Marketplace.

The main topics are as follows:

- How to prepare new or existing VM templates
- How to deploy VMs using Marketplace
- How to build up the parts of an Azure Resource Manager template to create an IaaS (VM) service

Understanding deployment of virtual machines in Azure Stack

There are two basic ways to provision a virtual machine. You may use the Marketplace at Azure Stack portal. If you go to **Marketplace** | **Virtual Machines**—you are able to offer your end user pre-defined virtual machines that are based on a (sysprepped) VHD with OS like Microsoft Windows Server 2012 R2 or Linux Ubuntu Server. You define which resources are available and/or required—like NIC for a virtual machine or in case of a multi-service application the required configuration settings. The end user has to use the gallery item as it is.

The alternative is to create Azure Resource templates and deploy them using PowerShell or CLI. This approach allows for automation of deployment and offers greater flexibility in (combining) resources offered.

An overview of the steps required to create and deploy an image of your choice using those different approaches are as follows:

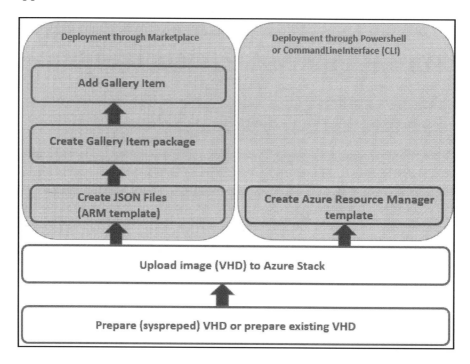

Preparing (sysprepped) VHD for Windows and Linux OS

Many of us might already have virtual machine templates used in System Center VMM and would like to reuse those. Unfortunately this is not possible directly. In case you used **Desired State Configuration (DSC)** for customization—then you might be able to re-use them as virtual machine extensions (customizations) may be done using DSC. We will look at virtual machine extensions in chapter 8, *Creating PaaS Services in Microsoft Azure Stack*.

In case you want to use an existing VHD to ensure that the requirements provided in this chapter are met. To maintain your accounts and other configurations do not run the `sysprep` command provided. To create a new image, install the required operating system and follow all the steps.

> In case you want to add a new image-several Linux and Windows images have been prepared for use in Azure Stack by the different vendors themselves. The link to those prepared VHD's are available in *There is more* at `http://www.azurestack.rocks/thereismore`. In this case, please go to the section *Upload image to Azure Stack* `http://www.azurestack.rocks/`.

There are a couple of important points to be aware of in order to succeed. At the time of writing these include:

- Generation 1 virtual machines have to be used as Azure Stack TP2 supports VHD only. The VHD must be of fixed size with a maximum size of 1.023 GB. The size must be multiples of 1 MB.
- Any drivers related to physical components like VMware tools or third party software related to physical components like transport interface filter driver used by network analyzation tools must be uninstalled.

There are additional requirements which are based on the installed OS. We will provide the exact steps for Linux Ubuntu Server and below that, steps for Windows Server 2012 R2, here.

So let's start out with Linux. There are some steps which are unique to each Linux derivate. Those are marked, only the Ubuntu Server commands are provided here. The section There is more... at `http://www.azurestack.rocks/thereismore`, provides links to configuration settings of additional Linux distributions including CentOS, Red Hat Enterprise Linux, Debian, SLES/openSUSE, and Oracle Linux. The Linux general and Ubuntu Server specific requirements are as follows:

- It is recommended to use standard partitions rather than LVM as it will avoid LVM name conflicts with cloned VMs.
- It is required that the kernel supports the UDF file system. During deployment of a VM, the Azure Linux agent must be able to mount a UDF formatted media containing the provisioning configuration.
- Ensure that the SSH server is installed and started at boot time which is usually the default setting.

- Ensure that the **Linux Integration Services (LIS)** for Hyper-V exists in the kernel. This should be the case for all recent Linux kernel versions based on 3.x.

Please be aware that on Red Hat 6.0 to 6.3 you will have to install LIS which is available at `http://go.microsoft.com/fwlink/p/?LinkID=254263clcid=0x409`.

- The next step is required on Ubuntu Linux Server only. The current repositories must be replaced to use the Azure ones. Therefore edit `/etc/apt/sources`. List using the following commands:

```
# sudo sed -i
"s/[a-z][a-z].archive.ubuntu.com/ azure.archive.ubuntu.com/g"
/etc/apt/sources.list
#sudo apt-get update
```

- The following step is required on Ubuntu Linux Server only. As the HWE kernel should be used to update the OS to the latest kernel using the following commands on Ubuntu 12.04 use:

```
#sudo apt-get update
#sudo apt-get install
linux-image-generic-lts-trusty linux-cloud-tools-generic-lts-trusty
#sudo apt-get install hv-kvp-daemon-init
#sudo apt-get dist-upgrade ## recommended only
On Ubuntu 14.04 use
#sudo apt-get update
#sudo apt-get install
linux-image-virtualc-lts-vivid linux-lts-vivid-tools-common
#sudo apt-get install hv-kvp-daemon-init
#sudo apt-get dist-upgrade ## recommended only
```

- Install the Azure Linux Agent on Ubuntu 12.04 or 14.04 the Azure Linux Agent should be available using the package repository by using the following commands:

```
#sudo apt-get update
#sudo apt-get install walinuxagent
```

Please be aware that this will remove the following two packages: `NetworkManager` and `NetworkManager-gnome`.

- The generic steps are, using the root user to get the agent from GitHub, unpack it, install the Python toolset, and lastly install the agent:

  ```
  #sudo apt-get install python3-setuptools
  ```

- Restart the Linux system and using root move forward with:

  ```
  #wget https://github.com/Azure/WALinuxAgent/archive/ v2.2.0.tar.gz
  #tar -vzxf v2.2.0.tar.gz
  #cd WALinuxAgent-2.2.0
  #python setup.py install -register-service
  #rm v2.2.0.tar.gz -f
  #rm WALinuxAgent -fR
  ```

- On the OS disk do not create a `swap` partition. Instead use the Azure Linux Agent to create one at the local resource disk (temporary disk) as shown. Edit `/etc/waagent.conf` using the following values:

  ```
  ResourceDisk.Format=y
  ResourceDisk.Filesystem=ext4
  ResourceDisk.MountPoint=/mnt/resource
  ResourceDisk.EnableSwap=y
  ResourceDisk.SwapSizeMB=XXXX ##note:replace XXXX with your
  required value like 4096
  ```

- Optional, for debugging, purpose console messages should be sent to the first serial port. Therefore, modify grub or grub2 with the following values:
    - Edit `/etc/default/grub` and on Ubuntu 12.04 and 14.04 change the following line (or add it in case it doesn't exist) to `GRUB_CMDLINE_LINUX="console=tty1 console=ttyS0,115200n8 earlyprintk=ttyS0,115200 rootdelay=300"` and generate a new config by issuing `#sudo update-grub`
    - In case you use an existing image that is not created on Hyper-V you may have to rebuild the initrd to ensure that `hv_vmbus` and `hv_storevsc` kernel modules exist. Using `mkinitrd` utility this could look as follows:

      ```
      #sudo mkinitrd -preload=hv_storvsc -preload=hv_vmbus
      -v -f initrd-`uname -r`.img `uname -r`.
      ```

- As a last step, `deprovision` (`sysprep`) the virtual machine by running the following commands:

```
# sudo waagent -force -deprovision
# export HISTSIZE=0
# logout
```

You are ready to upload your prepared Linux VHD.

> A Windows Server 2012 R2 images was added in Azure Stack Marketplace as part of the deployment. You may use or changes this one and the corresponding JSON files as a starting point.

To create a new Windows Server image or to check an existing image for compatibility the below steps are recommended, please use an administrative account with an elevated command console or PowerShell window to perform them:

1. Check for persistence routes by running: `route print`. If there is a route in the Persistent Routes section, remove it using `route delete`.
2. Remove the `WinHTTPproxy` by using:

```
netsh winhttp reset proxy
```

3. Configure the disk SAN policy by using: `diskpart san policy=onlineall`.
4. Configure UTC Time Zone and the startup type of the Windows time (`232time`) service:

```
REG ADD
HKLM\SYSTEM\CurrentControlSet\ Control\TimeZoneInformation
/v RealTimeIsUniversal /t REG_DWORD /d 1
sc config w32time start = auto
```

5. Ensure that the following Windows services are set to their default values. Then configure them use the following commands:

```
sc config bfe start= auto
sc config dcomlaunch start= auto
sc config dhcp start= auto
sc config dnscache start= auto
sc config IKEEXT start= auto
sc config iphlpsvc start= auto
sc config PolicyAgent start= demand
sc config LSM start= auto
sc config netlogon start= demand
```

```
sc config netman start= demand
sc config NcaSvc start= demand
sc config netprofm start= demand
sc config NlaSvc start= auto
sc config nsi start= auto
sc config RpcSs start= auto
sc config RpcEptMapper start= auto
sc config termService start= demand
sc config MpsSvc start= auto
sc config WinHttpAutoProxySvc start= demand
sc config LanmanWorkstation start= auto
sc config RemoteRegistry start= auto
```

Ensure that the Remote Desktop configurations are correct by doing the following:

1. Remove any self-signed certificates tied to the **Remote Desktop Protocol** (**RDP**) listener—open elevated command or PowerShell window:

    ```
    REG DELETE "HKLM\SYSTEM\CurrentcontrolSet\Control\
    Terminal Server\WinStations\RDP-Tcp\ SSLCertificateSHA1Hash"
    ```

2. Configure keep-alive values for RDP service:

    ```
    REG ADD
    "HKLM\SOFTWARE\Policies\Microsoft\Windows NT\Terminal Services"
    /v KeepAliveEnable /t REG_DWORD /d 1 /f
    REG ADD
    "HKLM\SOFTWARE\Policies\Microsoft\Windows NT\Terminal Services"
    /v KeepAliveInterval /t REG_DWORD /d 1 /f
    ```

3. Configure authentication mode values for RDP service:

    ```
    REG ADD "HKLM\SYSTEM\CurrentControlSet\Control\Terminal
    Server\WinStations\RDP-Tcp" /v UserAuthentication
    /t REG_DWORD  /d 1 /f
    REG ADD "HKLM\SYSTEM\CurrentControlSet\Control\Terminal
    Server\WinStations\RDP-Tcp" /v SecurityLayer /t REG_DWORD
    /d 1 /f
    REG ADD "HKLM\SYSTEM\CurrentControlSet\Control\Terminal
    Server\WinStations\RDP-Tcp" /v fAllowSecProtocolNegotiation
    /t REG_DWORD  /d 1 /f
    ```

4. Configure authentication mode values for RDP service:

    ```
    REG ADD "HKLM\SYSTEM\CurrentControlSet\Control\Terminal Server"
    /v fDenyTSConnections /t REG_DWORD  /d 0 /f
    ```

5. Ensure that PowerShell Remote service is available (through Windows firewall)—open administrative PowerShell windows and type:

```
Enable-PSRemoting -force
```

6. Ensure that the following Windows Firewall rules are configured for inbound/outbound connections:

```
netsh advfirewall firewall set rule group="Remote Desktop"
new    enable=yes
netsh advfirewall firewall set rule group="Core Networking"
new enable=yes
```

7. Ensure that the following Windows Firewall rules are configured for outbound connections:

```
netsh advfirewall firewall set rule dir=out
name="Network Discovery (LLMNR-UDP-Out)" new enable=yes
netsh advfirewall firewall set rule dir=out
name="Network Discovery (NB-Datagram-Out)" new enable=yes
netsh advfirewall firewall set rule dir=out
name="Network Discovery (NB-Name-Out)" new enable=yes
netsh advfirewall firewall set rule dir=out
name="Network Discovery (Pub-WSD-Out)" new enable=yes
netsh advfirewall firewall set rule dir=out
name="Network Discovery (SSDP-Out)" new enable=yes
netsh advfirewall firewall set rule dir=out
name="Network Discovery (UPnPHost-Out)" new enable=yes
netsh advfirewall firewall set rule dir=out
name="Network Discovery (UPnP-Out)" new enable=yes
netsh advfirewall firewall set rule dir=out
name="Network Discovery (WSD Events-Out)" new enable=yes
netsh advfirewall firewall set rule dir=out
name="Network Discovery (WSD EventsSecure-Out)" new enable=yes
netsh advfirewall firewall set rule dir=out
name="Network Discovery (WSD-Out)" new enable=yes
```

8. Ensure that the following Windows Firewall rules are configured for inbound connections:

```
netsh advfirewall firewall set rule dir=in
name="File and Printer Sharing (Echo Request - ICMPv4-In)"
new enable=yes
netsh advfirewall firewall set rule dir=in
name="Network Discovery (LLMNR-UDP-In)" new enable=yes
netsh advfirewall firewall set rule dir=in
name="Network Discovery (NB-Datagram-In)" new enable=yes
```

```
netsh advfirewall firewall set rule dir=in
name="Network Discovery (NB-Name-In)" new enable=yes
netsh advfirewall firewall set rule dir=in
name="Network Discovery (Pub-WSD-In)" new enable=yes
netsh advfirewall firewall set rule dir=in
name="Network Discovery (SSDP-In)" new enable=yes
netsh advfirewall firewall set rule dir=in
name="Network Discovery (UPnP-In)" new enable=yes
netsh advfirewall firewall set rule dir=in
name="Network Discovery (WSD EventsSecure-In)" new enable=yes
netsh advfirewall firewall set rule dir=in
name="Windows Remote Management (HTTP-In)" new enable=yes
netsh advfirewall firewall set rule dir=in
name="Windows Remote Management (HTTP-In)" new enable=yes
```

9. Ensure that the following **Boot Configuration Database (BCD)** values are configured:

```
bcdedit /set {bootmgr} integrityservices enable
bcdedit /set {default} device partition=C:
bcdedit /set {default} integrityservices enable
bcdedit /set {default} recoveryenabled Off
bcdedit /set {default} osdevice partition=C:
bcdedit /set {default} bootstatuspolicy IgnoreAllFailures
```

10. Ensure that **Windows Management Instrumentation (WMI)** repository is consistent by entering the following:

```
winmgmt /verifyrepository
```

11. Reboot virtual machine to ensure RDP connections are functional after all the previous configuration changes. Login by using the local administrator. In case local administrator does not have the correct permissions, open Group Policy editor and go to:

```
Computer Configuration\Windows Settings\Security
Settings\Local Policies\User Rights Assignment
```

12. And activate the following policy:

```
Allow log on through Remote Desktop Services
```

13. Optional, install the Azure virtual machine agent and run the installer. This is required in order to use VM extensions. The download link is `https://go.microsoft.com/fwlink/p/?LinkID=394789`.

14. Optional, there are several updates and hotfixes recommended to enhance stability of the virtual machine. These include: `KB2904100`, `KB3140410`, `KB313061`, `KB3033930`, and `KB3115224`.

15. As a last step, `sysprep` the virtual machine by running the following commands in the elevated command window:

```
%windir%\system32\sysprep\Sysprep.exe
```

16. In the **System Preparation Tool Window** under **System Cleanup Action** select **System Out-of-Box Experience** and ensure that **Generalize** is selected.

17. In **Shutdown** option, ensure that Shutdown is selected.

18. Click on the `OK` to start `sysprep`. You are ready to upload the VHD file.

Uploading the VHD via portal

In order to upload the VHD, we will create a Resource Group in which we will create a storage account using the Azure Stack portal. It is important to choose the **local** name or the name of the **region** you defined during installation as the location of your storage account as this will save your VHD image in the Azure Stack. After the storage account is created we will have to create a container where the image is temporarily stored until we upload it as a Marketplace item.

When uploading the image you will be asked for the URI to the image. The schema of the path is always the same `https://<azures storage account name>.blob.<Azure Stack domain as defined during deployment>/<container name>/<VHD name.vhd>` to upload it to Azure Stack.

 The Azure Stack domain may be defined during deployment of a multi-node installation. The default value is `azurestack.local`.

During the upload you will have to specify vendor specific information. As the Windows Server information are provided as default values in the Azure Stack portal—I will use Ubuntu Linux as an example in order to show which fields to customize when uploading a new image. To upload the image do the following thing:

1. Login to Azure Stack portal as administrator.
2. Go to **New** | **Data + Storage** | **Storage Account** to create a new one.
3. Enter a name for your storage account—for example, `stackvhds`. Create a new **Resource group**—for example, `DEV-AST2`. Leave the **Default Provider Subscription** or select **Standard_LRS** as **Replication** type as it is currently the only supported option. Choose **local** in **Location** and create the account:

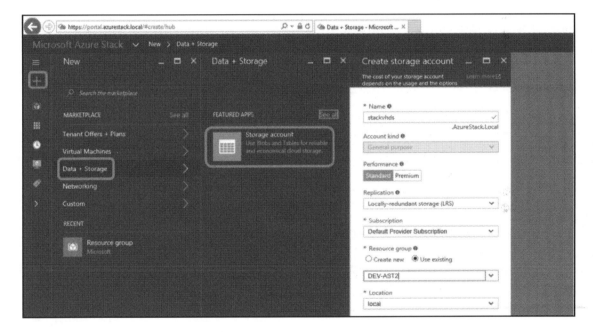

4. Go to **Resource groups** then select your resource group, in our case it's **DEV-AST2**. In the **Overview** window select your created storage account **stackvhds**.

5. To create a new container in the section **Blob Container** click on **Container**, then in the new window select **+Container**. Enter a name for the container, for example, images. Now select container as a **Public** in the **Access type** drop-down.

6. The **Overview** window of your storage account shows the created container images—including the URI of it—based on the previous input the URI in our case is https://stackvhds.blob.azurestack.local/images.

7. Now PowerShell is required to upload the local VHD to the container. Therefore go to your system that you prepared to connect to your Azure Stack environment. We will get the resource group we created, set the URI from step 6 to a variable $URI and providing the local path of our VHD. In my case the Ubuntu Server 16.04 VHD is residing at C:\instal\ubuntu-14-04-LTS.vhd. Therefor enter the following:

```
$RG = Get-AzureRMResoureGroup -Name 'DEV-AST2'
$URI =
'https://stackvhds.blob.azurestack.local/images/Ubuntu-14-04-disk1.vhd'
  $RG | Add-AzureRMVHD -Destination $URI
  -LocalFilePath "C:\instal\ubuntu-14-04-LTS.vhd"
```

8. You should see the following output in case of success:

```
MD5 hash is being calculated for the file  C:\instal\Ubuntu-14-04-LTS.vhd.
MD5 hash calculation is completed.
Elapsed time for the operation: 00:01:54
Creating new page blob of size 32212255232...
Detecting the empty data blocks in the local file.
Detecting the empty data blocks completed.
Elapsed time for upload: 00:00:15
```

9. To upload the VHD image go to **More Services | Region Management**.

10. In the new window select **local** now in the section **Resource Providers** select **Compute**. Now select **VM Images** in the **Content** section.

11. In the VM Images window, click on the **+Add** button. On the right hand side the new tab appears named **Add a VM Image**.

12. Enter the following information to adjust for Ubuntu Server upload:
    - **Publisher**: Canonical
    - **Offer**: UbuntuServer
    - **OS Type**: **Linux**
    - **SKU**: 14-04
    - **Version**: 1.0.0
    - **OS Disk Blob URI**:
      https://stackvhds.blob.azurestack.local/images/ubuntu-1
      4-04-disk1.vhd

13. Verify the details before clicking on the **Create** button to generate the Ubuntu VM image:

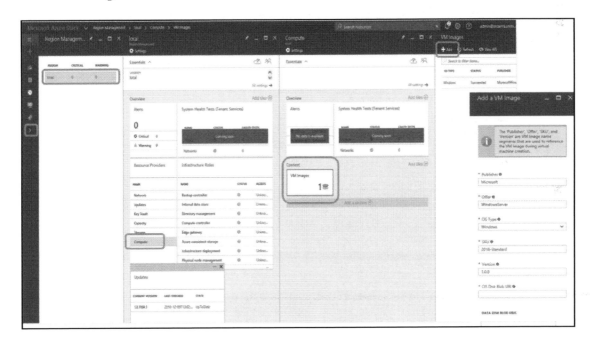

14. After the image is uploaded successfully it is visible at the VM Images section. Navigate to **More Services | Region Management | local |** in the **Resource Providers** section select **Compute | VM Images**.

The VHD gets uploaded and the `manifest.json` file gets created. After the job is successful you may view the VHD and manifest files at `C:\ClusterStorage\Volume1\Shares\SU1_Infrastructure_1\` `CRP\PlatformImages\<id of VHD upload>`.

It is possible to deploy a virtual machine using this image via PowerShell or JSON template. As we want to deploy it using the Azure Stack Marketplace we will have to create the gallery item package first.

Uploading the VHD via PowerShell

In this section we will perform the same steps as before using PowerShell. Please go to your system that is connected to your Azure Stack environment using an administrative account. We will use the same variable names as before. Do the following steps:

1. Create your Resource group `DEV-AST2`:

   ```
   $RG = New-AzureRmResoureceGroup -Name 'DEV-AST2' -Location local
   ```

2. Create your storage account `stackvhds`:

   ```
   $storeaccount = $RG | New-AzureRmStorageAcount -Name stackvhds
   -Type Standard_LRS
   ```

3. Create your container images within storage account `stackvhds`:

   ```
   $container = New-AzureStorageContainer -Name images
   -Permission Blob -Context $storeaccount.Context
   ```

4. Upload your local image:

   ```
   $uploadpath = $container | Set-AzureStorageBlobContent
   -File "C:\instal\ubuntu-14-04-LTS.vhd"
   ```

5. In case you want to simply add your Ubuntu Server 14.04 image without customization, use the provided `Add-VMImage` command. Otherwise move to the section *Preparing the Marketplace item* to create a customized one.

6. To add the image, first we will have to get the `$URI` path the VHD was uploaded to, and provide administrative credentials to your Azure Stack environment:

```
$URI = $uploadpath.ICloudBlob.StorageUri.PrimaryUri.AbsoluteUri
$passwd = ConvertTo-SecureString "<your AAD admin password>"
-AsPlainText -Force
$creds = New-Object PSCredential (<your AAD admin -
for example administrator@yourdomain.onmicrosoft.com, $passwd)
Add-VMImage -publisher "Canonical" -offer "UbuntuServer"
-sku "14-04" -version "1.0.0" -osDiskBlobURI $URI -osType Linux
-tenantID "yourdomain.onmicrosoft.com" -azureStackCredentials
$creds -location local
```

The Ubuntu Server images is now visible in the Azure Stack Portal at **+New** | **Virtual machines** | **Canonical-UbuntuServer-14-04** and may be used for deployment.

Preparing the Marketplace item

Every item, like a virtual machine image that you want to offer via Marketplace requires the following things in order to upload them:

- The Azure Resource Manager template which contains information on how to deploy it
- Metadata information like icons, classification information of the item you want to add
- Formatting information to display the item in the Marketplace

To offer an item via Marketplace two steps must be taken:

1. Create and upload the Marketplace item using the format of an Azure gallery package (`azpkg`)
2. Uploading the resources required by the Marketplace item like virtual machine image (as VHD), software (as ZIP) or code.

We already prepared the VHD with our virtual machine image and uploaded them. So we will focus on creating the required Azure Resource Manager template in order to create the Azure gallery package.

The whole process looks as follows:

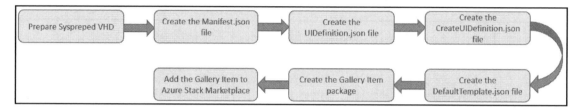

As Windows Server 2012 R2 gallery item is added by default in the Azure Stack we will use this as a starting point. This will make it easier to create the item as we just have to adjust the Linux specific values.

To prepare using the existing gallery item for Windows Server 2012 R2 that comes with the installation of Azure Stack TP2 do the following:

1. To get the existing gallery item go to
   `C:\ClusterStorage\Volume1\Shares\SU1_TenantLibrary_1\GalleryIma`
   `ges\Microsoft.Compute\local\MicrosoftWindowServer.WindowServer-`
   `2012-R2-Datacenter.1.0.0.azpkg` and copy it to a temporary folder like
   `C:\temp`.
2. Rename the file extension from `.aspkg` to `.zip`.
3. Create a folder named `UbuntuServer-16-04` and extract the following folders and files into this one—please keep the same hierarchy. The folders required are, `DeploymentTemplates`, `Icons`, `Strings` and the files are `Manifest.json` and `UIDefinition.json`. In the `DeploymentTemplates` folder delete the `_rels` folder. It should only hold the files `CreateUIDefinition.json` and `DefaultTemplate.json`.

We are now ready to configure the different JSON files.

Creating the Manifest.json file

Open the `Manifest.json` file. I am using the free **Visual Studio Code** from Microsoft but you may use other applications available to you. The `.json` file should look as shown here:

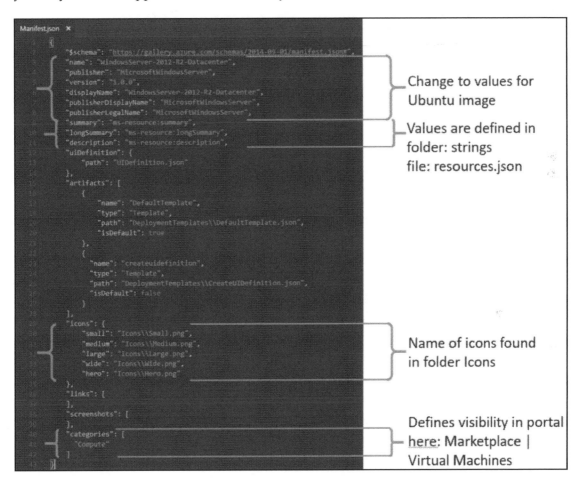

Change the following values to be valid for Ubuntu server:

- Value `name` changes to `UbuntuServer16-04`
- Value `publisher` changes to `Canonical`, please be aware that no spaces should be used in the name
- Value `displayName` changes to `Ubuntu Server 16-04`, this name will be visible to the customer in Marketplace
- Value `publisherDisplayName` changes to `Canonical`, this publisher name will be visible to the customer in Marketplace
- Value `publisherLegalName` changes to `Canonical`, this should be the legal name of the vendor/publisher

The other values do not have to change. To better understand the **Manifest.json** some further explanations of some values. The value path defines the paths to `UIDefinition`, `DefaultTemplate` and `CreateUIDefinition` JSON files. It should not be changed. As shown in the previous screenshot, the value for categories defines where your image is visible in the Marketplace. You may define several categories here.

Creating the UIDefinition.json file

Here you define which blade is used in the Azure Stack portal to deploy the virtual machine. At the time of writing, two blade types are known:

- `CreateVMWizardBlade`
- `DeployFromTemplateBlade`

In the Azure Stack portal the `CreateVMWizaredBlade` found at **New** | **Compute** | **Virtual machines** | **Create Virtual Machine Wizard**.

In the Azure Stack Portal the `DeployFromTemplateBlade` found at **New** | **Compute** | **Custom Image** | **Create From Custom Image**.

We do not have to adjust anything in this file as we want the user to use the **Create VM Wizard**.

Creating the resources.json file

The `resources.json` file may be found in the folder `Strings`. As with the `Manifest.json` files you will have to change several values to reflect the Ubuntu Server image. The following values must be changed:

- `summary:` Create an Ubuntu Server 16.04 image
- `longSummary:` Create an Ubuntu Server 16.04 image. Publisher:Canonical, Offer:Ubuntu, sku:16-04, Version:1.0.0
- `description:` Create an Ubuntu Server 16.04 image. Publisher:Canonical, Offer:Ubuntu, sku:16-04, Version:1.0.0

Change to values for Ubuntu image

Creating the CreateUIDefinition.json file

This JSON file defines what to deploy—in our case we want to deploy a single VM so we may leave the value handler as it is. The `osPlatform` value defines, where the image will be visible in Marketplace in regards to the OS. In addition, you are able to define the sizes recommended and offered to the user. If additional disks are required you would define them in value `dataDisks`.

As before you will have to change several values to reflect the Ubuntu Server image. The following values must be changed:

- `osPlatform`: Linux
- `recommendedSizes`: Can either be left as it is or remove all sizes which you do not want to offer
- `publisher`: Canonical
- `offer`: UbuntuServer
- `sku`: 16-04

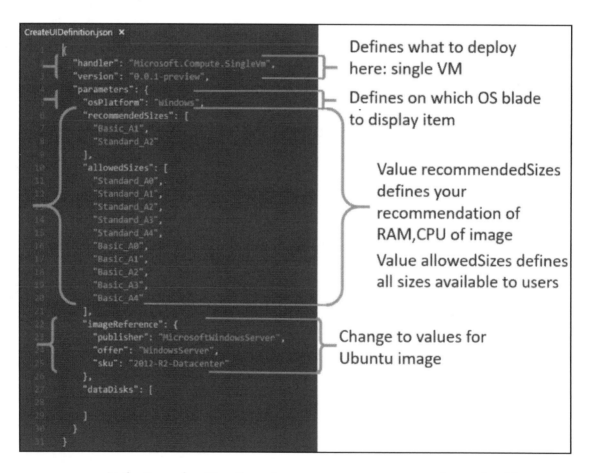

 At the time of writing the values `publisher`, `offer`, and `sku` should not contain any special values like / or spaces—also when using `Add-VMImage` do not use `"."`.

Creating the DefaultTemplate.json file

This may be found in the `DeploymentTemplates` folder. At the time of writing, no good scenario is known to change it. There leave this template as is.

Preparing the icons

The default Windows Server icons may be found in the folder, `Icons`. You will need to provide several icons that will be used in the Marketplace. I looked for an Ubuntu Server icon and used the program Windows Paint to create the correct sizes of them. But you could create your own icons. Just make sure to save them with the correct size and format. The required icons are:

Name	Size	Required
`Large.png`	115 x 115 px	Yes
`Medium.png`	90 x 90 px	Yes
`Small.png`	40 x 40 px	Yes
`Wide.png`	255 x 115 px	NA
`Hero.png`	815 x 290 px	NA

Creating the gallery item package

To create the gallery item package we have to use the **Azure Gallery Packager**. Run the following command:

```
AzureGalleryPackager.exe -m <path to manifest.json file>
-o <path to save the created package to>
```

In order to create the `.azpkg` file perform the following steps:

1. Download the Azure Gallery Packager from `http://aka.ms/azurestackmarketplaceitem`.
2. Extract it, for example in the same folder as the JSON files are in `C:\temp`.
3. Create a folder in `C:\temp\` with the name of `UbuntuServer`. If this folder does not exist next step will give you no results.

4. Open a PowerShell or Command Prompt to create the `GalleryItemPackage` and place it in the `UbuntuServer` folder. The path of the `Manifest.json` file was shown in the section *Creating the Manifest.json file*. Therefore enter the following:

```
cd C:\temp
.\AzureGalleryPackageGenerator\AzureGalleryPackager.exe
-m C:\temp\UbuntuServer16-04\Manifest.json
-o C:\temp\UbuntuServer
```

After the job finishes you should see the `.azpkg` file in the `UbuntuServer` folder. The name should be `publisher.name.version.azpkg`—in our case `canonical.ubuntuserver16-04.1.0.0.azpkg`.

Adding the gallery item

I am assuming you are already connected to the Azure Stack environment. We will reuse the resource group storage account that we created in the step, *Uploading the VHD via PowerShell* and create a new container named `galleryitem`. In order to upload the `.azpkg` file do the following steps:

1. Create a new container for the temporary gallery item:

```
$RG = Get-AzureRmResourceGroup -Name 'DEV-AST2'
$storeaccount = $RG | Get-AzureRmStorageAccount -Name "stackvhds"
$galleryItemContainer = New-AzureStorageContainer
-Name galleryitem -Permission Blob -Context $storeaccount.Context
```

2. Upload the `.azpkg` file to the container `galleryitem`:

```
$galleryitempath = $galleryitemcontainer |
Set-AzureStorageBlobContent -File
"C:\UbuntuServer\Canonical.UbuntuServer16-04.1.0.0.azpkg"
```

3. Get the URI path to the uploaded gallery item package and get the subscription ID available. After that add the gallery item for Ubuntu Server to the Marketplace:

```
$URIGalleryItem =
 $galleryitempath.ICloudBlob.StorageUri.PrimaryUri.AbsoluteUri
$subscriptID = (Get-AzureRmSubscription -SubscriptionName
'Default Provider Subscription').SubscriptionId
Add-AzureRMGalleryItem -SubscriptionId $subscriptID
-GalleryItemUri $URIGalleryItem -Apiversion "2015-04-01"
```

`-Verbose`

4. If it succeeds a status message of **OK** appears.
5. Go to Azure Stack portal—you may have to wait several minutes before you are able to see the Ubuntu Server as administrator and/or as a tenant. The image is available at **+New** | **Virtual machines** | **Canonical-UbuntuServer-16-04**.
6. You are now ready to deploy the VM using the **Create Virtual Machine** wizard.

It is recommended to delete the `.apkzg` file in the storage account we uploaded it in, as it has been added to the Marketplace.

Please be aware of the following two things when deploying a VM image: In *step 1* at OS disk type the value HDD must be selected otherwise you will get a failure for location local.

In *step 3* at **Setting** configure optional features | **Monitoring** | **Boot diagnostics** is set to **Enabled** as default value. As we have not uploaded the diagnostics files to Azure Stack please set this to **Disabled**.

Resource Manager template

After we focused on using the Azure Stack portal GUI and the Marketplace to upload and deploy images we will focus on Azure Resource Manager templates and PowerShell to create and deploy a virtual machine manager image.

We will go into more details starting with basic steps like creating a storage account and finish with a virtual machine template.

Azure Resource Manager template, provides declarative statements to deploy objects from the resource providers available in Azure Stack. This could be a network, storage, or in regards to compute something like a (multi-service) IaaS and/or PaaS services. Focusing on an IaaS service means, you define the deployment and configuration settings for your virtual machine or application. Therefore, each template will contain some combination of the following components:

- Resource Provider (mandatory)
- Template functions like parameters, variables to define resources
- Template functions like (VM) extensions for in guest OS or application customization

A resource could be just a storage account (storage resource provider) or a multi-VM service like a SharePoint Farm (compute resource provider).

Azure Resource Manager performs the necessary process orchestration honoring defined dependencies like in which sequence to perform actions. For example to deploy a virtual machine (compute) a dependency exists to the storage account (storage) as it is required to store the virtual disks. In addition Azure Resource Manager will convert those declarative statements to REST API operations of the correct Resource Provider so that it gets called to create the resources as described in the template. This will ensure the resources are in the correct state and deployed or updated as defined in the template.

Especially the update process of resources is greatly simplified. During an incremental deployment, if a resource like a NIC in a virtual machine already exists, it will be updated as described in the template. If it isn't created yet, the deployment process will create the NIC.

Azure and Azure Stack use the same Azure Resource Manager template model. You could create templates for use in Azure Stack and Azure. Just keep in mind that not all resource providers and template functions available in Azure exist in Azure Stack.

There are several ways to deploy templates. Just like templates the tools to deploy the templates in Azure or Azure Stack work in the same way. Those tools are:

- Azure portal
- Command Line Interface
- Visual Studio
- PowerShell

The only difference is how you connect to the environment, like using the Azure portal for Azure, or Azure Stack portal for Azure Stack deployments.

Understanding the template format

Before starting with creation and deployment of a simple virtual machine using the Azure Resource Manager template we will start with the basic template structure and explain those elements. As mentioned before, at the time of writing there are several hundred sample Azure resource provider templates available. In order for you to adopt those templates to your environment or to your requirements a basic understanding of the Azure Resource Manager template structure and elements is required.

The template is a JSON file where the basic structure looks as follows:

```
{
  "$schema": http://schema.management.azure.com/schemas/2015-01-
01/deploymentTeplate.json#,
  "contentVersion": "",
  "parameters": { },
  "variables": { },
  "resources": [ ],
  "outputs": { }
}
```

The elements are used as follows:

Element name	Mandatory	Description
$schema	Yes	Defines the location of the JSON schema file which describes the version of the template language—that is, which resource type or parameter and so on are available.
contentVersion	Yes	Defines the template version. You may specify any value like 1.0.0.0. This value helps to ensure that the correct template is deployed.
Parameters	No	To allow for flexible deployment, values are defined either as default value or allowed values in order to customize the resource deployment.
Variables	No	To simplify complex expressions, values are defined often based on parameter values.
Resources	Yes	Defines the resource type that are deployed or updated within a resource group.
Outputs	No	Defines values that are returned after deployment.

When working with Azure Resource Manager templates you will come across the terms, expressions and functions. Therefore, a short explanation: expressions and functions are used to extend the basic structure of JSON. Using an expression with a function, could be used to configure a resource a certain way. For example to deploy two network interfaces (network resource) for a VM we could use the copyIndex() function and define a numberOfInstances variable with a value of 2. We will show a complete example using this later on.

Understanding the parameter format

Parameters are not required but they are greatly recommended. Defining parameters allows for user input thus adding flexibility to the deployment process. For example we could use parameters to define the storage account for different environments like development, test, or production. The parameter `storageaccountname` could be defined with a `defaultValue` to ensure that deployment runs through even without any user interaction. In addition, adding `allowedValues` ensures that the user is choosing existing or standardized values only. Otherwise you might end up with different values for the same thing like value `developmentLinux` while the next administrator will define the `DEV-Linux` string.

The basic parameter structure looks as follows:

```
{
"$schema": http://schema.management.azure.com/schemas/2015-01-
01/deploymentTeplate.json#,
"contentVersion": "1.0.0",
"parameters": {
  "NameOfParameter":{
    "type": "string",
    "defaultValue": "value if no interaction occurs",
    "allowedValues": [
      "first_Value",
      "second_Value"
]
    },
    "NameOfNextParameter":{
      "type": "string",
      "metadata": {
        "description": "This structure is used when value will be added
either through parameter json file or when deploying resource like VM by
using the nameofnextparameter = <actual value> "
      }
    }
},
"variables": { },
"resources": [ ],
"outputs": { }
}
```

The elements are used as follows:

Element name	Mandatory	Description
Name of Parameter	Yes	Unique identifier of parameter within the template.
Type	Yes	Must be one of the allowed types. Those are: `string`, `secureString`, `int`, `Boolean`, `object`, or `array`.
`defaultValue`	No	Default value which will be used if nothing is provided in the parameter file or at time of deployment by user.
`AllowedValues`	No	Array of allowed values for parameter to ensure only correct/valid entries are made.

Let us look at an example, in the section *Uploading the VHD via PowerShell* we already created a storage account with location of local and containers. In addition we used the `storageendpoint` of `blob.azurestack.local` to upload things to the Azure Stack environment. The unique way Azure Resource template handles resources, is that we are able to reuse the templates without affecting the current deployed resources. That means the storage account `stackvhds` that we already created will not be overwritten when referenced in our template here. Instead, when using PowerShell and re-using the same template we are informed that the resource group already exists, and asks if an update should be run. If we provide a storage account name which doesn't exist yet, it will be created.

In this example we will also provide the parameter `vmname` for the name of VM. We do not provide a value here. Therefore, a value must be provided at deployment time. On the other hand the parameter for the allowed sizes is defined within the ARM template. Therefore, if no further value is provided during deployment time the default value of `Standard_A2` will be used; otherwise one of the **allowed values** may be chosen. If *PowerShell ISE* or similar tools are used for deployment—the allowed values are displayed. In order to use those we declare them in ARM template as follows:

```
"parameters": {
 "ResoureceGroup":{
 "type": "string",
 "metadata": {
    "Description": "Type name of existing Resource Group containing the
storage account"
    }
  },
"vmName":{
"type": "string"
}
```

```
"vmSize":{
    "type": "string",
    "defaultValue": "Standard_A2",
    "allowedValues": [
    "Standard_A1",
    "Standard_A2",
    "Standard_A5"
    ]
},
"adminUserName":{
"type": "string"
},
"adminPassword":{
"type": "securestring"
},
"storageAccountName":{
    "type": "string",
    "defaultValue": "stackvhds"
    },
    "storageAcountContainerName":{
      "type": "string",
      "defaultValue": "images"
    },
    "storageendpoint":{
      "type": "string",
      "defaultValue": "blob.azurestack.local"
    },
},
```

Understanding the variables format

Variables are either provided by the author within the template or referenced in other parts of the template. We will show this in the section *Understanding the resources format*. Another great point is that you are able to specify the same variable across multiple resources. For example the location local is required to define the storage container that should be created in Azure Stack and not in Azure. At the same time we need to define the deployment location of the VM itself as well. The following are several examples which we need in:

```
"variables": {
    "location": "local", "osType":{ "publisher": "Canonical",
    "offer": "UbuntuServer", "sku": "16-04", }
    "nicName": "vNic", "OSdiskName": "UbuntuServer-16-04",
    "subnetName": "devsubnet01", "addressPrefix": "10.0.0.0/16",
    "subnetPrefix": "10.0.0.0/24",
    "storageAccountType": "Standard_LRS",
    "publicIPnicName": "myPublicIP", "publicIPAddressType": "Dynamic",
```

```
    "virtualNetworkName": "devNET", "storageID":
    [resourceId(parameters('ResourceGroup'),
    'Microsoft.Storage/storageAccounts',
    parameters('storageAccountName')]", "vnetID": "
    [resourceId((parameters('ResoureceGroup'),
    'Microsoft.Network/virtualNetworks',
    variables('virtualNetworkName'))]",  "subnetRef": "
    [concat(variables('vnetID'),'/subnets/',variables('subnetName'))]"
},
```

The first values are just a combination of variable names and values. The last three examples use more advanced template functions. The variable storageID and vnetID use resourceID function. This function returns the unique identifier of a resource. We are using it at this point because we want to use our existing storage account stackvhds in our existing resource group DEV-AST2. This resource is not provisioned within this template; therefore, we are referencing it by using the resourceID.

The variable subnetRef is created using concat. The concat allows us to create a variable by taking the variable vnetID and combine it with the value provided in the variable subnetName.

Understanding the resources format

In this section of the template we define what we are deploying or updating. Usually we define the resources and their configuration values here. The configuration values could be defined within this section or you could reference values that are already added in the parameter or variables section.

The basic resource structure looks as follows:

```
"resources": [
  {
   "apiVersion": "apiVersion of Resourece",
   "type": "ResoureceProviderNamespace/ResoureceTypeName",
   "name": "Name Of Resource",
   "location": "Location Of Resource",
   "tags": "Name value pairs"
   "dependsOn": [
     "Array of Related Resource"
 ],
 "properties": "settings of the resource",
 "resources": [
 "Array of dependint Resources"
   ]
```

```
    }
  ],
```

The elements are used as follows:

Element name	Mandatory	Description
apiVersion	Yes	API version that supports this resource.
Type	Yes	Defines the type of resource.
Name	Yes	Name of the resource
Location	No	Resources providers are available at Azure Stack (local) or at Microsoft Azure locations like **West Europe**. This element defines which to call.
Tags	No	Tags could be used to group resources. Then if you want to delete or update a certain group you could select all of the resources using the defined tag.
dependsOn	No	Defines dependencies of resources. Configuring the virtual NIC with IP, gateway and so on depends on the availability of a virtual NIC when the VM is created. Therefore, it defines the deployment order as a virtual NIC is required first before configuring it. Another example is storage account. If no storage account exists, it must be created first before deploying the VM to it. If no dependsOn is defined resources will be created in parallel.
Properties	No	Resource specific configuration settings.
Resources	No	Defines child resources that depend on the resources that are currently defined.

Let us look at two examples. The first one is the resource to create a vNIC for a VM. In type, we define that a network interface should be created. The name of this vNIC is already defined in the variable section with a value of nicName. Another important part within Resources is the dependsOn elements. As mentioned before, this allows you to define dependencies during deployment as resources are created in parallel for faster deployment. Therefore, to create a vNIC for a VM at least the virtual network to which the VM should be connected to must exist prior to configuration of the vNIC itself The resource section for the network interface looks as follows:

```
    "resources": [
    {
```

```
          "apiVersion": "2015-05-01-preview",
          "type": "Microsoft.Network/networkInterfaces",
          "name": "[variables('nicName')]",
          "location": "[variables('location')]",
          "dependsOn": [
            "[concat('Microsoft.Network/publicIPAdresses/',
             variables('publicIPnicsName'))]",
            "[concat('Microsoft.Network/virtualNetworks/',
             variables('virtualNetworkName'))]"
          ],
        ],
```

Also in the resource section we will add the resource provider compute to configure our virtual machine. All the parameters and variables defined before will be used in this section to configure the settings of our virtual machine. In the parameter section we defined vmname. In the resource section we just referenced name to the previous defined parameter vmName. As another example we will use the value storageAccountName we defined in the parameter section and use this parameter to place our VHD into this existing storage account. Therefore, the resource provider will look as follows:

```
      "resources": [
    {
        "apiVersion": "2015-05-01-preview",
        "type": "Microsoft.Compute/virtualMachines",
        "name": "[parameters('vmName')]",
        "location": "[variables('location')]",
        "dependsOn": [
          "[concat('Microsoft.Network/networkInterfaces/',
           variables('nicName'))]"
        ],
        "properties": {
          "hardwareProfile": {
            "vmSize": "[parameters('vmSize')]"
          },
          "osProfile": {
            "computername": "[parameters('vmName')]",
            "adminUsername": "[parameters('adminUsername')]",
            "adminPassword": "[parameters('adminPassword')]",
        "windowsConfiguration": "{
    "enableAutomaticUpdates": true,
    "provisionVMAgent": true
    }
          },
          "storageProfile": {
            "imageReference": {
              "publisher": "[variables('osType').publisher]",
              "offer": "[variables('osType').offer]",
```

```
            "sku": "[ variables('osType').sku]",
            "version": "latest"
        },
        "osDisk": {
            "createOption": "fromImage",
"name":"[parameters('vmName')]",
"vhd": {
                "uri":
"[concat('http://',parameters('storageAccountName'),'.'
parameters('storageendpoint'),'/',parameters('storageAccountContainerName')
,'/',variables('OSDiskName'),'.vhd')]"
        },
            "caching": "ReadWrite"
        }
    }
],
```

Understanding the output format

In this section, we will define possible outputs from this template. Outputs could be passed into another deployment. One example is when deploying a SQL server you might need connection value as input to create the application server. The basic structure looks as follows:

```
"outputs": {"outputName":{      "type": "type of output value",
"value": "output value",
 }
}
```

The elements are used as follows:

Element name	Mandatory	Description
outputName	Yes	Name of the output value.
Type	Yes	Defines the type of resource. Those are: string, secureString, int, Boolean, object, or array.
Value	Yes	Output value.

Providing complete example using previous values

Following is a complete Azure Resource Manager template to create a single virtual machine. Several parameters and variables were explained previously but more are required to create a VM.

The following example is available for testing the link <URL to example – not yet available>. Save the following example as vmdeploy.json to use in the section Deploy a VM using ARM template. The example looks as follows:

```
{
"$schema": http://schema.management.azure.com/schemas/2015-01-
01/deploymentTeplate.json#,
 "contentVersion": "1.0.0",
 "parameters": {
"ResoureceGroup":{
"type": "string",
"metadata": {
    "Description": "Type name of existing Resource Group containing the
storage account"
    }
},
"vmName":{
"type": "string"
}
"vmSize":{
  "type": "string",
  "defaultValue": "Standard_A2",
  "allowedValues": [
  "Standard_A1",
  "Standard_A2",
  "Standard_A5"
  ]
},
"adminUserName":{
"type": "string"
},
"adminPassword":{
"type": "securestring"
},
"storageAccountName":{
  "type": "string",
  "defaultValue": "stackvhds"
  },
  "storageAcountContainerName":{
```

```
    "type": "string",
    "defaultValue": "images"
  },
  "storageendpoint":{
    "type": "string",
    "defaultValue": "blob.azurestack.local"
  }
  },
  "variables": {
      "location": "local",
      "osType":{
    "publisher": "Canonical",
    "offer": "UbuntuServer",
    "sku": "16-04",
      }
      "nicName": "vNic",
       "OSdiskName": "UbuntuServer-16-04",
     "subnetName": "devsubnet01",
  "addressPrefix": "10.0.0.0/16",
  "subnetPrefix": "10.0.0.0/24",
  "storageAccountType": "Standard_LRS",
  "publicIPnicsName": "myPublicIP",
  "publicIPAddressType": "Dynamic",
  "virtualNetworkName": "devNET",
  "storageID":
"[resourceId(parameters('ResourceGroup'),'Microsoft.Storage/storageAccounts
',parameters('storageAccountName'))]",
  "vnetID":
"[resourceId((parameters('ResoureceGroup'),'Microsoft.Network/virtualNetwor
ks',variables('virtualNetworkName'))]",
  "subnetRef":
"[concat(variables('vnetID'),'/subnets/',variables('subnetName'))]"
},
  "resources": [
{
    "apiVersion": "2015-05-01-preview",
    "type": "Microsoft.Network/PublicIPAdresses",
    "name": "[variables('publicIPnicsName')]",
    "location": "[variables('location')]",
    "properties": {
        "publicIPAllocationMethode": "[variables('publicIPAddressType')]"
  }
      },
{
    "apiVersion": "2015-05-01-preview",
    "type": "Microsoft.Network/virtualNetworks",
    "name": "[variables('virtualNetworkName')]",
    "location": "[variables('location')]",
```

```
            "properties": {
                  "addressSpace": {
"addressprefixes": [
    "[variables('addressPrefix')]"
]
            },
    "subnets": [
        {
"name": "[variables('subnetName')]",
"properties": {
"addressprefixes":"[variables('subnetPrefix')]"
}
                }
        ]
        }
        },
        {
        "apiVersion": "2015-05-01-preview",
        "type": "Microsoft.Network/networkInterfaces",
        "name": "[variables('nicName')]",
        "location": "[variables('location')]",
        "dependsOn": [
          "[concat('Microsoft.Network/publicIPAdresses/',
variables('publicIPnicsName'))]",
        "[concat('Microsoft.Network/virtualNetworks/',
variables('virtualNetworkName'))]"
        ],
"properties": {
            "ipConfiguration": [
        {
"name": "ipconfig1",
"properties": {
"privateIPAllocationMethode":"Dynamic",
"publicIPAdress": {
    "id": "[resoureceID('Microsoft.Network/publicIPAddresses',
variables('publicIPnicsName'))]"
}
"subnet": {
"id": "[variables('subnetRef')]"
}
                }
        }
        ]
        }
        },
        {
        "apiVersion": "2015-05-01-preview",
        "type": "Microsoft.Compute/virtualMachines",
```

```
      "name": "[parameters('vmName')]",
      "location": "[variables('location')]",
      "dependsOn": [
        "[concat('Microsoft.Network/networkInterfaces/',
variables('nicName'))]"
      ],
      "properties": {
        "hardwareProfile": {
          "vmSize": "[parameters('vmSize')]"
        },
        "osProfile": {
          "computername": "[parameters('vmName')]",
          "adminUsername": "[parameters('adminUsername')]",
          "adminPassword": "[parameters('adminPassword')]",
      "windowsConfiguration": "{
    "enableAutomaticUpdates": true,
    "provisionVMAgent": true
    }
        },
        "storageProfile": {
          "imageReference": {
            "publisher": "[variables('osType').publisher]",
            "offer": "[variables('osType').offer]",
            "sku": "[ variables('osType').sku]",
            "version": "latest"
          },
          "osDisk": {
            "createOption": "fromImage",
  "name":"[parameters('vmName')]",
  "vhd": {
              "uri":
 "[concat('http://',parameters('storageAccountName'),'.'
parameters('storageendpoint'),'/',parameters('storageAccountContainerName')
,'/',variables('OSDiskName'),'.vhd')]"
            },
            "caching": "ReadWrite"
          }
        },
    "networkprofile": {
      "networkinterfaces": [
        {
          "id": "[resoureceID('Microsoft.Network/networkinterfaces',
variables('vicName'))]"
        }
        ]
      }
    }
     }
```

```
    ],
    "outputs": {
    }
}
```

Providing a parameter file for deployment

All parameters that we created without a default value must be specified during deployment. For example, we added the parameter ResourceGroup without providing one, therefore, we will be asked to provide a value during deployment. Instead of providing the values during deployment we could create a JSON file containing those parameters and their values. Thus we could create different parameter files for different environment like for production, test, or development. In case we need to update a new value for a specific parameter we just have to change it in the given parameter file.

Save the below example as parameter.vmdeploy.json file to use it in the next section. An example looks as follows:

```
{
"$schema": http://schema.management.azure.com/schemas/2015-01-
01/deploymentTeplate.json#,
"contentVersion": "1.0.0",
    "parameters": {
   "ResoureceGroup":{
   "value": "DEV-ATS2"
   },
   "vmName": {
"value": "DEV-LX01"
},
"adminUserName": {
"value": "myNameDEV"
}
    }
}
```

Deploying a VM using ARM template

As mentioned in the section Resource Manager template, there are several ways to prepare and especially deploy ARM templates. As we have focused on PowerShell we will continue to do so. To deploy the template to Azure Stack you have to be connected to your Azure Stack environment. We will use the `vmdeploy.json` and the `parameter.vmdeploy.json` holding to create the VM. First upload the `vmdeploy.json` and the `parametervmdeploy.json` to your container. Please follow the steps:

1. Using PowerShell create a new container for the temporary JSON files:

   ```
   $RG = Get-AzureRmResourceGroup -Name 'DEV-AST2'
   $storeaccount = $RG | Get-AzureRmStorageAccount -Name "stackvhds"
   $jsonContainer = New-AzureStorageContainer -Name vmdeploy
   -Permission Blob -Context $storeaccount.Context
   ```

2. Upload the `vmdeploy.json` file to the container `vmdeploy` and do the same for the parameter `vmdeploy.json` file:

   ```
   $vmdeploypath = $jsonContainer | Set-AzureStorageBlobContent
   -File "C:\instal\vmdeploy.json"
   ```

3. Get the URI Path to the uploaded JSON file and repeat this step for the `parametervmdeploy.json`—as an example I am assuming `$vmdeployURI` and `$parameterVMdeployURI` are created. Therefore, do the following:

   ```
   $vmdeployURI =
   $vmdeploypath.ICloudBlob.StorageUri.PrimaryUri.AbsoluteUri
   ```

4. Create the VM using ARM template via PowerShell. As we did not define a value for password anywhere but it is defined in the parameter section it has to be provided now by doing the following:

   ```
   New-AzureRMResourceGroupDeployment -Name devLX01
   -ResourceGroupName $RG -TemplateURI $vmdeployURI
   -templateparameterURI $parametervmdeployURI -adminPassword
   "myPassword" -verbose
   ```

We do not have to use the `-templateURI` path as there is a `-templateFile` parameter as well. When using the `-templateFile`—it is most likely that the file resides at a local storage like C partition of your client VM you are connected to the Azure Stack environment. Therefor I would recommend to upload the resources you want to work with to Azure Stack. That way you can ensure that they are available regardless from where you are connected.

Summary

In this chapter we learned how to create, add, and deploy on of the most basic services of Azure Stack—virtual machines. We saw that there are two options to add and deploy them, either as a Marketplace item or as a custom virtual machine image using Azure Resource Management template.

In the next chapter we will learn how this virtual machine image or Marketplace item may be offered to your tenants.

6

Creating a Private Cloud Solution

The previous chapters of this book focused on the components of Azure Stack to define and configure infrastructure/fabric and services of the private cloud. Just as with **Virtual Machine Manager** (**VMM**) and Azure Pack, those underlying components are not visible to the end user (tenant). They see an abstraction of them. The benefits of this approach are self-service, quick allocation, and the deallocation of pooled resources, standardization and automation/optimization.

In this chapter we will introduce the mechanism on how to make those components we created/configured in previous chapters available to the end user (tenants). The main topics are as follows:

- Considerations for creating a Plan and Offer
- Creating a Plan and an Offer
- Short introduction to Subscription

Considerations for creating a Plan and Offer

We will start with a short definition of Plan, Offer, and Subscription to create a basic understanding of those terms.

- Plans are used to group services together that you want to Offer your end users (tenants).
- Offers are created by the Azure Stack service administrator and include one or more Plans. Therefore all the services that are grouped into a Plan are then Offered to the end user through your Offer.

- Subscription is the method used by an end user (tenant) to get (subscribe to) the services the end user wants to use. The end user creates a Subscription in the Azure Stack portal and selects your public Offers. Another approach is for you to approve each Subscription in cases where your Offer is private. Billing is part of a Subscription so that all services/resources used by the end users Subscription is billed to them.

The following diagram provides an overview of the relationship between **Plan** | **Offer** | **Subscription**. There is a large community available at GitHub providing examples for add-ons that you are able to include in your Plan:

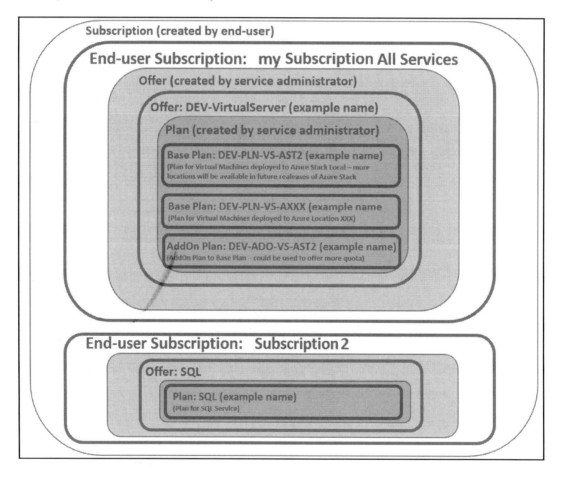

As mentioned before an end user (tenant) creates one or more Subscription based on an Offer that you as the provider created and make public. An alternative is a private Offer where you manage (approval of) Subscriptions for your end users. Each Offer contains one or more Plan(s). Each Plan contains the services, defines the region, and might contain quotas for those services within their specific regions. You could also Offer add-ons to add more quota to a Plan or to Offer services such as for monitoring or billing.

The following table provides an overview of all the elements within a Plan and their ramifications:

Element name	Mandatory	Description
Services	Yes	Each Plan must contain one or more services that you want to Offer. A service could be a storage or virtual NIC but it could be a more complex service like virtual machine or SQL services. Within a Plan you must select all resource providers that are necessary for your service. For example, to offer a storage service you require the `Microsoft.Storage` resource provider, but to offer a virtual machine as a service you require `Microsoft.Storage`, `Microsoft.Network`, and `Microsoft.Compute`.
Quota	No	If active, only a certain amount of your resources will be allocated to this Plan. This allows you some measure of resource management. Please keep in mind that the Quota is per end user Subscription. Default Quotas already exist for each resource provider—so you do not have to configure them.
Region	Yes	Please be aware that each service within a Plan may be configured for one region. If you want to Offer services deployed to Azure Stack and the same service deployed to Azure—you will have to create 2 different services within your Plan with the specific region.
Plan	Yes	You must select a base Plan within your Offer. This defines which services at which location you want to make available to your end user.

Status	Yes	Offers follow the normal life cycle Plan of planning | making an Offer available | decomposing the Offer. The following statuses are available: • **Private**: Offer is visible to service administrator. Used during planning/creating an Offer. If you want to keep an overview of resource allocation, you may use this state, as each Subscription must be approved by service administrator. • **Public**: Visible to end user (tenant). Each end user may subscribe to this Offer. • **Decommissioned**: New Subscriptions cannot be created based on this Offer. All existing Subscription are not affected and will keep running. This is usable to phase out your plans/services.

The key to successfully identifying what Plans and Offers your organization require is a clear understanding of the requirements your end users (tenants) have or which services your organization wants to Offer and how.

Ask the right questions to get an understanding on what to Offer and how.

Using a general approach, those could be:

- What end user groups do you want to Offer which services to?
- How flexible are you with resource allocation within your infrastructure?
- Or what is your largest possible resource allocation for a certain Offer?
- Where do you want to deploy those services to?

Build on the example questions to define the scope of your Offer. Depending on the target end user group, the answers could be quite different.

The first question is the most important one, as it has an influence on the following questions. Who is your end customer and what kind of requirements do they have? Do you provide services to your company or do you Plan to Offer services to the general public or limit it to certain business (partners)?

Let us assume you want to Offer services in your own company. You might have a development team that is writing or adopting applications. This department needs a permanent development environment for programming. For testing purposes they will need additional virtual machines which they will spin off, perform their tests and destroy. Those test machines may not have the same requirements as production machines. For example requirements for I/O performance or high availability of storage, host and network might differ compared to production virtual machines. Based on the requirements of your end user (group) create a Plan that Offers a virtual machine service. For the development team, you may have to create two Plans offering virtual machines but targeting different region. One region contains Hyper-V cluster(s) with the above mentioned lower performance for test virtual machines only and one targeting a standard environment for the development environment. I would recommend to add Quotas to limit the resources used by the development team. This will force them to do some housekeeping. Otherwise the test team might simply deploy new VMs for testing without deleting the older ones even if they are no longer used. This Plan may be used by the whole development team so they will have to decide who may use how many resources assigned to their Plan.

For your operations department you will probably have different requirements and different priorities in regards to the deployment environment and resource allocation. So create a different Plan for this department that will Offer virtual machines as service and might not have any resource quotas assigned. In addition this Plan might be private. Private Plans are not visible to your end users. Therefore you will have to approve the Subscription. Therefore you are able to ensure that your department is involved with every new Subscription/resource allocation or project started by your operations department.

A more general approach for a provider is to create base Plan based on the services Offered. So you might have a Plan offering the service virtual machines and could Offer add-on Plans for location targeting a high performance environments like CPU with higher GHz or storage with higher I/O and shorter latency. Just keep in mind that you will have to create a storage service targeting a high performance storage and a storage service targeting a standard storage in those regions before creating the Plan. Please be aware that within Azure Stack—at the time of writing local is the only Region possible. You may target different location at Azure.

Creating a Plan

As mentioned before, all components required for a service you want to include in your Plan should already exist.

The steps to create a Plan are as follows:

1. Log in to the Azure Stack portal at
   `https://portal.local.azurestack.external/` using an account belonging to the service administrator—for example, the admin account you provided during installation.

2. To create a new Plan, go to **+New** | select **Tenant Offers + Plans** | select **Plan**, as shown in the following screenshot:

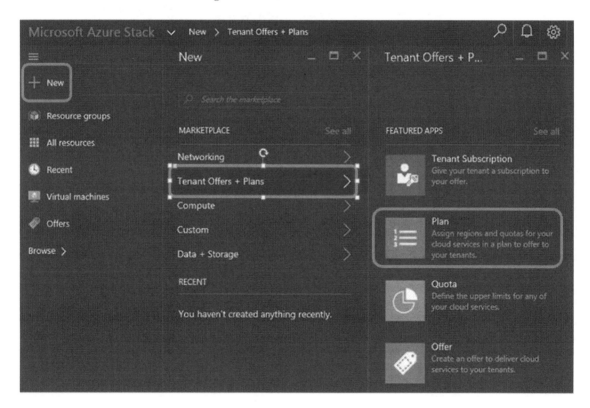

3. In the tab **New Plan**, enter a name for your Plan in the **Display Name** field. This name will be visible to your end user, for example: DEV-VS-PLN. Enter a name in **Resource Name**, which will be visible to administrators only:

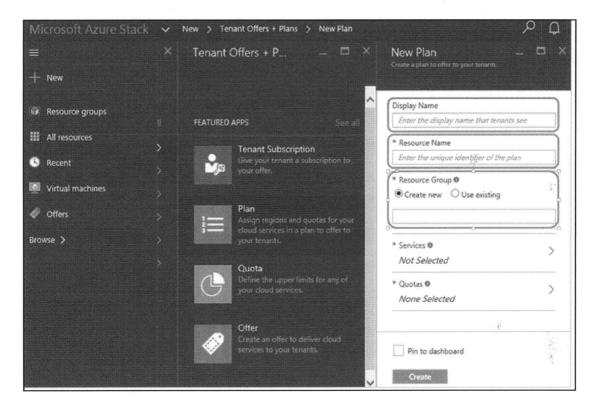

4. Under **Resource Group**, select **Create new** one as container for the Plan or select **Use existing**. Following the structure used in this chapter, the name of my resource group here is DEV-PLN-AST2.

5. Click on **Services**. A new tab opens. Here you must select all resource providers required to deploy your service. In our case we must select **Microsoft.Storage**, **Microsoft.Network**, and **Microsoft.Compute** then press **Select**:

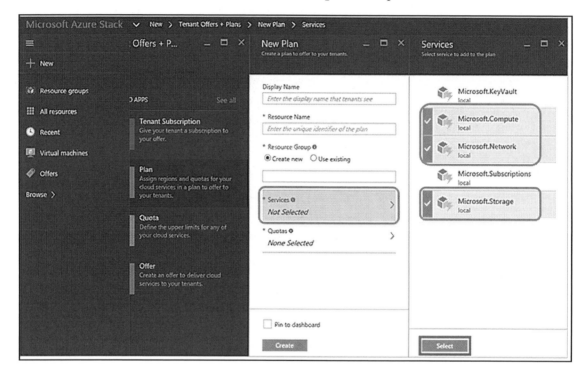

6. Next click on **Quotas** if you want to limit the resource allocated to this Plan. A new tab opens. For each Resource, you are able to set a Quota as shown in the following screenshot:

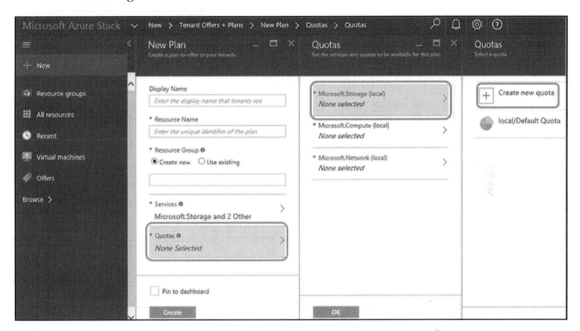

7. Click on **Microsoft.Storage (local)** to open the new tab **Quotas**—see the previous screenshot. Click on **Create new quota**. In the new tab **Create new Quota** provide a **Name** for your Quota rule then select **Quota Settings** to configure the actual Quota. Enter a value in **Maximum capacity (GB)**. I will limit each Subscription to 500 of storage. Therefore, all VMs running within the same Subscription based on this Plan/Offer cannot exceed 500 GB. To limit the storage accounts, enter a value in **Total number of storage accounts**. Click on **OK** to create the settings and **Create** in the **Create new Quota** tab:

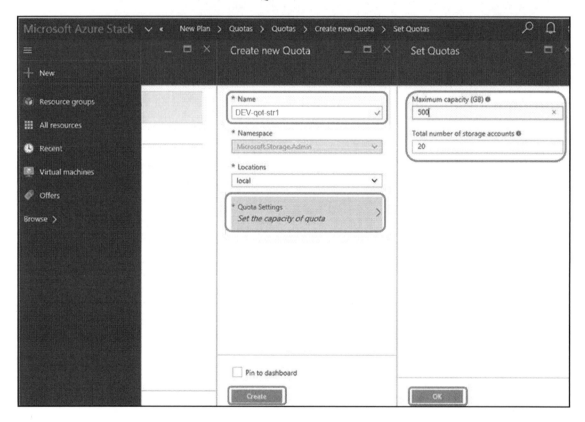

8. Click on **Microsoft.Network (local)** to open the new tab **Quotas**. Click on **Create new quota**. In the new tab **Create new Quota**, provide a **Name** for your quota rule then select **Quota Settings** to configure the actual Quota. In the new tab **Set Quotas**, enter values that you require. The possible values are shown in the following screenshot. Click on **OK** to set these values and in the tab **Create new Quota**, click on **Create** button:

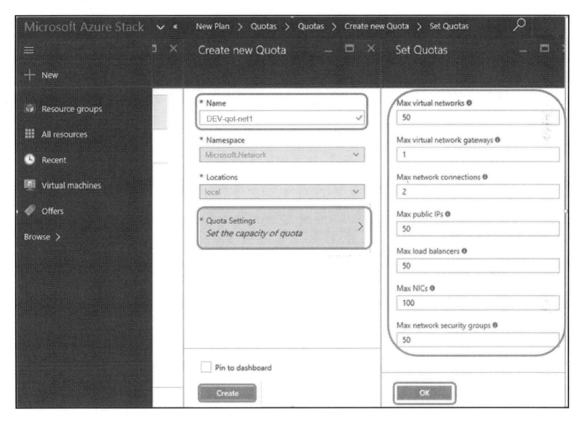

9. Click on **Microsoft.Compute (local)** to open the new tab **Quotas**. Click on **Create new quota**. In the new tab **Create new Quota** provide a **Name** for your Quota rule | select **Quota Settings** to configure the actual Quota. In the new tab Set **Quotas** enter values to limit the number of virtual machines and/or the total number of RAM and vCores for all VMs within this Plan/Offer. Click on **OK** to set this values and in tab **Create new Quota** click on the **Create** button:

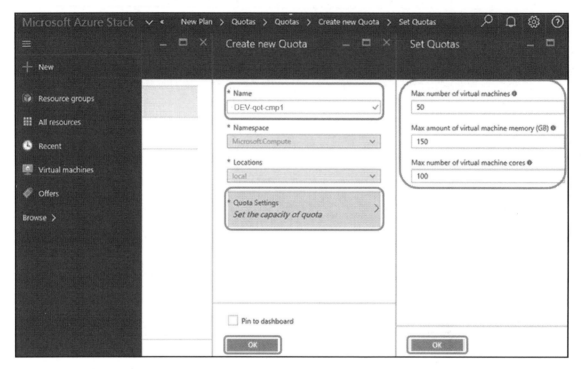

10. After all resource provider that you wanted to set Quotas for are configured click on **OK** in the tab **Quotas** and click **Create** in the tab **New Plan** to create the Plan.

11. Your new Plan DEV-VS-PLN is visible in the portal at **All resources**.

You do not have to set Quota for every resource provider. There is a default Quota available that you could use. In case you want to configure your own Quota, please be aware that you do not have to configure all values. For example in Microsoft.Compute you could limit the number of VMs that may be deployed per description but leave the maximum amount of RAM or vCores open.

Creating an Offer

As mentioned before Offers are displayed to your end user (tenants) which they can subscribe to. You should have created one or more Plans by now as you will include one or multiple Plans in your Offer.

The steps to create an Offer are as follows:

1. Login to the Azure Stack portal at `https://portal.local.azurestack.external/` using an account belonging to service administrator—for example the admin account you provided during installation.

2. To create a new Offer go to **+New** | select **Tenant Offers + Plans** | select **Offer** as shown in the following screenshot:

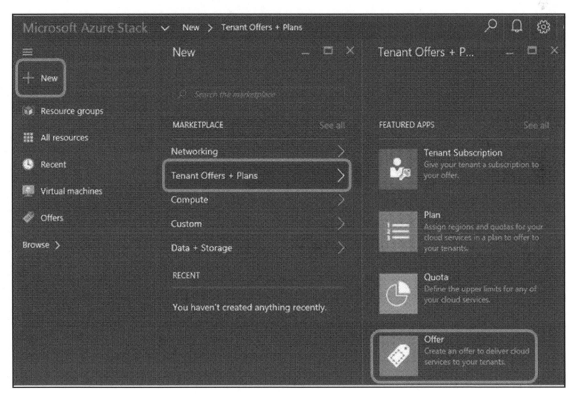

3. In the tab **New Offer** enter a **Display Name** for your Plan I will be using `DEV-VirtualServer` as a name. This name will be visible to your end user. As mentioned in Plans—the **Resource Name** is visible to administrators, only and may be used as an ARM resource.

4. Under **Resource Group** either create a new one as container for the Offer or select an existing one. Following the structure used in this chapter, the name of my resource group here is `DEV-RG-AST2`:

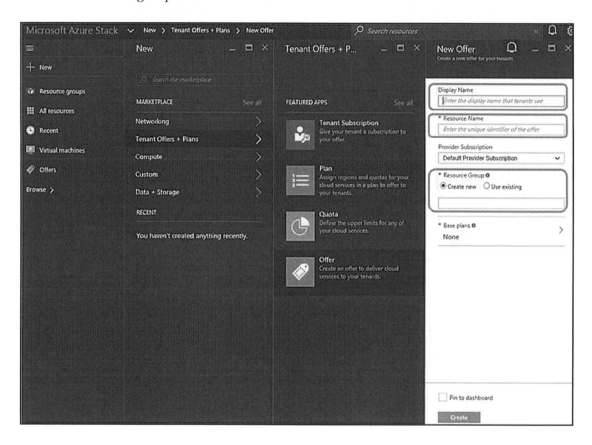

5. Select **Base plans**. The new tab **Plan** opens. Here you are able to select all Plans already created. Select the Plan or Plans you want to include in this Offer and click on **Select** button. In the tab **New Offer** click on **Create** button to create your Offer:

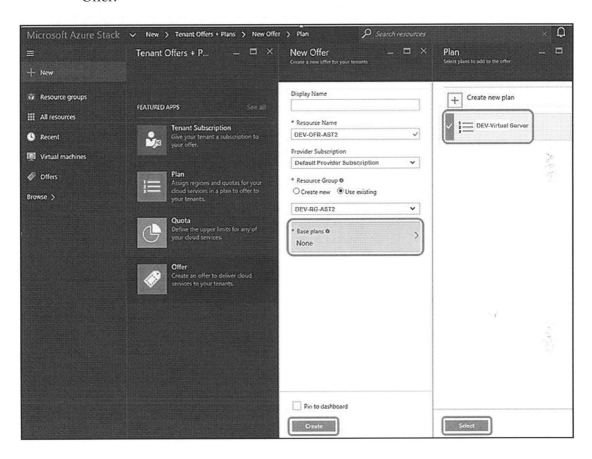

6. In the main navigation menu select **Offers** then select the created Offer—in my example, DEV-VirtualServer:

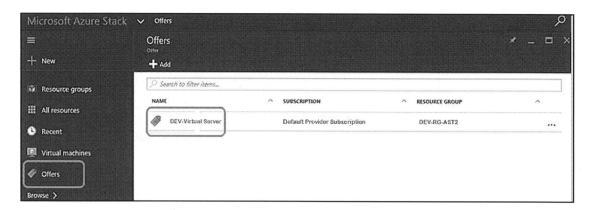

7. A new tab **Offers** opens providing details on your Offer. Go to **Change State** then select the state you want for this Plan either **Public** or leave it at **Private**:

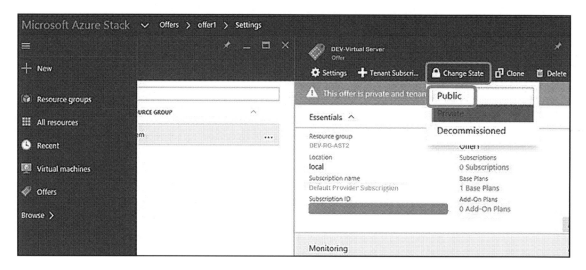

8. The new Offer is not visible to your end user (tenants) until next login. Therefore to view the Offer immediately they would have to logout/login again.

9. The next step is for your tenants to create a Subscription based on your Offer `DEV-VirtualServer`. To do this the end user (tenant) using an account that is part of the Azure Stack domain, has to login to `https://portal.azurestack.local` then in the dashboard select **Get a Subscription** | in the new tab **Get a Subscription** enter a name for it and select **Offer** and choose the Offer you created before, then click on the **Create** button.

Now the end user is able to create their virtual machines—for example the ones available in **Marketplace**, which we added in this chapter.

Summary

In this chapter, we learned about the components required to make the virtual machines service available to our end user (tenants). The virtual machine template, we created in the previous chapter are now available to them.

The next chapter will provide details on how to manage the Azure Stack fabric in addition to the Private Cloud we created previously. In addition, we will look at the tenant perspective for administrating their environment.

7

Understanding Automation in Microsoft Azure Stack

In the previous chapters, you have seen how to create cloud environments in Azure Stack and how to create one or more virtual machines in there. As you have recognized, this all is done with ARM templates and Azure Resource Manager. The ARM template defines the parameters for your resource, and Azure Resource Manager deploys them to the environment. The result of an ARM deployment is one or more virtual machines that are working in the same environment and define a solution in Azure Stack. As you have also already seen, there may be hybrid setups where parts of a solution are from another Azure based-cloud solution such as Azure public.

If we have a look at common solution design scenarios, a solution with various resources contains of default solutions (such as a VM template) and specifications dedicated to a customer environment. How could we set these specifications in the dedicated resources if a VM has been deployed? That is the point where automation comes in. After a resource has been created (using ARM), the automation jumps in, modifies an environment and configures services and roles, modifies a default VM, and adds customizations. With VMs, we have different ways of doing that, depending on the operating system of the VM (such as Windows or Linux). We will have to talk about custom scripts and **DSC** (knows as **Desired State Configuration**) PowerShell configurations.

Another type of automation task is any task that needs to run periodically or is event based. This is where Azure automation provides a solution (as part of the Microsoft Operations Management Suite or as a single solution). You can run scripts (so-called **runbooks**) based on a schedule or an event trigger. With Azure Stack, as of today, this is impossible. Therefore, we will need to talk about Azure Stack hybrid automation. This means that we will need to create a hybrid solution and set up a configuration to fire up PowerShell scripts from Azure public to an Azure Stack environment that needs to be connected to Azure.

In this chapter, we will cover the following topics:

- VM extensions
- Azure Stack hybrid automation

VM extensions

VM extension is some kind of script that will run after the ARM deployment has finished. You can set up a VM extension in the ARM Portal, depending on the operating system, as follows.

Windows VM extensions

A Windows VM provides three different solutions:

- **Custom Scripts Extension**
- **Microsoft Antimalware** extension
- **PowerShell Desired State Configuration** extension

In the following screenshot the three different resources are illustrated:

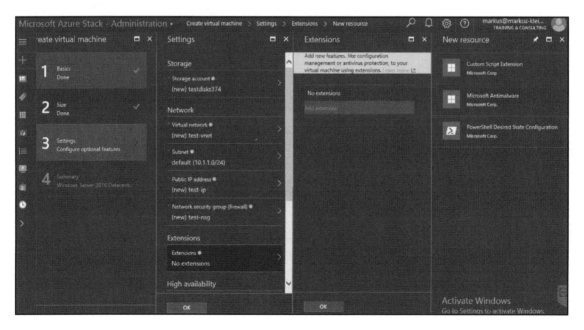

Microsoft Antimalware extensions

The easiest VM extension is one that installs a **Microsoft Antimalware** extension:

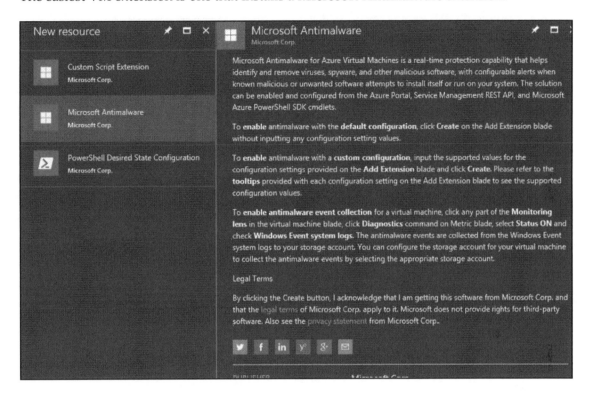

With **Microsoft Antimalware**, you will get a valid solution for antimalware and antivirus on your Windows Server instance that provides an industrial standard with valid antimalware and antivirus patterns. You will not have to use any other third-party vendor solution for it. As of today, with Azure Stack, it is only available for Windows VMs.

Custom Script Extension

A custom script is anything that could be executed inside a VM:

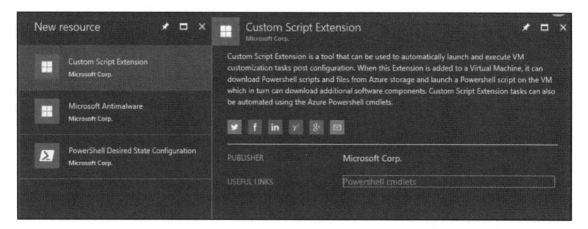

As you can see, a custom script is more or less a PowerShell script that turns on additional software components or installs third-party software solutions after the VM has been installed.

Let's look at the concept of minimizing the TCOs of setting up and updating individual VMs. We talked about downloading a generic VM template for Windows from Azure and defining the portions of a VM to make it your VM; this is the correct point to run the corresponding scripts to make a default VM template specific to your company.

PowerShell Desired State Configuration extensions

As a third option, there is a way to run PowerShell DSC extensions on your VM:

DSC is a powerful solution to declaratively define a configuration for a VM using a JSON file, and PowerShell DSC makes sure that it will be configured as defined and--if you want it like that--it will be mandatory. This means that if somebody were to change it to something else, the system would automatically change it back.

Samples from real-world DSC configurations could be as follows:

- Enabling roles or features on your VM
- Setting network configurations (such as IP address, gateway, and static routes)
- Installing third-party software (such as your company's defined security solution)

The requirement for DSC is an operating system that supports **Windows Management Framework (WMF)** 4.0 or 5.0.

A full list of supported OSes can be found here:
https://blogs.msdn.microsoft.com/powershell/2014/11/20/release-h
istory-for-the-azure-dsc-extension/

The DSC extension for Windows VMs uses the Azure Agent VM framework to interact with and report on DSC configurations. A DSC extension itself is a `.zip` file that contains the configuration document and the parameters provided by the Azure PowerShell SDK or the Azure portal itself.

To get a full list of Azure VM extensions, the following PowerShell will help:

```
Get-AzureRmVmImagePublisher -Location local | `
Get-AzureRmVMExtensionImageType | `
Get-AzureRmVMExtensionImage | Select Type, Version
```

The output should look something like this:

```
PS C:\> Get-AzureVMAvailableExtension -ExtensionName IaaSDiagnostics

Publisher                      : Microsoft.Azure.Diagnostics
ExtensionName                  : IaaSDiagnostics
Version                        : 1.2
Label                          : Microsoft Monitoring Agent Diagnostics
Description                    : Microsoft Monitoring Agent Extension
PublicConfigurationSchema      :
PrivateConfigurationSchema     :
IsInternalExtension            : False
SampleConfig                   :
ReplicationCompleted           : True
Eula                           :
PrivacyUri                     :
HomepageUri                    :
IsJsonExtension                : True
DisallowMajorVersionUpgrade    : False
SupportedOS                    :
PublishedDate                  :
CompanyName                    :
```

As only one extension per VM is possible, you will have to use nesting to add more than one. A sample of template nesting is as follows:

```json
    },
    {
      "comments": "Extension to install additional Software",
      "name": "Software",
      "type": "Microsoft.Resources/deployments",
      "apiVersion": "2015-01-01",
      "dependsOn": [
        "[concat('Microsoft.Compute/virtualMachines/', variables('vmName'), '/extensions/Microsoft.Azure.Diagnostics.IaaSDiagnostics')]"
      ],
      "properties": {
        "mode": "Incremental",
        "templateLink": {
          "uri": "[variables('ArtifactLocationInstall')]",
          "contentVersion": "1.0.0.0"
        },
        "parameters": {
          "ArtifactLocationInstall": {
            "value": "[variables('ArtifactLocationInstall')]"
          },
          "vmName": {
            "value": "[variables('vmName')]"
          }
        }
      }
    }
  ]
```

This is how it looks:

```json
{
  "$schema": "https://schema.management.azure.com/schemas/2015-01-01/deploymentTemplate.json#",
  "contentVersion": "1.0.0.0",
  "parameters": {
    "ArtifactLocationInstall": {
      "type": "string"
    },
    "vmName": {
      "type": "string"
    }
  },
  "resources": [
    {
      "type": "Microsoft.Compute/virtualMachines/extensions",
      "name": "[concat(parameters('vmName'),'/CustomScriptExtension')]",
      "apiVersion": "2015-06-15",
      "location": "[resourceGroup().location]",
      "properties": {
        "publisher": "Microsoft.Compute",
        "type": "CustomScriptExtension",
        "typeHandlerVersion": "1.8",
        "autoUpgradeMinorVersion": "true",
        "settings": {
          "commandToExecute": "powershell (parameters('ArtifactLocationInstall'),'InstallSoftware.ps1'"
        }
      }
    }
  ]
}
```

To work with nested templates, you will have to run the following steps:

1. Create the corresponding PowerShell scripts.
2. Create the parent ARM template.
3. Create the nested ARM template.
4. Upload the PowerShell scripts.
5. Upload nested ARM template.
6. Execute the PowerShell deployment script.

As you may have seen before, DSC is a powerful toolset to define a configuration inside a VM in the same way you do with ARM templates: the declarative way. The options that are available with DSC are unbelievable. It starts with setting up roles and features of a VM, comes to configuration tasks, and goes on to setting up and configuring third-party software, as soon as it provides a way for scripting.

Linux-based VM extensions

If you are deploying a Linux-based VM, the following extensions are available:

- **Custom Script for Linux**
- **Docker**

As illustrated in the following screenshot:

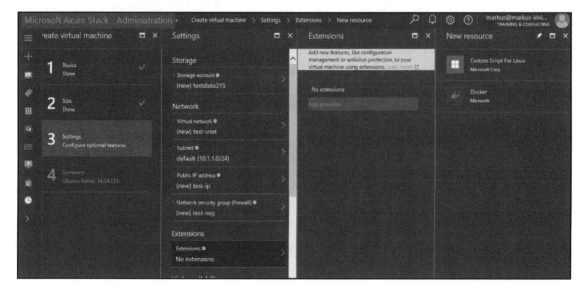

Custom Script for Linux

To enable **Custom Script for Linux** using the VM extensions feature, you will have to have the Azure (Stack) VM agent running on your virtual machine. It will be enabled in the following conditions:

- When you create a VM using the ARM portal and select an image from the marketplace.
- When you create a VM using the `New-AzureVM` or `New-AzureQuickVM` cmdlets.
- When you manually create a VM, you will need to set the `ProvisionGuestAgent` property to `true`. This can be done via the following script:

```
$vm = Get-AzureVM -ServiceName $svc -Name $name
$vm.VM.ProvisionGuestAgent = $TRUE
Update-AzureVM -Name $name -VM $vm.VM -ServiceName $svc
```

 If you need to install the agent manually, you can find it here: `https://github.com/Azure/WALinuxAgent`

You could add the custom scripts as follows:

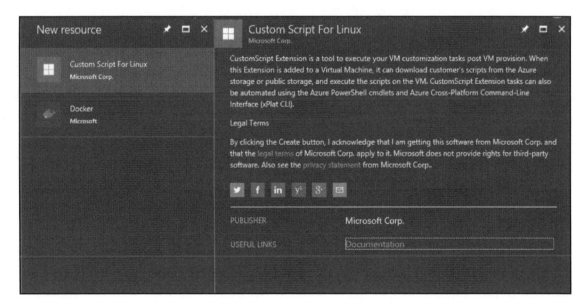

Using scripts, a lot of customization is possible.

 The following URL shows some sample Linux scripts running as extensions:
`https://blogs.msdn.microsoft.com/linuxonazure/2017/02/12/extensi`
`ons-custom-script-for-linux/`

As you can see, we are currently missing the DSC extension for Linux, although it's technically possible to make one.

As of now, it is not fully supported and tested with Azure Stack. You could add it using the following how-to:

`https://github.com/Azure/azure-linux-extensions/tree/master/DSC`

Also have in mind that--as of today--Linux DSC is just at its start, and time will show how it will develop and provide better experiences than Linux scripts.

Linux Docker extension

The Linux **Docker** extension provides the Docker daemon and installs and configures it on the VM to listen to the Docker client:

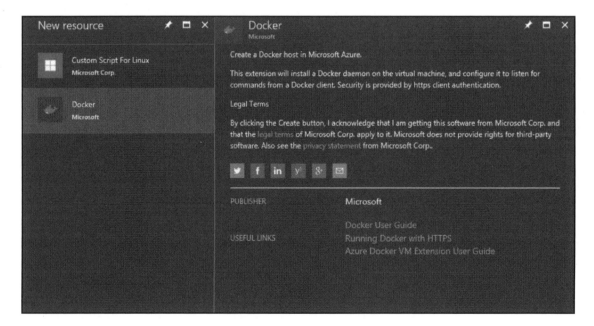

Docker is a popular virtualization approach that uses Linux containers as a way of isolating data and computing on shared resources. You can use the Docker VM extension and the Azure Linux agent to create a Docker VM that hosts any number of containers for your applications on Azure.

For more details on Docker, the following link could help
`https://channel9.msdn.com/Blogs/Regular-IT-Guy/Docker-High-Level-Whiteboard`.

After having successfully deployed the Docker-enabled VMs in Azure Stack (or even Azure in a hybrid setup), we could start and add these VMs to a Docker orchestrator such as Swarm, Kubernetes, or DCOS.

The following URLs describe how to connect Docker VMs to their orchestrator:
`https://docs.microsoft.com/en-us/azure/container-service/kubernetes/container-service-kubernetes-walkthrough`
`https://docs.microsoft.com/de-de/azure/container-service/dcos-swarm/container-service-docker-swarm`

Azure Stack hybrid automation

As I have already mentioned, Azure Stack as of today does not provide any fully integrated automation feature compared to public Azure. When do you need automation like this? Do you want any scripts that have to run on a regular basis? Do you need scripts that start if a specific event occurs? This is the appropriate use case for Azure automation.

One solution is using other runbook automation tools on premises, such as System Center Orchestrator, and using them for your Azure Stack automation tasks. Alternatively, you could use the most powerful toolset Microsoft ever developed: PowerShell. You will find a solution using these tools for most of your scenarios, and if you are in a disconnected scenario with your Azure Stack setup, this is the right way of doing it.

If you are running Azure Stack in a connected scenario, there are other ways to solve this without providing any additional orchestration and automation solution: we could plug Azure Stack to Azure automation and use the features directly. We could call this Azure Stack hybrid automation.

To use Azure automation, we would need to set it up at first, if it is not already being used. This could be done in different ways. If we do it using the Azure portal, this is how to do it:

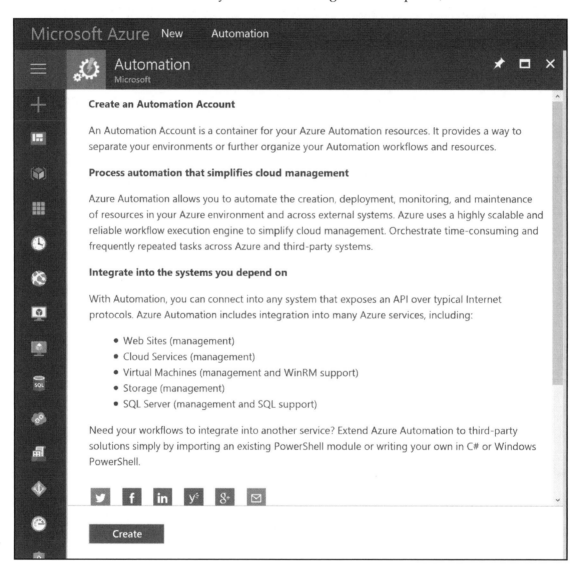

After hitting the **Create** button, we would need to set the properties for it:

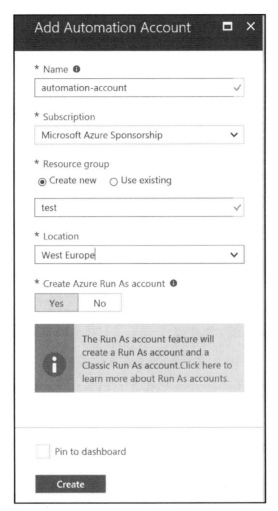

 The important part is choosing an appropriate **Resource group** name based on your naming convention and the Azure region (such as **West Europe**).

After it has been created, you will find the following view in Azure:

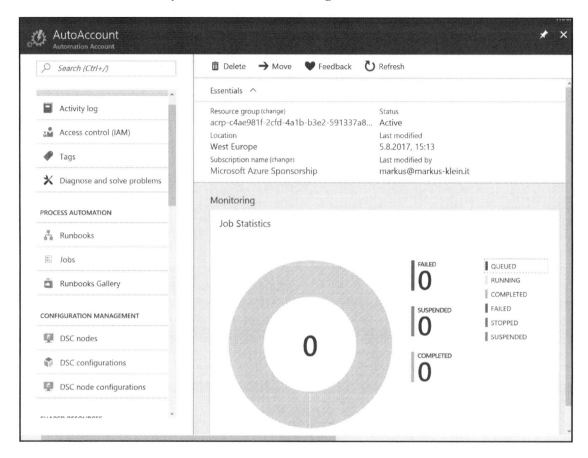

In this overview, we see a monitoring pane with all jobs that are completed, suspended, or failed. This gives a good overview. On the left, there are the two main parts automation works with:

- Process automation
- Configuration management

Process automation

Process automation deals with runbooks. You can see all of it in this pane:

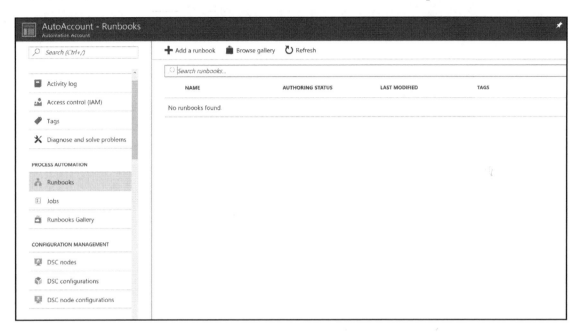

You could add your (existing) runbook manually or using the gallery:

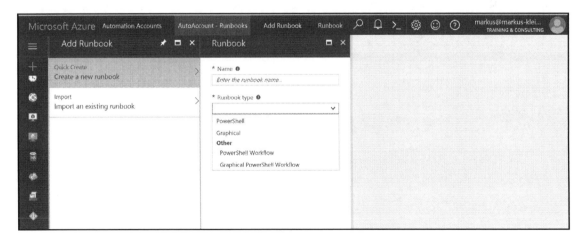

As you can see, a runbook could be created in two ways: using a text editor or a graphical editor for setting up the basic structure:

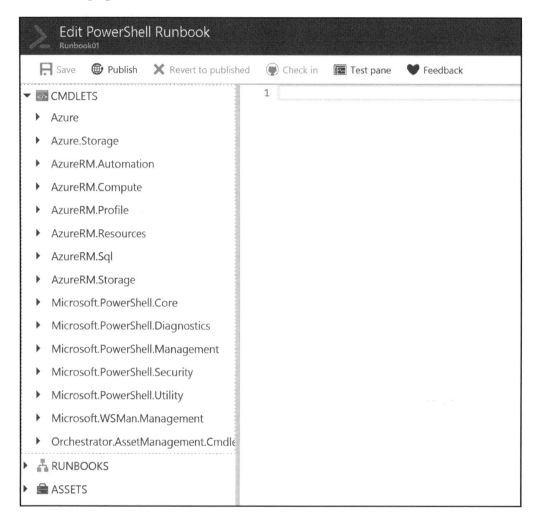

It could be a **PowerShell workflow**, too. If you have your existing workflows from Orchestrator or anything else, you just could add them with minor modifications.

If you choose a gallery, you will have to choose the gallery target first:

This could be either **PowerShell Gallery** or the **Script Center**:

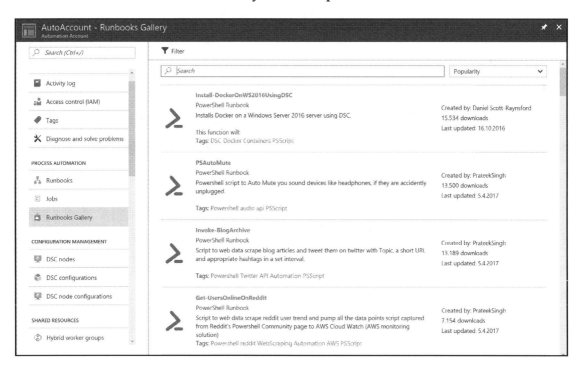

As you can see, there are different basic scripts that could be added and used directly or with small modifications:

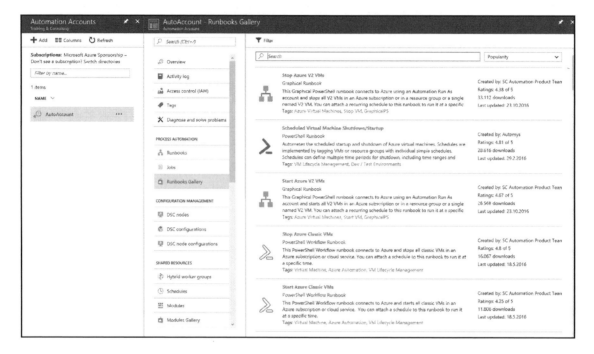

If you will not be using a runbook, you could even use DSC for this. This means that you could set up DCS nodes (responsible for DSC) in Azure or on premises in Azure Stack. This is where all automation finally becomes hybrid:

As you can see, each VM (in Azure or on premises) is supported as a DSC node unless it is a Linux VM, as this is currently unsupported.

Summary

As you have seen in this chapter, there are different ways to provide automation with Azure Stack. If we talk about something that needs to happen in a VM as the last step after it has been deployed, we could do this with the VM extension feature. As things become more complex and we need a fully orchestrated and automated setup, the well-known old-school automation tools could help, but the smoother way (if we are in a connected scenario) would be to use Azure automation as a hybrid solution and provide on-premises Azure Stack automation using a connected scenario running and orchestrating automation tasks from Azure public.

8
Creating PaaS Services in Microsoft Azure Stack

The goal of Azure Stack is not **Infrastructure as a Service (IaaS)**, as there are better solutions in the market just running VMs. If you just want to run some VMs somewhere and not in your data center, you may even think of a Hyper-V cluster with Virtual Machine Manager as the management solution.

A cloud solution always starts to invoice itself and start gaining money if you think about more than a lift and shift scenario (which means migrating each VM on premise 1:1 to the cloud). Often, it even costs more than running the same VMs in your data center. As most of the cloud solutions provide a solution to power off VMs when you are not using them and power them on when you really need them, but it is that one you are really willing to use? Do you run VMs in your data center and power them on only if you need them? From a pay as you go model perspective, this will reduce the costs and drive your cloud solution to a more economical one from the business perspective. Costs will start decreasing when you start using multi-tenant solutions on a PaaS basis.

Platform as a service (PaaS) means that in regard to shared responsibility in cloud environments, you are not responsible for the VM and the OS; you are running your services (for example, a SQL database) on an existing SQL Server cluster. You are responsible for the database and the cloud provider is responsible for running the VM plus OS plus basis application (for example, SQL Server) itself:

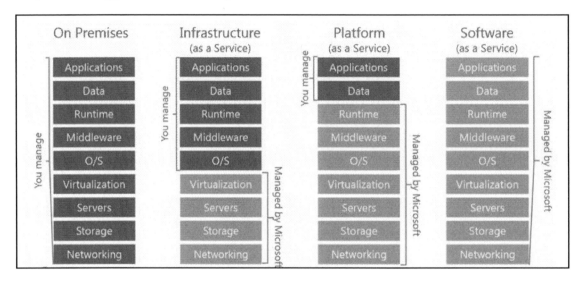

Source:
https://acomdpsstorage.blob.core.windows.net/dpsmedia-prod/azure.microsoft.com/en-us/documentation/articles/azure-security-best-practices-software-updates-iaas/20151102073235/sec-cloudstack.png

The example SQL Server is a good way to explain even the business aspects a little more. In general, everybody knows how expensive a SQL Server license is and what resources you really need for a powerful database of an application. If you could just use an existing SQL Server with your database, that would cost lesser per database for sure, and if you think about your IT infrastructure, how many SQL Server are actually running with only a single database on it? How many resources could be set free if you would start using these databases on a single SQL Server cluster?

If we take a step forward and move this story to a private cloud environment with hybrid connectivity, you will have to rethink the story a little bit. If you are running the Azure Stack environment, it means that you will have to run the SQL Server environments yourself. If you are using an Azure Stack environment at a service provider, you would not have to run the environment as your responsibility. This needs to be considered when planning your hybrid cloud environment.

As Azure Stack owns the concept of resource providers, you will note that each additional resource provider will follow the same concept to interact with the ARM technology. In general, you will see that each new PaaS solution from Azure Stack will bring its own virtual machines (a minimum of one) with its own web service and some ARM integrations.

For GA, you will find three additional resource providers with PaaS solutions; these are as follows:

- Microsoft SQL resource provider
- MySQL resource provider
- App Service resource provider

On the following pages, we will describe these resource providers and discuss their installation, requirements, and features in depth. You will learn how to add them to your Azure Stack environment and which administrative processes are required.

Microsoft SQL resource provider

From a design perspective, the resource providers should be the same as with Azure microservices, which will be possible in general. As of today, there is only one different resource provider in comparison to Azure, which is the Microsoft SQL resource provider. In Azure, it automatically spins up VMs in the background on the existing SQL Server farms Azure relies on. The Azure Stack resource provider is a little bit different as it does not automatically scale out the SQL Server environment. It just manages them, but you will need to add them as dedicated environments.

The Azure Stack resource provider is, therefore, more or less compatible with the old Azure Pack resource provider as it has the same functionality. Elastic database pools and the ability to scale database performance up and down automatically are unavailable. However, it does support create, read, update, and delete operations in SQL.

The resource provider consists of three components:

- SQL resource provider adapter VM, which is a Windows VM running the provider services
- SQL resource provider itself, which processes requests and exposes database resources
- Servers that host SQL Server, which provides capacity for databases

Preparations

To prepare the installation of the Microsoft SQL resource provider, you will have to meet the following requirements on the host:

- Windows Server 2016 image or SQL Server 2016 image
- The SQL Server Extension for Windows VMs

You can find these images on the Azure Marketplace if you have enabled the Marketplace syndication feature.

In addition, the most important requirement is to plan the SQL Server databases offerings you would like to integrate in your Azure Stack offerings.

A good practice is to plan based on t-shirt sizes, which means *small, medium, large* and *x-large* in regard to availability, performance, and **Service Level Agreement (SLA)**.

You will have to set up the SQL hosting servers in advance in order to be able to provide these offers to your customers:

Name	SQL hosting server	SLA
Small	SQL on HDD storage	95%
Medium	SQL on SSD storage	99%
Large	SQL on Always On cluster	99.5%
x-Large	SQL on HA cluster	99.9%

Based on these offerings, you will need to size the machines where the SQL instances reside and which SLA you are willing to offer on the sizes and for how many databases you are planning to host on.

In regard to SQL Server editions, SQL Server 2012 and higher are supported with the resource provider.

In addition, you will have to plan all SQL Server instances in regard to authentication as Azure Stack Microsoft SQL services because it does not support Active Directory authentication. Therefore, you will have to enable SQL Server authentication on the servers. If the server setup itself will have Active Directory authentication enabled, you would have to design a mixed authentication environment.

Installation

When installing the Azure Stack Microsoft SQL resource provider, this needs to be done from a computer where Azure Stack and Azure PowerShell has been installed. If you have installed any versions of the AzureRM or Azure Stack PowerShell modules other than 1.2.9 or 1.2.10, you will need to remove them. This includes versions 1.3 or higher.

Now we need to download the resource provider. The download location for the Microsoft SQL resource provider is `https://aka.ms/azurestacksqlrp`.

After you have downloaded the file, you will need to log on as the AzureStackAdmin account and extract it on the deployment VM.

On the development toolkit, the resource provider is extracting the root CA certificate and creating a self-signed one for the deployment itself. On multi-node deployments, you need to provide your own certificates and copy to a local directory. You need the following certificates:

- A wildcard certificate for `*.dbadapter.<region>.<external fqdn>` needs to be created. This certificate must be trusted and the certificate chain must work properly.
- The root certificate used by your Azure Resource Manager instance. If it is not available, it will be extracted.

While preparations are now finished, we can start the deployment by running the following deployment script called `DeploySqlProvider.ps1` from an elevated PowerShell prompt.

During the deployment, the following steps are performed:

- Upload the certificates to a storage account on your Azure Stack system
- Publish gallery packages to the gallery
- Deploy a VM using the Windows Server 2016 image and install the resource provider on it
- Register a local DNS entry that maps to the resource provider VM
- Register the resource provider with the Azure Stack Resource Manager (tenant and admin)

 The installation of the resource provide may take more than 90 minutes; if there are any issues, the deployment behavior is the same as with Azure Stack itself: you will see an error message, the error will be logged, and the installation will try to rerun from the failed step once you run the deployment again.

With the following PowerShell script, provided by Microsoft, the installation will run through, if you would change the accounts and REST endpoints, if needed before:

```
# Install the AzureRM.Bootstrapper module
Install-Module -Name AzureRm.BootStrapper -Force

# Installs and imports the API Version Profile required by Azure Stack into
the current PowerShell session.
Use-AzureRmProfile -Profile 2017-03-09-profile
Install-Module -Name AzureStack -RequiredVersion 1.2.10 -Force

# Download the Azure Stack Tools from GitHub and set the environment
cd c:\
Invoke-Webrequest
https://github.com/Azure/AzureStack-Tools/archive/master.zip -OutFile
master.zip
Expand-Archive master.zip -DestinationPath . -Force

# This endpoint may be different for your installation
Import-Module C:\AzureStack-Tools-master\Connect\AzureStack.Connect.psm1
Add-AzureRmEnvironment -Name AzureStackAdmin -ArmEndpoint
https://adminmanagement.local.azurestack.external

# For AAD, use the following
$tenantID = Get-AzsDirectoryTenantID -AADTenantName <your directory name> -
EnvironmentName AzureStackAdmin

# For ADFS, replace the previous line with
# $tenantID = Get-AzsDirectoryTenantID -ADFS -EnvironmentName
```

```
AzureStackAdmin

$vmLocalAdminPass = ConvertTo-SecureString P@ssw0rd1 -AsPlainText -Force
$vmLocalAdminCreds = New-Object System.Management.Automation.PSCredential
(sqlrpadmin, $vmLocalAdminPass)

$AdminPass = ConvertTo-SecureString P@ssw0rd1 -AsPlainText -Force
$AdminCreds = New-Object System.Management.Automation.PSCredential
(admin@mydomain.onmicrosoft.com, $AdminPass)

# change this as appropriate
$PfxPass = ConvertTo-SecureString P@ssw0rd1 -AsPlainText -Force

# Change directory to the folder where you extracted the installation files
and adjust the endpoints
<extracted file directory>\DeploySQLProvider.ps1 -DirectoryTenantID
$tenantID -AzCredential $AdminCreds -VMLocalCredential $vmLocalAdminCreds -
ResourceGroupName SqlRPRG -VmName SqlVM -ArmEndpoint
https://adminmanagement.local.azurestack.external -TenantArmEndpoint
https://management.local.azurestack.external -DefaultSSLCertificatePassword
$PfxPass
```

As per https://www.microsoft.com, the DeploySQLProvider.ps1 has the following parameters that you can modify for a different installation behavior:

Parameter name	Description	Comment or default value
DirectoryTenantID	The Azure or ADFS Directory ID (GUID).	required
AzCredential	Provide the credentials for the Azure Stack service admin account. You must use the same credentials as you used for deploying Azure Stack.	required
VMLocalCredential	Define the credentials for the local administrator account of the SQL resource provider VM. This password is also used for the SQL sa account.	required

ResourceGroupName	Define a name for a resource group in which items created by this script will be stored, for example, `SqlRPRG`.	required
VmName	Define the name of the virtual machine on which to install the resource provider, for example, `SqlVM`.	required
DependencyFilesLocalPath	Your certificate files must be placed in this directory as well.	optional
DefaultSSLCertificatePassword	The password for the `.pfx` certificate.	required
MaxRetryCount	Define how many times you want to retry each operation if there is a failure.	2
RetryDuration	Define the timeout between retries in seconds.	120
Uninstall	Remove the resource provider and all associated resources (refer to the following notes).	No
DebugMode	Prevents automatic cleanup on failure.	No

Table source: https://docs.microsoft.com/en-us/azure/azure-stack/azure-stack-sql-resource-provider-deploy#deploy-the-resource-provider

Verifying the resource provider deployment

To verify the installation, you should double-check the following points in the admin portal of Azure Stack:

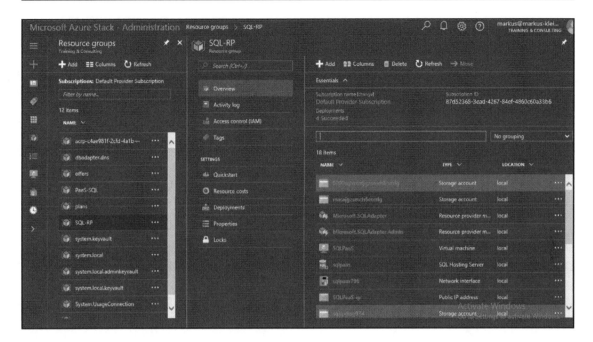

If the resource group in Azure Stack whose name you have provided during the deployment of the resource provider exists and the resources are created, the deployment should be fine.

> Based on my experiences, it is good to wait 1-2 hours before starting the next steps and creating offers with the Microsoft SQL resource provider, as some steps need to be done internally with Azure Stack before completely enabling the new resource provider.

Adding a SQL hosting server capacity

If you have played with the **Technical Previews (TP)** of this **resource provider (RP)**, you should keep in mind that after the deployment of the RP, you would have to install a SQL hosting server. This is not done anymore as the TP release did.

As already mentioned in the beginning, you should set up your design for SQL Server PaaS offerings (the t-shirt sizes keyword).

If you want to add a virtual machine with SQL Server installed, you would have to deploy a VM from an existing template that might have been synchronized earlier from Azure Marketplace using the Syndication feature. If you create the deployment, you should keep in mind the following requirements for a SQL Server:

- Enable SQL Server authentication
- Create local accounts on the Windows VM underneath

After the deployment is successful, we need to add it to Azure Stack as the SQL capacity for PaaS:

Now we will need to fill in the hosting server properties:

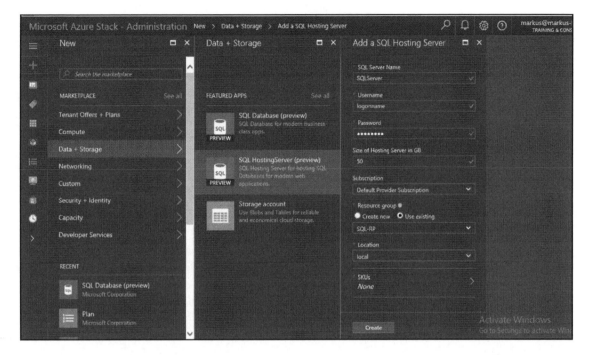

The important properties are as follows:

- The size of hosting server in GB
- Resource group
- **Stock Keeping Unit (SKU)**

The SKU can be used to describe the offering (the t-shirt sizes keyword):

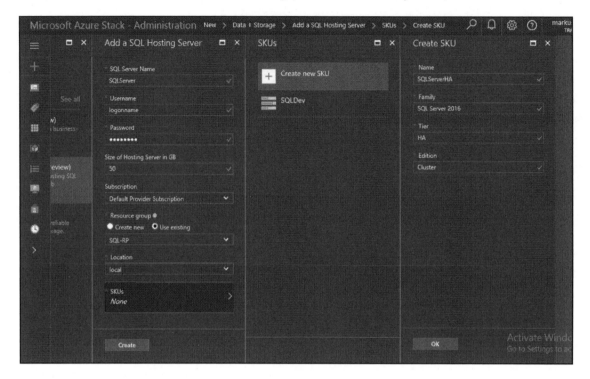

The SKU will be displayed later when a customer is ordering a database.

 Again, based on my experiences, it is good to wait up to 60 minutes before it is visible in the portal because a new SKU needs some time for internal synchronization too.

Creating a new database in Azure Stack PaaS

To set up a new DB, you would need to perform the following steps:

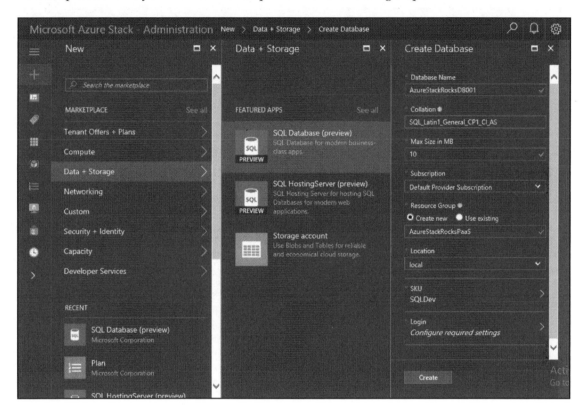

In regard to the login, that is the login, your customer needs to know hoe to access the database:

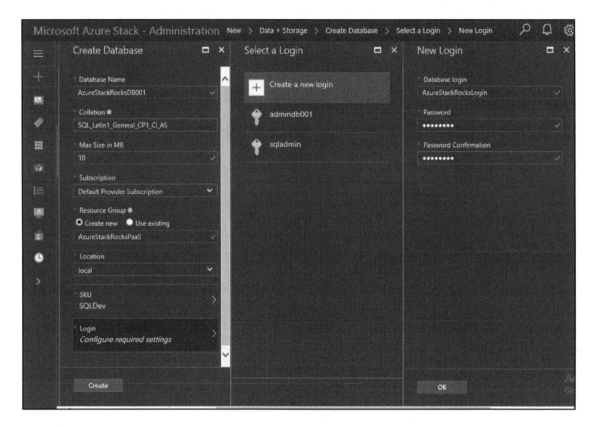

 Keep in mind that the login needs to be unique in the complete hosting environment. So I prefer to set up a process that makes sure that it is unique and no other customer is able to create new logins with the same properties. The resource provider does not check before the deployment. It just fails with an error message stating that duplicate logins are not allowed on a single SQL Server environment.

Enabling SQL PaaS for the tenants

As the features a tenant may order are bound to plans, we now need to update our plans or even create new ones to add SQL PaaS to it. This will be done as follows:

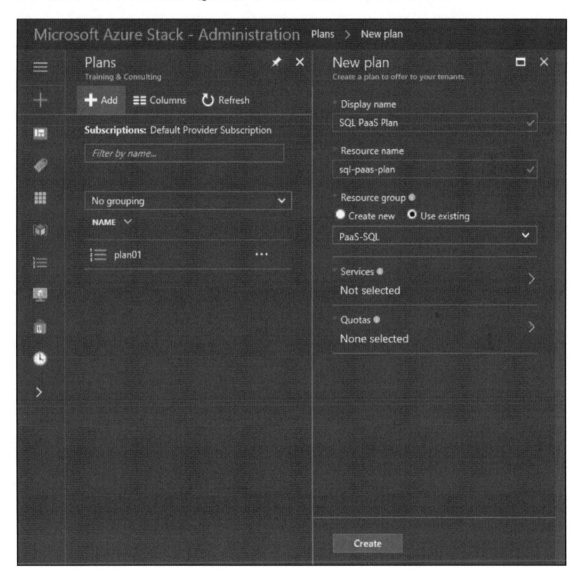

Now we will need to define the services and enable the SQL adapter:

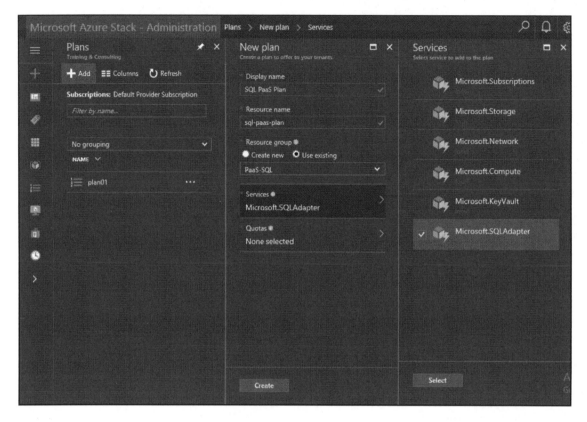

And finally, we need to define the quotas.

MySQL resource provider

A second resource provider, which is available for Azure Stack, is the MySQL resource provider. As a lot of services, specifically for web apps, are using a MySQL database to host all the details of their configuration and all the content they have in a website with some CMS systems (for example, WordPress, Drupal, or Joomla). In addition, lots of the small services that run with a SQL database work with MySQL.

That is one of the main reasons why a MySQL offering with your Azure Stack should be a valid option to prepare and offer services.

The resource provider consists of three components:

- The MySQL resource provider adapter VM that is a Windows virtual machine running the provider services.
- The resource provider itself, which processes requests and creates the database resources.
- Servers that provide capacity for MySQL server, called **hosting servers**.

Preparations

To prepare the installation of the MySQL resource provider, you will have to meet the following requirement on the host:

- Windows Server 2016 image or SQL Server 2016 image

You can find these image on the Azure Marketplace if you have enabled the Marketplace syndication feature.

Installation

When installing the Azure Stack MySQL resource provider, this needs to be done from a computer where Azure Stack and Azure PowerShell have been installed. If you have installed any versions of the AzureRM or Azure Stack PowerShell modules other than 1.2.9 or 1.2.10, you will need to remove them. This includes versions 1.3 or higher.

Now we need to download the resource provider. Download the location for the MySQL resource provider at `https://aka.ms/azurestackmysqlrp`.

After you have downloaded the file, you will need to log on as `AzureStackAdmin` account and extracted it on the deployment VM.

On the development toolkit, the resource provider is extracting the root CA certificate and creating a self-signed one for the deployment itself. On Multi-Node Deployments, you need to provide your own certificates and copy to a local directory. You need the following certificates:

- A wildcard certificate for `*.dbadapter.<region>.<external fqdn>` needs to be created. This certificate must be trusted and the certificate chain must work properly.

- The root certificate used by your Azure Resource Manager instance. If it is not available, it will be extracted.

While preparations are now finished, we can start the deployment by running the following deployment script called `DeployMySqlProvider.ps1` from an elevated PowerShell prompt.

During the deployment, the following steps are performed:

- Upload the certificates to a storage account on your Azure Stack system
- Publish gallery packages to the gallery
- Deploy a VM using the Windows Server 2016 image and install the resource provider on it
- Register a local DNS entry that maps to the resource provider VM
- Register the resource provider with the Azure Stack Resource Manager (tenant and admin)

The installation of the resource provide may take more than 90 minutes, if there are any issues, the deployment behavior is the same as with Azure Stack itself: you will see an error message; the error is logged and the installation will try to rerun from the failed step once you run the deployment again.

With the following PowerShell script, provided by Microsoft, the installation will run through if you change the accounts and REST endpoints:

```
# Install the AzureRM.Bootstrapper module
Install-Module -Name AzureRm.BootStrapper -Force

# Installs and imports the API Version Profile required by Azure Stack into
the current PowerShell session.
Use-AzureRmProfile -Profile 2017-03-09-profile
Install-Module -Name AzureStack -RequiredVersion 1.2.10 -Force

# Download the Azure Stack Tools from GitHub and set the environment
cd c:\
Invoke-Webrequest
https://github.com/Azure/AzureStack-Tools/archive/master.zip -OutFile
master.zip
Expand-Archive master.zip -DestinationPath . -Force

# This endpoint may be different for your installation
Import-Module C:\AzureStack-Tools-master\Connect\AzureStack.Connect.psm1
Add-AzureRmEnvironment -Name AzureStackAdmin -ArmEndpoint
https://adminmanagement.local.azurestack.external

# For AAD, use the following
$tenantID = Get-AzsDirectoryTenantID -AADTenantName <your directory name> -
EnvironmentName AzureStackAdmin

# For ADFS, replace the previous line with
# $tenantID = Get-AzsDirectoryTenantID -ADFS -EnvironmentName
AzureStackAdmin

$vmLocalAdminPass = ConvertTo-SecureString P@ssw0rd1 -AsPlainText -Force
$vmLocalAdminCreds = New-Object System.Management.Automation.PSCredential
(mysqlrpadmin, $vmLocalAdminPass)

$AdminPass = ConvertTo-SecureString P@ssw0rd1 -AsPlainText -Force
$AdminCreds = New-Object System.Management.Automation.PSCredential
(admin@mydomain.onmicrosoft.com, $AdminPass)

# change this as appropriate
$PfxPass = ConvertTo-SecureString P@ssw0rd1 -AsPlainText -Force

# Change directory to the folder where you extracted the installation files
# and adjust the endpoints
<extracted file directory>\DeployMySQLProvider.ps1 -DirectoryTenantID
$tenantID -AzCredential $AdminCreds -VMLocalCredential $vmLocalAdminCreds -
ResourceGroupName MySqlRG -VmName MySQLRP -ArmEndpoint
https://adminmanagement.local.azurestack.external -TenantArmEndpoint
```

```
https://management.local.azurestack.external -DefaultSSLCertificatePassword
$PfxPass -DependencyFilesLocalPath
```

DeployMySQLProvider.ps1 has the following parameters that you can modify for a different installation behavior:

Parameter name	Description	Comment or default value
DirectoryTenantID	The Azure or ADFS Directory ID (GUID).	required
ArmEndpoint	The Azure Stack Administrative Azure Resource Manager endpoint.	required
TenantArmEndpoint	The Azure Stack Tenant Azure Resource Manager endpoint.	required
AzCredential	Azure Stack service admin account credential (use the same account as you used to deploy Azure Stack).	required
VMLocalCredential	The local administrator account of the MySQL resource provider VM.	required
ResourceGroupName	Resource group for the items created by this script.	required
VmName	Name of the VM holding the resource provider.	required
AcceptLicense	Skips the prompt to accept the GPL license (http://www.gnu.org/licenses/old-licenses/gpl-2.0.html).	
DependencyFilesLocalPath	Path to a local share containing mysql-connector-net-6.9.9.msi. If you provide them, certificate files must be placed in this directory as well.	optional
DefaultSSLCertificatePassword	The password for the .pfx certificate.	required
MaxRetryCount	Each operation is retried if there is a failure.	2

RetryDuration	Timeout between retries in seconds.	120
Uninstall	Removes the resource provider.	No
DebugMode	Prevents automatic cleanup on failure.	

Table source: https://docs.microsoft.com/en-us/azure/azure-stack/azure-stack-mysql-resource-provider-deploy#deploy-the-resource-provider

Verifying the resource provider deployment

To verify the installation, you should double-check the following points in the admin Portal of Azure Stack:

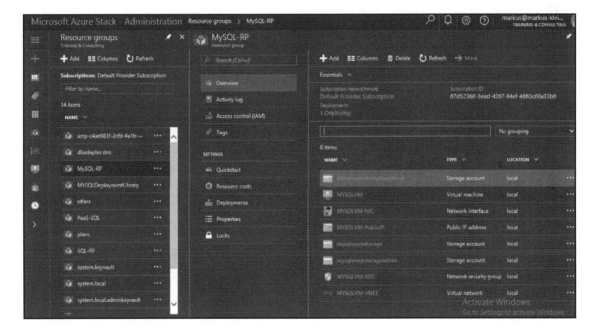

If the resource group in Azure Stack whose name you have provided during the deployment of the resource provider exists and the resources are created, the deployment should be fine.

 Based on my experiences, it is good to wait 60-90 minutes before starting the next steps and creating offers with the MySQL resource provider, as some steps need to be done internally with Azure Stack before completely enabling the new resource provider.

Adding a MySQL hosting server capacity

If you have played with the TP of this RP, you should have in mind that after the deployment of the RP, you would have to install a SQL hosting server. This is not done anymore as the TP release did.

As already mentioned at the beginning, you should set up your design for MySQL Server PaaS offerings (the t-shirt sizes keyword).

If you want to add a virtual machine with MySQL Server installed, you would have to deploy a VM from an existing template that might have been synchronized earlier from Azure Marketplace using the Syndication feature.

 Another location for the MySQL templates is the quick start template GitHub, which can be found here: `https://github.com/Azure/AzureStack-QuickStart-Templates/tree/master/mysql-standalone-server-windows`.

After the deployment is successful, we need to add it to Azure Stack as the SQL capacity for PaaS.

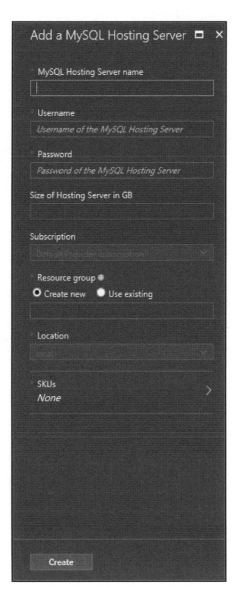

Finally, we will need to create the SKU in the Azure admin portal, as follows:

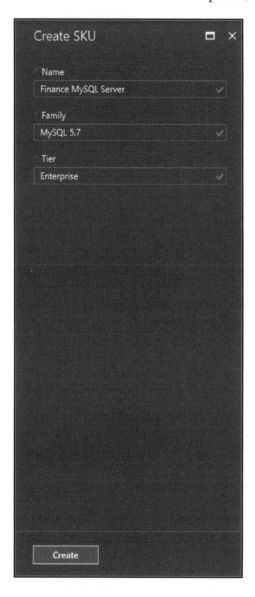

 Again, as stated with the Microsoft SQL resource provider, based on my experiences, it is good to wait up to 60 minutes before it is visible in the portal because a new SKU needs some time for internal synchronization too.

Creating a New Database in Azure Stack PaaS

Now we can test and create a first MySQL database with Azure Stack MySQL PaaS:

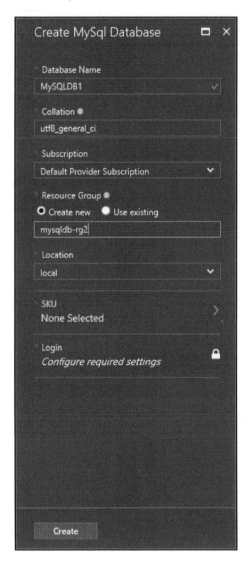

For the points **SKU** and **Login**, the same requirements are in place as with Microsoft SQL resource provider.

Enabling SQL PaaS for the tenants

To give the tenants access to the new offering, we would need to modify the plan again, and the new offering will be ready to use.

App Service resource provider

Azure Stack App Services is the first resource provider that has been brought directly to Azure Stack. It provides the following instances:

- Controller
- Management (two instances are created)
- Frontend
- Publisher
- Worker (in the Shared mode)
- File server

At first, we will need to create an App Service resource provider. The pricing container for applications is called an **App Service plan**, and it is a set of dedicated VMs used to present the apps. The resource provider administrators are able to define the worker tiers they want to make available. This can be multiple sets of shared workers or different sets of dedicated workers.

Preparations

App Service requires two databases to run the App Service resource provider. During the installation, it is possible to choose and define the SQL Server instance. The question is whether you should use the Microsoft SQL resource provider for these databases or a dedicated one. The answer to this question is quite easy as it depends (like always) on the workloads that you or your customers are planning to run on it.

Installation

Before you can start with the installation, you will have to download the required components. This can be done with the following URLs.

App Service on Azure Stack installer: `http://aka.ms/`
`appsvconmasrc1installer`
App Service on Azure Stack deployment helper scripts: `http://aka.ms/`
`appsvconmasrc1helper`

After having extracted the helper scripts, the following file and folder structure should exist:

- Create-AppServiceCerts.ps1
- Create-IdentityApp.ps1
- Modules
  - AzureStack.Identity.psm1
  - GraphAPI.psm1

Before starting the deployment, we would need to create the certificates required for this service using the Create-AppServiceCerts.ps1 script in this container, which has the following parameters.

Parameter	Required/optional	Default value	Description
pfxPassword	Required	Null	Password used to protect the certificate private key
DomainName	Required	local.azurestack.external	The Azure Stack region and domain suffix
CertificateAuthority	Required	AzS-CA01.azurestack.local	The certificate authority endpoint

Source: https://docs.microsoft.com/en-us/azure/azure-stack/azure-stack-app-service-deploy

The installer can be run online and can download the required components during its runtime, or you can download them early on. After you start it, it completes the following steps:

- Collecting the Azure Stack environment data
- Creating a blob container in Azure Stack
- Downloading the sources for the App Service resource provider
- Uploading the sources to the storage account
- Deploying the resource provider itself
- Creating the DNS zone and entries for RP
- Registering the App Service resource provider in Azure Stack
- Deploying the App Service gallery items

To run the installer, you will have to start `appservice.exe` as Azure Stack admin and choose to deploy the resource provider:

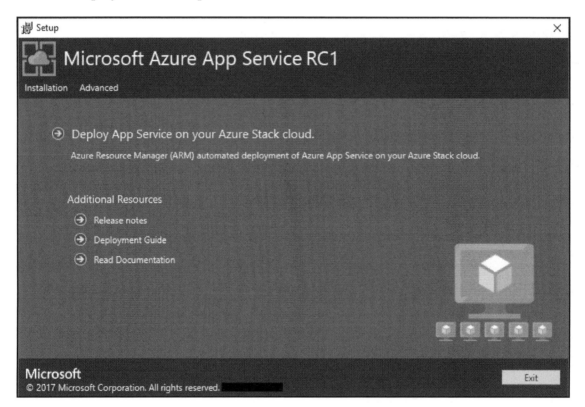

After having collected lots of details on the REST endpoints and authentication information locally in and Azure AD (if you are using the connected scenario), you will have to define the VM sizes for each VM instance and the corresponding numbers:

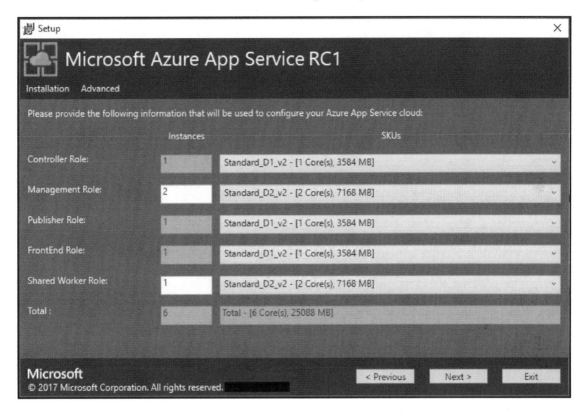

These are the predefined sizes; if you expect more load on the system because your tenants are using App Services heavily, you should think of adding more powerful VMs here or modifying the number of workers.

As the installation may take its time, you should inspect the following output to get to know the actual status of the deployment:

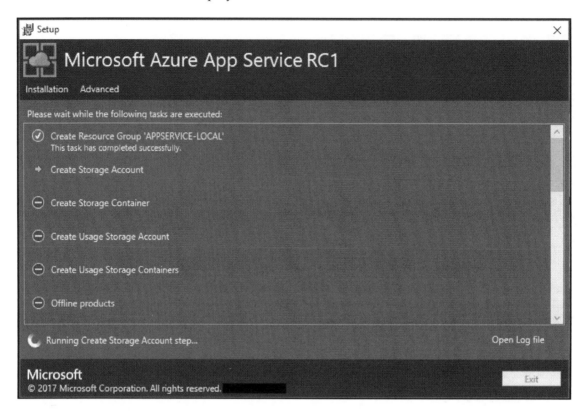

To check whether the installation is finished, you should run the admin tool called **web cloud management console** on the VM called **CN0-VM**. It should look somehow like this:

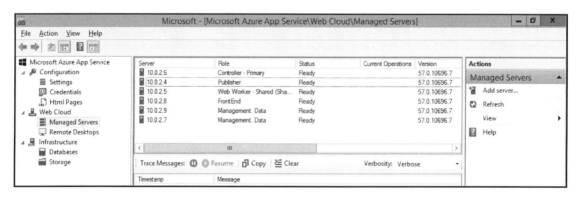

A minimum of one worker is needed deploy a web, mobile, or API app or Azure Functions.

After having done this, we would need to create the single-sign-on feature, which will be done as follows:

1. Run the `CreateIdentityApp.ps1` script as Azure Stack admin in the elevated mode. (If you are running a disconnected scenario, the Azure AD tenant ID will be ADFS. The registration steps with Azure AD will not appear).

2. Enter the path and the password to the certificate created earlier. The script will now create a new certificate for the DNS name: `sso.appservice.local.azurestack.external`.

3. Finally, a new application in the tenant Azure AD and PowerShell script named `UpdateConfigOnController.ps1` will be created.

4. Copy this script and the certificate to the VM called **CN0-VM**.

5. Log on to Azure portal and navigate to the Azure AD pane.

6. Add a new **App Registration** with the ID created by the script in *step 3*.

7. Add a new key called `Description - Functions Portal` and set **Expiration Date** to **Never Expires**.

8. Click on **Save**.

9. In **Application Registration** in Azure AD, navigate to **Required Permissions | Grant Permissions | Yes**.

10. Go to the **CN0-VM** and open the web cloud management console again.

11. Select **Settings** node on the left-hand side pane and search the **ApplicationClientSecret** setting.

12. Right-click and select **Edit**. Paste in the key generated in *step 7* and save it by clicking on **OK**.

13. Finally, log on to the **CN0-VM** and run the script called `UpdateConfigOnController.ps1`, which updates the services using the repair option. This script has the following parameters:

Parameter	Required/optional	Default value	Description
`DirectoryTenantName`	Mandatory	Null	The Azure AD tenant ID. Provide the GUID or string, for example, `myazureaaddirectory.onmicrosoft.com`
`TenantAzureResourceManagerEndpoint`	Mandatory	`management.local.azurestack.external`	The tenant Azure Resource Manager endpoint
`AzureStackCredential`	Mandatory	Null	The Azure AD administrator
`CertificateFilePath`	Mandatory	Null	The path to the identity application certificate file generated earlier
`CertificatePassword`	Mandatory	Null	The password used to protect the certificate private key
`DomainName`	Required	`local.azurestack.external`	The Azure Stack region and domain suffix
`AdfsMachineName`	Optional	Ignored in the case of Azure AD deployment but required in AD FS deployment. The AD FS machine name, for example, AzS-ADFS01.azurestack.local	None

Source: https://docs.microsoft.com/en-us/azure/azure-stack/azure-stack-app-service-deploy

To test the deployment, the following steps are required:

1. As a tenant, go to your portal and navigate to **New** | **Web + Mobile** | **Web App**.
2. Set a name in the **Web App** box.
3. Create a new resource group.
4. Create a new **App Service** plan.
5. Set a name for the **App Service** plan.
6. Click on **Pricing tier** | **Free-Shared** or **Shared-Shared** | **Select** | **OK** | **Create**.
7. After the **Web App** has been created, you can browse to open the default website.

Adding capacity to App services

To create new workers, you can use the Azure Stack portal to scale up in the **Roles** setting:

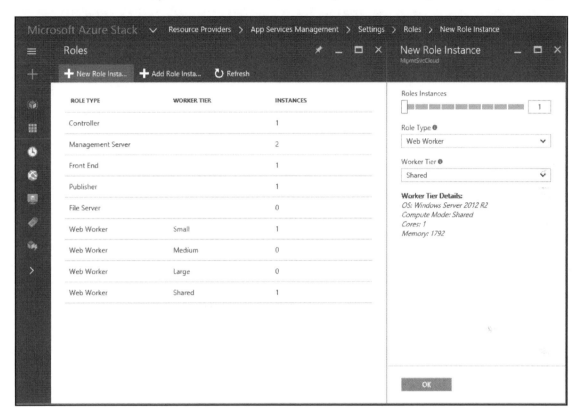

A maximum of 10 role instances is possible.

The following deployment sources are possible by default:

- GitHub
- Bit Bucket
- OneDrive
- Dropbox

 To set your preferred deployment source, visit this following URL for the steps on how to enable it: https://docs.microsoft.com/en-us/azure/ azure-stack/azure-stack-app-service-configure-deployment- sources.

The second option is to enable FTP on the corresponding website. This needs to be done as follows:

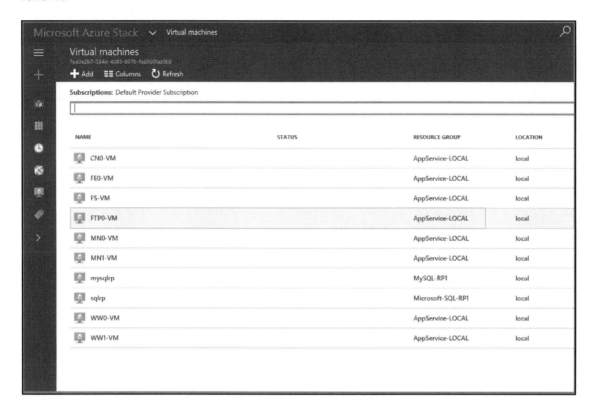

Log on to **FTP0-VM** VM and enter the public IP address to the hosting FTP site in IIS:

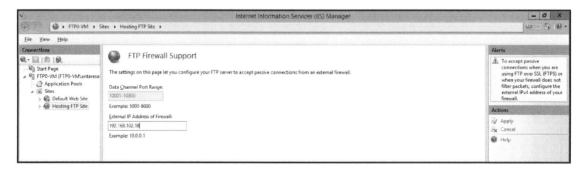

From a security perspective, FTP is not the best choice and maybe other options may fit better.

Summary

As you have seen in this chapter, there is already a wide variety of PaaS solutions available with Azure Stack in GA. You have the options for Microsoft SQL, MySQL, or App Services, which already provide you with great features. As you may have recognized, there is a bunch of tasks that you will need to fulfill in order to enable these features. But in regard to documentation, there is a lot available, and it is more or less a walkthrough and within a time of configuration, it is available.

As already mentioned in the other chapters, Microsoft has already promised that we will see more and more of PaaS solutions, which will come to Azure Stack in the future after GA on a regular basis.

The next chapter will provide you with guidance on how to prepare your Azure Stack environment for your tenant by preparing plans, offers, and subscriptions.

9

Managing and Administering Private Clouds with Microsoft Azure Stack

In the last eight chapters, we got an overview of the design, setup, and basic technology features of Azure Stack. This is more or less the technology. With this chapter, we go a little deeper into how you should do things, so we will talk about the following:

- Naming management
- Subscription management
- Resource management
- Security management

To design, manage, and administer private clouds with Azure Stack, you will need to align all these topics in a concept for your tenants and design offered based on these principles. Otherwise, you will be lost in the middle of nowhere at a certain point of time, but as tenants are already online and productive, you will have no chance to modify this *wild design* anymore. This is not only important for enterprise customers, it is more important for **Hosting Service Providers (HSP)** offering Azure Stack to tenants.

As HSP, you will have the chance to standardize your environments when you design the service offerings. As you should never do things manually with the Azure Stack portal, you should do them using PowerShell scripts. This makes sure that you will not make a mistake when configuring steps manually as humans make errors, which is normal. A PowerShell script with most of the configuration properties predefined makes sure that there will not any human mistake. More or less, this chapter talks about Azure Stack cloud governance, so we will set up some standards and defaults on which all operations in Azure Stack will be based. These design principles will define and take care.

Naming management

Before creating anything in Azure Stack, we need a good naming convention in place. A naming convention ensures that all the resources have a predictable name, which helps lower the administrative burden associated with managing these resources.

You might choose to follow a specific set of naming conventions defined for your entire organization or for a specific Azure subscription or account. Although it is easy for individuals within organizations to establish implicit rules when working with Azure Stack, when a team needs to work on a project on Azure Stack, that model does not scale well. The good thing is that you will maybe already have these conventions with Azure and as Azure Stack is relying on the same design concepts, they may be already set and just need to be modified to fit to Azure Stack design specifications.

Agree on a set of naming conventions up front; there are some considerations regarding naming conventions that cut across that sets of rules.

You should have naming conventions for the following Azure Stack resources:

- Subscriptions
- Storage accounts
- Virtual networks
- VPN gateway
- Subnets
- Availability sets
- Resource groups
- Virtual machines
- Network security groups
- Public IP address name

You also should consider some abbreviations for Azure Stack resources in common use.

We recommend that you follow abbreviations for some of the common Azure Stack resources listed earlier:

Resource or artifact	Abbreviation	Sample
Availability sets	`avset`	`avset01 - n`
Azure Resource Manager	`arm`	None
Environment	`prod, stg, tst, dev`	`prod=Production; stg=Staging; tst=Testing; dev=Development.`
Network security group	`nsg`	`nsg01 - n`
Resource groups	`rg`	`rg01 - n`
Storage accounts	`sa`	`sa01 - n`
Subscription	`sub`	`sub01 - n`
Subnets	`subnet01`	`subnet01 - n`
Virtual networks	`vnet`	`vnet01 - n`
Virtual machines	`vm`	`vm01 - n`
VPN gateway	`vpngw`	`vpngw01 - n`

Subscriptions

A **subscription** is a billing container for deployed Microsoft Azure Stack services. Azure Stack subscriptions provide you with the cloud services themselves, such as the following:

- Virtual machines
- Cloud services
- Azure Active Directory
- Virtual networks

Multiple subscriptions allow you to easy view the billing for each subscription and limit who can access the Microsoft Azure services associated with that subscription.

In an enterprise enrollment, the subscription naming convention should be separated on development and production environment. Therefore, we recommend the following naming conventions:

- Company name
- Environment
- Tier
- Subscription consecutive number *1-n*

Examples for subscriptions naming conventions are presented in the following table:

Subscription/Region	Examples
Subscription Company prod	compprodt1s1-n
Subscription Company dev	compdevt1s1-n

Storage account and storage services

Storage accounts have special rules governing their names. Be aware that you can only use lowercase letters and numbers and the name must be unique within Azure Stack. Within Azure Stack storage account, there are four three storage services, as listed here:

- Blob storage stores unstructured object data
- Table storage stores structured datasets
- Queue storage provides reliable messaging for workflow processing and for communication between components of cloud services

Each of the Azure Storage services have different naming restrictions, as listed in the following table:

Storage account/Kind	Context/Scope	Case	Valid character set	Length
Storage account	Global	Lowercase	Alphanumeric	3-24
Blob storage	Container	Sensitive	URL characters	10-24
Storage queue	Storage account	Lowercase	Alphanumeric and hyphen	3-63
Storage table	Storage account	Insensitive	Alphanumeric	3-63

There are two primary use cases for storage accounts: backing disks for VMs and storing data in blobs (general purpose), queues, and tables. Therefore, we recommend that you separate the storage account naming convention according to the use case. We recommend the following naming convention for storage account itself: company name; environment; use case/account kind; performance; encryption; consecutive number:

Company	Environment	Use case	Performance	Encryption	Storage account consecutive number
Comp1	Prod/Dev	VM disk/General purpose	*Standard = std* *Premium = pm*	*Enabled = enc* *Disabled = blank*	*Storage account = sa* *Consecutive number = 01 -n*

Virtual networks

Azure Stack **virtual networks** (**VNets**) should have following naming conventions while considering casing and valid character lengths:

Category	Scope	Casing	Valid characters	Length
VNet	Resource group	Case-insensitive	Alphanumeric, dash, underscore, and period	2-64

Subnets

Azure Stack virtual network subnets should be easily allocated to the associated VNet. Therefore, we recommend the following naming convention:

- Company
- VNet
- Subnet consecutive number *1-n*

VPN gateway

For Azure Stack VPN gateway, we recommend the same naming convention principles as virtual networks and subnets:

- Company
- VPN gateway (`vpngw01-n`)
- Subnet consecutive number *1-n*

Availability sets

In Azure Stack, **virtual machines (VMs)** can be placed in a logical grouping called an **availability set**. When you create VMs within an availability set, the Azure Stack platform distributes the placement of these VMs across the underlying infrastructure. Naming convention should follow almost the same principle as virtual networks. Therefore, we recommend the following naming convention:

- Company
- Region
- Availability sets (`avset01 - n`)
- Application or VM

Resource groups

Azure Stack resource group is a container that holds related resources. In Azure Stack, you logically group related resources such as storage accounts, virtual networks, VMs in resource groups:

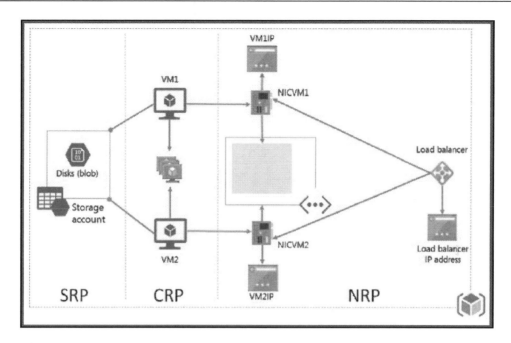

You can deploy, manage, and maintain them as a single entity. The naming conventions for **Azure Resource Manager** (**ARM**) should also follow the principles for an easy association with the tenants' naming guidelines:

Category	Service	Scope	Casing	Valid characters	Length
Resource group	Resource group	Global	Case-insensitive	Alphanumeric, underscore, and hyphen	1-64
Resource group	Availability Set	Resource group	Case-insensitive	Alphanumeric, underscore, and hyphen	1-80

Therefore, we recommend the following naming conventions:

- Company
- Resource group (`rg01 -n`)
- Resource group usage

Virtual machines

Azure Stack virtual machines should also be separated on the workloads they are used for. Therefore, we recommend the naming conventions separated on the workloads and applications they are being used for:

Category	Service	Scope	Casing	Valid characters	Length
Virtual machine	Resource group	Resource group	Case-insensitive	Alphanumeric, hyphen	1-15

We also recommend separated abbreviations for virtual machines, which would help fast identification of the virtual machine usage and function:

Server	Function
S - Windows	DCxx: Domain Controller
S - Linux	AVxx: Antivirus server
None	Fxx: File server
None	SQLxx: SQL Server
None	APxx: Application server

Network security groups

A **network security group (NSG)** contains a list of ACL rules that allow or deny network traffic to your VM instances in a virtual network. NSGs can be associated with either subnets or individual VM instances within that subnet. With the naming convention for NSGs, you should be able to easily identify which resource group or VMs the NSGs belong to.

Therefore, we recommend the following naming conventions:

- Company
- Resource group consecutive number
- Virtual machine
- Network security group consecutive number (nsg01 - n)

Subscription design management

Subscriptions should be designed in reference to good practice. One good practice for enterprise-level companies is to design subscriptions based on tiers. One important reason for design Azure Stack subscriptions in tiers is the possibility to scale the Azure Stack services based on your needs. During the deployment, the *default subscription provider* is being created. This one should be used to manage Azure Stack, deploy resource providers, and create tenant offers and plans. It should not be used to run customer workloads and applications.

As Azure Stack can be designed in an Azure-connected scenario and a disconnected one, the subscription design management has to rely on that model.

Subscriptions in connected scenarios

In a connected scenario, you have the possibility to connect Azure Stack to an Azure subscription. If you choose to set up Azure Stack based on an Azure subscription and you need to change this in future times, you will have to redeploy Azure Stack completely.

In Azure, a subscription can be created via the enterprise agreement portal with **administrator account** permissions:

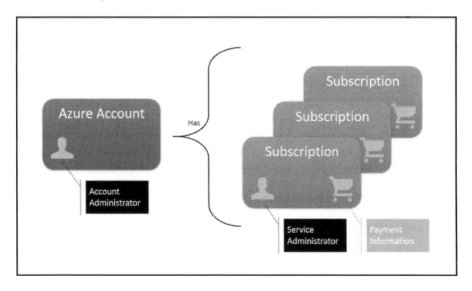

Source: https://docs.microsoft.com/en-us/azure/active-directory/media/active-directory-understanding-resource-access/ic707931.png

This means we can install Azure Stack into one of these subscriptions created via the EA-portal. From the business model perspective, it is best to be a cloud service provider with Microsoft:

Cloud Solution Provider components

Direct Billing & Provisioning
- Order & provision cloud services
- Manage billing & payments
- Monthly billing options available
- Manage cloud subscriptions
- CSP platform API integration available
- Commerce marketplace through partner offers

Technical Support
- Pre-sales tech support
- Post-sales T1 & T2 tech support
- Technical advisory services
- Usage & adoption services
- Cross-sell & upsell services

Migration Services
- Onboarding & activation
- Data migration
- Platform readiness services
- Partner automation toolsets available

Managed Services & Solutions
- Management solutions
- SaaS aggregation
- Security & regulatory services
- Integration apps
- Functional extensions
- Workflow & dashboards

Key: Required | Recommended |

Source:
https://image.slidesharecdn.com/plumchoicemicrosoftcspwebinarpres18nov2015-151118173240-lva1-app6891/95/microsoft-csp-partner-program-get-cloud-solutions-to-market-faster-more-profitably-through-cloud-enablement-services-13-638.jpg?cb=1447881772

If you add Azure Stack to a new or pre-existing Azure Stack subscription, it is even possible to set up an **Azure billing bridge**. This means that usage data is sent from Azure Stack to Azure through the Azure bridge. In Azure, the commerce system processes the usage data and creates one bill. After the bill is generated, the Azure subscription owner can view and download it from the Azure account center (`https://account.windowsazure.com/Subscriptions`):

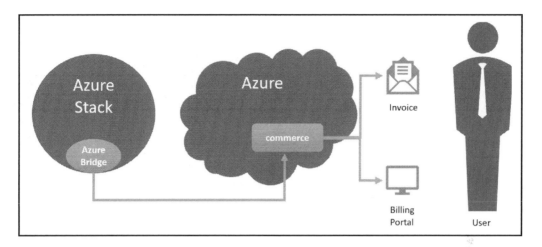

If you need to transfer billing data directly toward your billing system, there are some API references available for it:

- **Provider usage API:** `https://docs.microsoft.com/en-us/azure/azure-stack/azure-stack-provider-resource-api`
- **Tenant usage API:** `https://docs.microsoft.com/en-us/azure/azure-stack/azure-stack-tenant-resource-usage-api`

To create new subscriptions for Azure Stack connected scenarios, you will need to follow this procedure in the ARM portal:

1. Log in to your Azure portal (`https://portal.azure.com`).
2. In Azure, go to **Azure Active Directory**.
3. In Azure AD, choose your Azure Stack directory or create a new one.
4. Click on **Users**.
5. Click on **Add a user**.
6. In this wizard, select **New user** in your organization.
7. Enter the username.
8. Choose the e-mail address.
9. On the next page, fill in **First name**, **Last name**, and **Display name**.
10. Select the **User Role**.
11. Choose to create a temporary password.

12. Copy the **New password** to the clipboard.
13. Log in to the Azure portal with that new account and change the password.
14. Now you are able to log in to `https://portal.local.azurestack.external` with the new account.

With PowerShell, the following script can be used to set up a new account:

```
# Provide the AAD credential you use to deploy Azure Stack Development Kit
$msolcred = get-credential

# Add a tenant account "Tenant Admin <username>@<yourdomainname>" with the
initial password "<password>".
connect-msolservice -credential $msolcred
$user = new-msoluser -DisplayName "Tenant Admin" -UserPrincipalName
<username>@<yourdomainname> -Password <password> Add-MsolRoleMember -
RoleName "Company Administrator" -RoleMemberType User -RoleMemberObjectId
$user.ObjectId
```

You can configure Azure Stack to support users from multiple **Azure Active Directory (Azure AD)** tenants to use services in Azure Stack.

Onboarding guest directory tenants

To onboard a guest directory tenant, you will have to run the following PowerShell script:

```
Import-Module .\Connect\AzureStack.Connect.psm1
Import-Module .\Identity\AzureStack.Identity.psm1
$adminARMEndpoint = "https://adminmanagement.local.azurestack.external"

## Replace the value below with the Azure Stack directory
$azureStackDirectoryTenant = "contoso.onmicrosoft.com"

## Replace the value below with the guest tenant directory.
$guestDirectoryTenantToBeOnboarded = "fabrikam.onmicrosoft.com"

Register-AzSGuestDirectoryTenant -AdminResourceManagerEndpoint
$adminARMEndpoint `
 -DirectoryTenantName $azureStackDirectoryTenant `
 -GuestDirectoryTenantName $guestDirectoryTenantToBeOnboarded `
 -Location "local"
```

Next, register Azure Stack with the guest directory:

```
$tenantARMEndpoint = "https://management.local.azurestack.external"
## Replace the value below with the guest tenant directory.
$guestDirectoryTenantName = "fabrikam.onmicrosoft.com"
Register-AzSWithMyDirectoryTenant `
 -TenantResourceManagerEndpoint $tenantARMEndpoint `
 -DirectoryTenantName $guestDirectoryTenantName `
 -Verbose
```

 Finally, the users from the guest Azure AD can sign in to the Azure Stack portal using the following URL:
`https://portal.local.azurestack.external/<MSDomn>.onmicrosoft.com`

Subscriptions in disconnected scenarios

In disconnected scenarios, the user management is a little bit simpler as you would just have to create a new user account your ADFS linked directory service and the account is available to log on to the Azure Stack portal.

 If possible, it is always recommended that you set up Azure Stack in a connected scenario as there are quite more possibilities than without connectivity.

Resource management

After having theoretic access to Azure Stack resources using your subscriptions, we now have to talk about how to allow/restrict access to resources.

This is where it comes to:

- Quotas
- Plans
- Offers

 In comparison to Azure public, you are responsible for the resource management. This is why we need to set up Quotas, Plans, and Offers. With Azure public, this is responsibility of Microsoft.

Quotas

If we have one or more active subscriptions, we can order resources from Azure Stack based on our Quotas. A Quota defines the limits of resources that a tenant subscription can consume. It can be configured per service and per location and gives the administrators a way to control the usage of resources in Azure Stack. Quotas for a service can be created from the resource provider administration blade in the administrative portal:

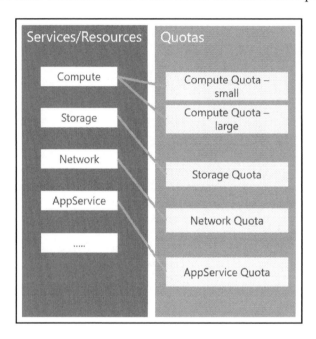

As per the resource provider, there is a default Quota, which means no restrictions to the resources that are available, as you can see in the following table:

Type	Default value	Description
Max number of virtual machines	50	The maximum number of virtual machines that a subscription can create in this location.
Max number of virtual machine cores	100	The maximum number of cores that a subscription can create in this location (for example, an A3 VM has four cores).

Max amount of virtual machine memory (GB)	150	The maximum amount of RAM that can be provisioned in megabytes (for example, an A1 VM consumes 1.75 GB of RAM).

Source: https://docs.microsoft.com/de-de/azure/azure-stack/azure-stack-setting-quotas

The following screenshot illustrates **Create new Quota** wizard:

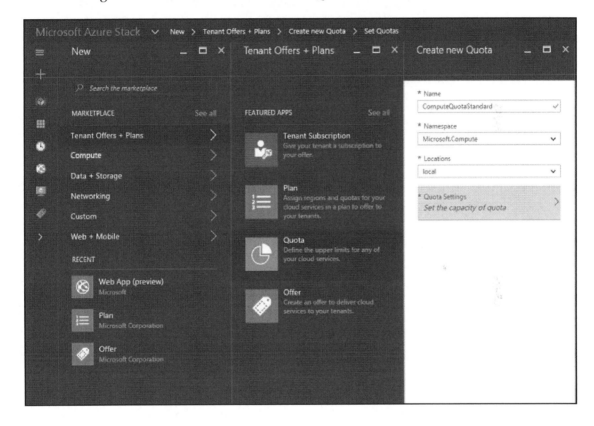

As you can see, you can set the Quota in the portal and define the **Quota Settings** in detail, in this example, for the computer resource provider:

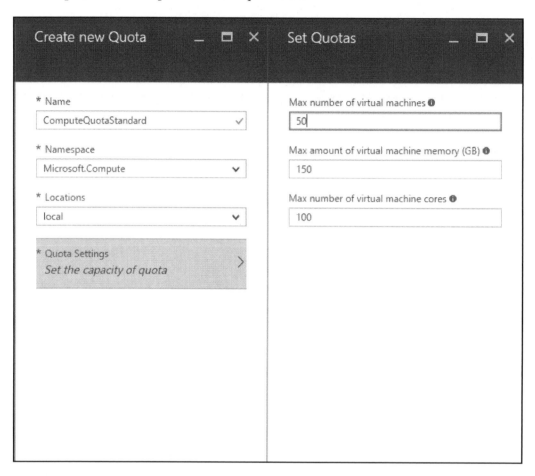

Now the Quota is available in global for this Azure Stack resource provider and can be used for all tenants.

 If you want to create Quotas via PowerShell, that is unavailable right now, but it will be tested and made available with the API (`https://docs.microsoft.com/en-us/rest/api/index`).

As there are three basic resource provider that Azure Stack is working with: computer, storage and network. Each of these Quotas has its own default Quota that is available and that you are able to add. The following screenshots will show these Quotas in detail:

- Compute

Type	Default value	Description
Max number of virtual machines	50	The maximum number of virtual machines that a subscription can create in this location.
Max number of virtual machine cores	100	The maximum number of cores that a subscription can create in this location (for example, an A3 VM has four cores).
Max amount of virtual machine memory (GB)	150	The maximum amount of RAM that can be provisioned in megabytes (for example, an A1 VM consumes 1.75 GB of RAM).

- Storage

Item	Default value	Description
Maximum capacity (GB)	500	Total storage capacity that can be consumed by a subscription in this location.
Total number of storage accounts	20	The maximum number of storage accounts that a subscription can create in this location.

- Network

Item	Default value	Description
Max public IPs	50	The maximum number of public IPs that a subscription can create in this location.
Max virtual networks	50	The maximum number of virtual networks that a subscription can create in this location.
Max virtual network gateways	1	The maximum number of virtual network gateways (VPN Gateways) that a subscription can create in this location.
Max network connections	2	The maximum number of network connections (point-to-point or site-to-site) that a subscription can create across all virtual network gateways in this location.
Max load balancers	50	The maximum number of load balancers that a subscription can create in this location.
Max NICs	100	The maximum number of network interfaces that a subscription can create in this location.
Max network security groups	50	The maximum number of network security groups that a subscription can create in this location.

 You can find more on Quotas here: https://docs.microsoft.com/en-us/azure/azure-stack/azure-stack-setting-quotas.

Plans

The next level of resource restriction we need to talk about is Plans. They are used to group several Quotas as logical units. You can compare it a little with the plan for a mobile phone provider where a plan puts Quotas for SMS, voice, and data together. This is a similar concept to Plans in Azure Stack. Plans are levels of service capacity that you, as an internal or external provider, can offer to your tenants:

 Users are not assigned to Plans directly.

Quotas are the technical controls, and Plans put them into a more general mapping:

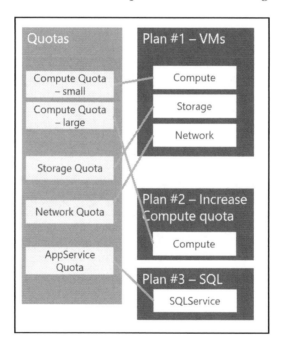

In real-world scenarios, Plans are often tied together as a technical basis for IaaS, PaaS, or even SaaS services that you might theoretically offer to your tenants.

To create a new plan in Azure Stack, you will have to ensure the following steps. At first, we need to navigate to **New** | **Tenant Offers + Plans** | **Plan**:

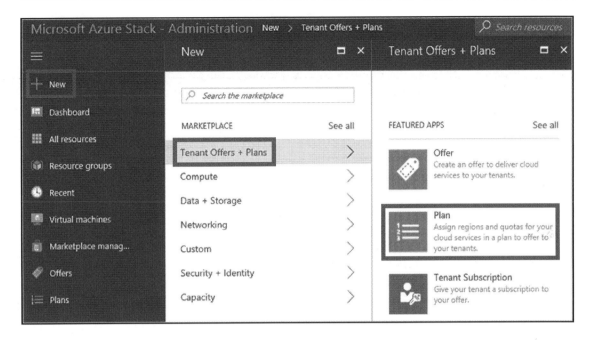

Next, set a **Display name** and a **Resource name**:

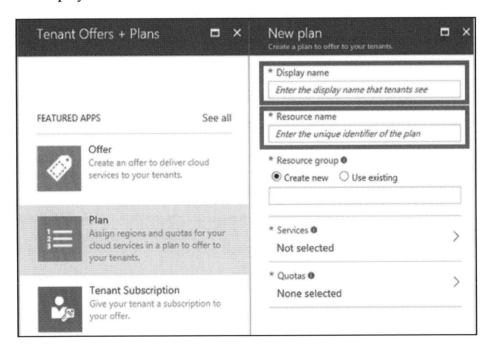

Finally, we need to set the resource providers:

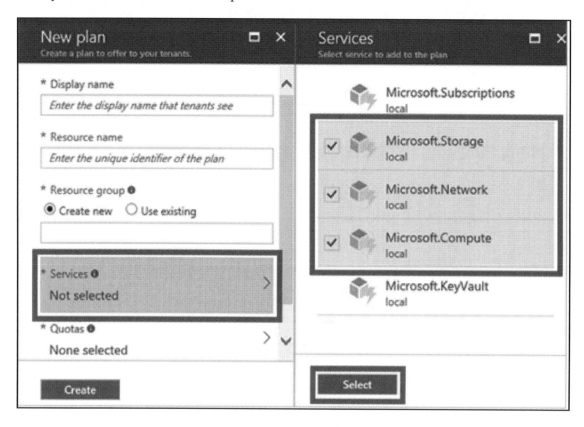

As a last step, we need to define the appropriate **Quotas** for the services:

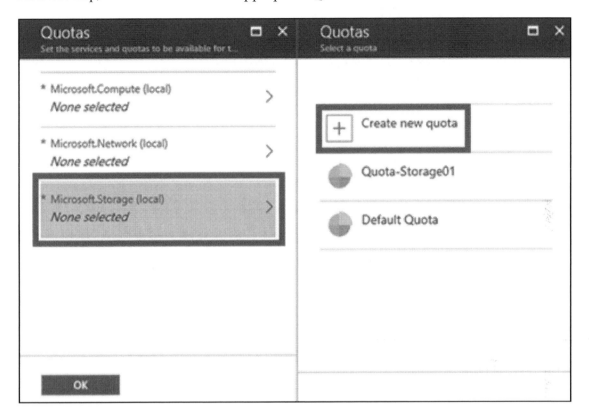

If more PaaS services (for example, SQL, MySQL, or App Service) are deployed, you will find them in the resource provider list too.

 If you want to allow a tenant to act as a provider, you will need to add the resource provider for Microsoft Subscriptions too.

Offers

An offer in Azure Stack is a group of one or more Plans to present the offering for a tenant from the **hosting service provider's** perspective. This is used to make the Plans available to users. An offer has a price tag and can have a so-called **base plan** and one or more **add-on plans** associated with it. This means that you can include multiple Plans in one offering. An Offer is what the tenant users will see when they sign up to Azure Stack and where their Subscription has been subscribed to as well:

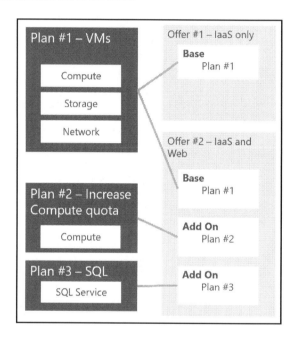

From real-world scenarios, you will find offerings such as:

- IaaS Silver
- IaaS Gold
- IaaS Platinum
- SQL Gold
- SQL Platinum

More or less, you combine a service of resources, which are provided by Azure Stack with a **Service Level Agreement (SLA)** that finally defines the availability of the service and the performance on Azure Stack and even the helpdesk if things do not run as expected.

To create an offer in Azure Stack, you will need to take the following steps. At first, we need to go to **New** | **Tenant Offers + Plans** | **Offer**:

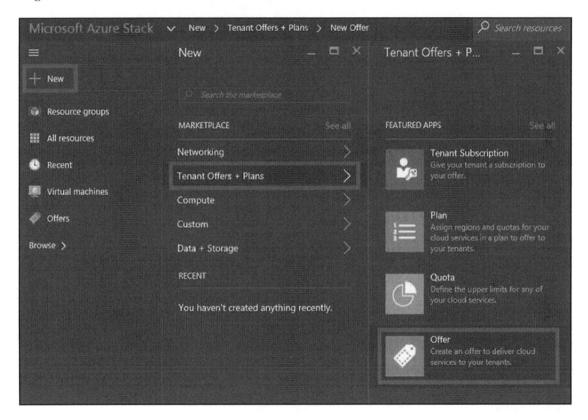

Then, we need to set up a **Display Name** and a **Resource Name**:

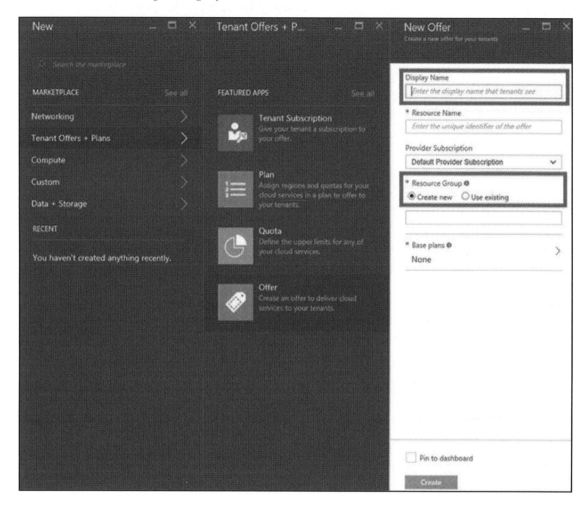

Then, we need to add the corresponding Azure Stack **Offer**:

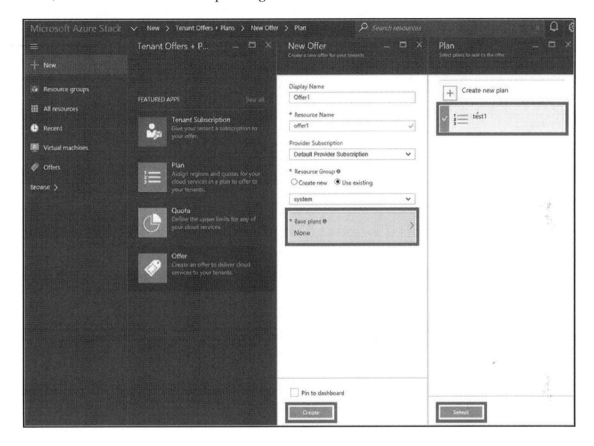

If an offer has been created, it will go to the type **Private**. This means that it is unavailable to the tenants. This means we will have to set it to the type **Public** to enable them for them:

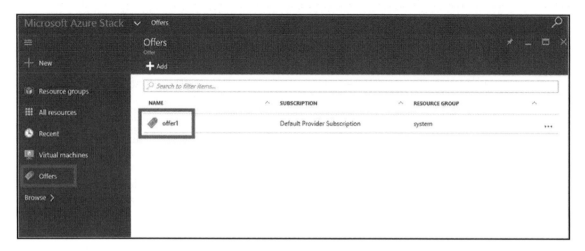

Offers can have different levels:

- **Private offers**: These are visible only to cloud administrators
- **Public offers**: These are visible to tenants
- **Depreciated offers**: These are not enabled for new subscribers

Putting it all together, the following structure of Subscriptions, Plans, and Offers define the hosting service provider's offerings that are available with Azure Stack:

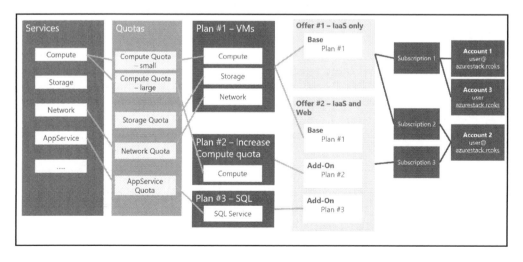

Security management

As Azure Stack provides a variety of resources to the tenants based on the Offers, Plans, and Quotas, the question that is always there is this: how do we secure our resources?

Tagging

At first, one of the best things to provide a first level of security is to tag the resources to the corresponding customers and resource groups.

Resource manager enables you to logically organize resources by applying tags. The tags consist of key/value pairs that identify resources with properties that you define. To mark resources as belonging to the same category, apply the same tag to those resources. Tags can be applied to Resource groups or resources directly. Tags can then be used to select resources or Resource groups from the console, web portal, PowerShell, or the API.

Tags can be helpful when you need to organize resources for billing or management. Each tag you add to a resource or Resource group is automatically added to the Subscription-wide taxonomy. Each resource can have a maximum of 15 tags. The tag name is limited to 512 characters, and the tag value is limited to 256 characters.

We recommend tagging based on company name and cost center:

Tag name	State	Description	Tag value
EnvironmentType	Required	Provides information on what the resource group is used for (useful for maintenance, policy enforcement, chargeback, and so on).	Dev, Test, Prod

MaintenanceWindow	Optional	Provides a window during which patch and other impacting maintenance can be performed.	Window in UTC `day:hour:minute-day:hour:minute`
Cost center `LOCxxxx`	Required	Cost center customer 1	4711
Cost center `CUSTxxx`	Required	Customer name customer 1	Customer number

Tagging resources is possible in different ways. At first, we will look at the portal:

Now we need to define the tag **Name** and the **Value**:

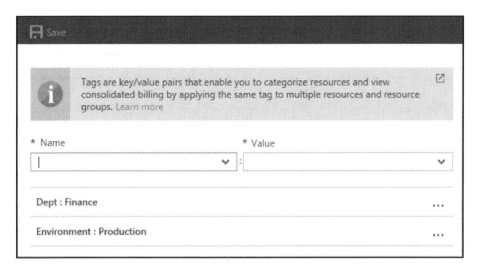

You can even filter based on **Tags**, as follows:

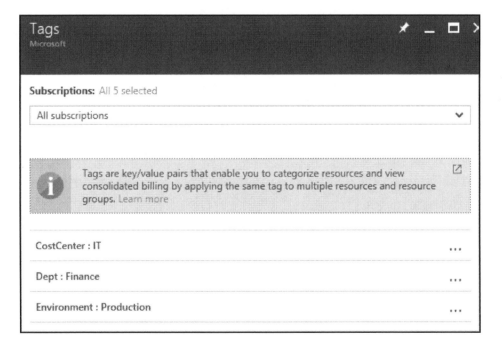

To filter all resources with a specific tag, you will have to run the following PowerShell command:

```
(Get-AzureRmResourceGroup -Name AzureStackRocks-RG).Tags
```

To set a tag to a resource group without existing tags, the following PowerShell is fine to run:

```
Set-AzureRmResourceGroup -Name AzureStack-RG -Tag @{Dept="IT";
Environment="Test"}
```

To set a tag directly from the ARM template, the following syntax needs to be used:

```
{
  "$schema": "https://schema.management.azure.com/schemas/2015-01-01/
  deploymentTemplate.json#",
  "contentVersion": "1.0.0.0",
  "resources": [
    {
      "apiVersion": "2016-01-01",
      "type": "Microsoft.Storage/storageAccounts",
      "name": "[concat('storage', uniqueString(resourceGroup().id))]",
      "location": "[resourceGroup().location]",
      "tags": {
        "Dept": "Finance",
        "Environment": "Production"
      },
      "sku": {
        "name": "Standard_LRS"
      },
      "kind": "Storage",
      "properties": { }
    }
  ]
}
```

As there are lot of more possibilities with PowerShell, CLI, and the API, this URL will help you: https://docs.microsoft.com/en-us/azure/azure-resource-manager/resource-group-using-tags.

Resource locks

It is strongly recommended that you use Azure Stack resources locks. Locking Azure Stack resources helps you avoid accidental deletion or modifying of Azure Stack resource and Resource groups. You can set resource locks on subscription, resource group, and resource level.

You can set the lock level to **CanNotDelete** or **ReadOnly**.

- **CanNotDelete** means authorized users can still read and modify a resource, but they can't delete the resource.
- **ReadOnly** means authorized users can read a resource, but they can't delete or update the resource. Applying this lock is similar to restricting all authorized users to the permissions granted by the **Reader** role.

We recommend that you set the resource lock on the Subscription level for the production environment. For dev/test Subscriptions, you can set the resource lock on the resource group level. So, the development/test teams would be able to delete the tested resources by themselves.

Resource locking could look like the examples in the following table:

Resource lock name	Lock type	Scope	Notes
CanNotDelete subscription01	Delete	Subscription	Deny delete any resources in subscription01
CanNotDelete subscription dev-test	Delete	Resource groups	Deny delete RG in subscription dev-test

You can set resource **Locks** in Azure ARM portal, JSON template, with Azure PowerShell as well as with the Azure REST API.

Using the Azure Stack portal, resource logs are created, as follows:

Now we can define the required resource locks directly:

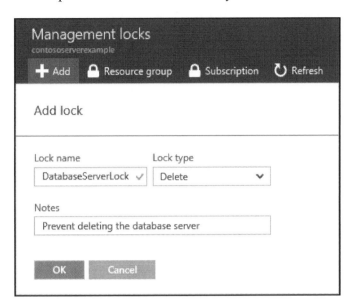

To delete the existing resource locks, you will have to choose the following highlighted point in the portal:

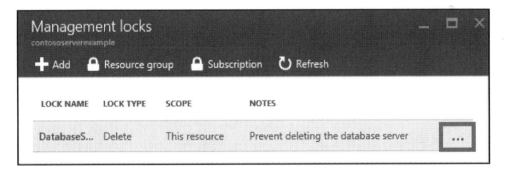

The following PowerShell command sets a resource lock in your Azure Stack environment:

```
New-AzureRmResourceLock -LockLevel CanNotDelete -LockName LockSite `
-ResourceName examplesite -ResourceType Microsoft.Web/sites `
-ResourceGroupName exampleresourcegroup
```

To get all resource logs for a resource group, the following PowerShell command will help you:

```
Get-AzureRmResourceLock -ResourceName examplesite -ResourceType
Microsoft.Web/sites `
-ResourceGroupName exampleresourcegroup
```

If you need to set a lock in your ARM template, you will have to fulfill the following syntax:

```
{
  "$schema": "https://schema.management.azure.com/schemas/2015-01-01/
  deploymentTemplate.json#",
  "contentVersion": "1.0.0.0",
  "parameters": {
    "lockedResource": {
      "type": "string"
    }
  },
  "resources": [
    {
      "name": "[concat(parameters('lockedResource'),
'/Microsoft.Authorization/myLock')]",
      "type": "Microsoft.Storage/storageAccounts/providers/locks",
      "apiVersion": "2015-01-01",
      "properties": {
        "level": "CannotDelete"
      }
    }
  ]
}
```

Firewalls and network security groups

The questions for a lot of HSPs is this: do we need to set up firewalls in the customer environments to secure the provided services or do network security groups suffer?

As per the definition, a **network security group** (NSG) is more or less a firewall on the network layer of a VM, and it is suitable to secure VMs from outside your network environment on a port level. From real-world scenarios, the NSG is the basis for securing resources, and often enough, if we do not need any further network inspection.

A firewall in your environment as the entry level for security provides a higher level of security because it secures resources and provides a network inspection on the IP packages. It is your choice which firewall provider you would like to choose as a firewall on IaaS; the good thing is that you could just choose your defined firewall OEM and use it in cloud environments too. From the level of customer engagements, a good practice is to enable a firewall VM as soon as the number of VMs is more than only a few ones and especially high secure workloads are running on them and there are some services that need to be available from the internet.

Summary

As you saw in this chapter, there are a lot of things that you should have in mind before starting to offer services from your Azure Stack environment. As soon as you put into practice the topics discussed in this chapter, you can provide cloud environments to your customers as a good practice. You will always have a good overview of what is going on in your Azure Stack environment and what your customers are really using.

In the next chapter, we will see what can be done with Azure Stack if you add valued services from the Azure public to your environment and start to go hybrid instead of private.

10
Integrating Public Cloud Services with Microsoft Azure Stack

In previous chapters, we talked about what is possible from a technical point of view and how to design and configure all the details regarding Azure Stack in a multinode deployment or development toolkit. With this chapter, we will try to bring it all together and design a solution and not a mere feature. As basically 98% of all Azure Stack customers have company services running in public Azure already, their plan is to design a hybrid cloud solution with some percentage of services from public Azure, some from Azure Stack, and some as a combination of both since a hybrid cloud solution will either consist of different cloud solutions or different cloud vendors. But all this involves some kind of internet connectivity, so we will not talk about hybrid solution designs within disconnected scenarios.

If we talk about all the different solutions in hybrid cloud, you may also think about adding third-party solution frameworks such as Cloud Foundry, Docker containers (with Kubernetes), and Apache DC/OS (also known as **Mesos**) if you plan on adding container solutions to your offering. Depending on the solution design, your offering may be a recipe out of the best of breeds of public and private Azure clouds.

Another thing we will need to design is a secure IAM solution. Azure Stack in a connected scenario talks about Azure Active Directory as an IAM solution. As AAD relies on public Azure and is not available with Azure Stack itself, this is just a hybrid solution.

In detail, we will talk about the following hybrid cloud solutions designs in this chapter:

- VPN connectivity
- Azure Active Directory
- Azure Container Services
- Third-party Azure cloud services

VPN connectivity

To be able to connect to services from another cloud solution or from your private cloud environment, you will need to set up a VPN connection to your Azure Stack environment. As a technical basis, the Virtual Network Gateway will connect you. With the Azure Stack Development Toolkit, all connectivity will go through one public IPv4 address; with the multinode environment, you will have different public IPs, and you will have to choose the IP address that fits into your Azure Stack resources.

To prepare connectivity, you will have to prepare the connecting machine with:

- Azure PowerShell
  (https://docs.microsoft.com/de-de/azure/azure-stack/azure-stack-powershell-install)
- Azure Stack PowerShell
  (https://docs.microsoft.com/de-de/azure/azure-stack/azure-stack-powershell-download)

Now let the PowerShell magic begin; configure a VPN:

```
Set-ExecutionPolicy RemoteSigned
Import-Module .\Connect\AzureStack.Connect.psm1
```

Let's extract and configure the certificates:

```
#Change the IP address in the following command to match your Azure
Stack host IP address
$hostIP = "<Azure Stack host IP address>"
# Change the password in the following command to the
administrative password that is provided when deploying Azure
Stack.
$Password = ConvertTo-SecureString `
  "<Administrator password provided when deploying Azure Stack>" `
  -AsPlainText -Force
#Add host IP and certificate authority to the to trusted hosts
Set-Item wsman:\localhost\Client\TrustedHosts -Value $hostIP
-Concatenate
```

Import the VPN entry to your computer:

```
Add-AzsVpnConnection -ServerAddress $hostIP -Password $Password
```

You will now see a proper VPN connection entry with your computer and should be able to start with the hybrid solution designs that follow.

Azure Active Directory

Azure Active Directory (**AAD**) is a multi-tenant Active Directory service developed by Microsoft and provided via Microsoft public Azure:

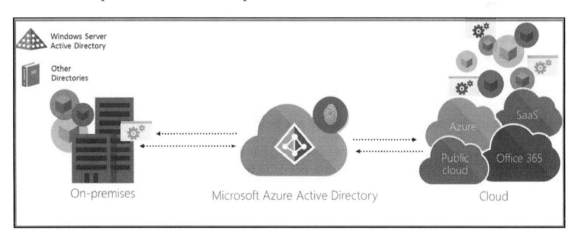

Source: https://docs.microsoft.com/en-us/azure/active-directory/media/hybrid-id-design-considerations/hybridid-example.png

The goal of AAD is to have one single cloud-based identity management solution that provides **Single Sign On** (**SSO**) features for every cloud service that is being consumed. Mainly, Azure AD provides the following capabilities:

- Multi-factor authentication
- Self-service password and group management
- Role-Based Access Control
- Privileged account management
- Application usage monitoring
- Security auditing, monitoring, and alerting

One of the most interesting design goals is that by default, each directory's information is being saved three times, which means that two copies of all directory data exist in different Azure regions spread all around the world. This provides a highly available and scalable directory service compared to most on-premise Active Directory services.

As AAD provides a synchronization mechanism to leverage your on-premises Active Directory accounts and transfer them to AAD using AD Connect, you will just have to define the details of the synchronization (which accounts) and to choose whether only accounts or even passwords should be synchronized.

As most of the companies in Europe rely on higher security expectations, the majority only synchronize the accounts and not the passwords. This means we are back to **Active Directory Federation Services** (**ADFS**). The access token will be generated from a local ADFS instance and transferred to Azure Active Directory:

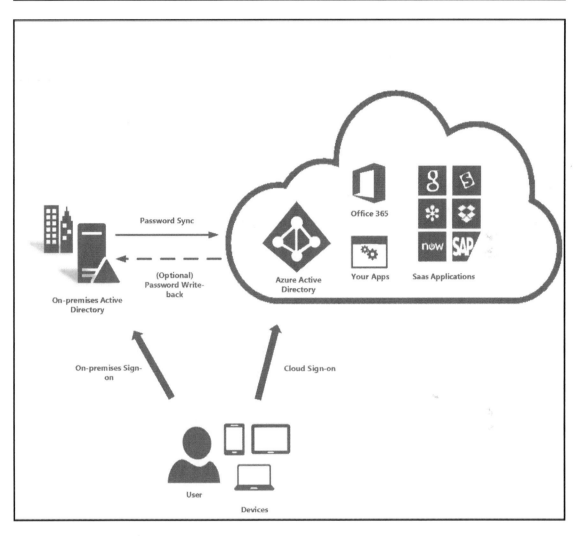

Regarding firewall security, the following ports need to be configured:

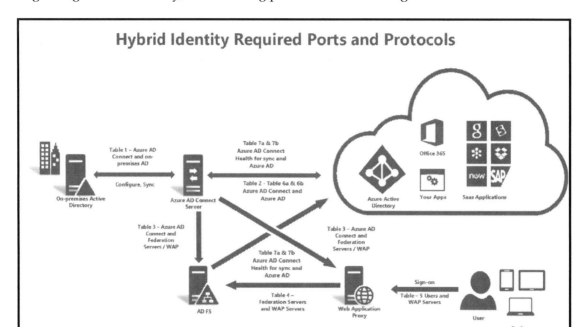

Source: https://docs.microsoft.com/de-de/azure/active-directory/connect/media/active-directory-aadconnect-ports/required3.png

When choosing your Azure AD features, you will have a choice between four options:

- Azure AD Free
- Azure AD Basic
- Azure AD Premium P1
- Azure AD Premium P2

 For a complete feature overview between these options, you should visit the following link:
`https://www.microsoft.com/en-us/cloud-platform/azure-active-directory-features`.

As Azure Stack connected scenarios rely on Azure AD only and no other features than Azure AD Free are required, the choice is up to the company's regulations for authentication; different options may be better suitable.

Preparing Azure AD for Azure Stack

If your company as of today does not have Azure AD already deployed, you will need to prepare it now. This can be done quite easily using the Azure Resource Manager portal (`http://portal.azure.com`), and you can choose to create a new Azure AD as follows:

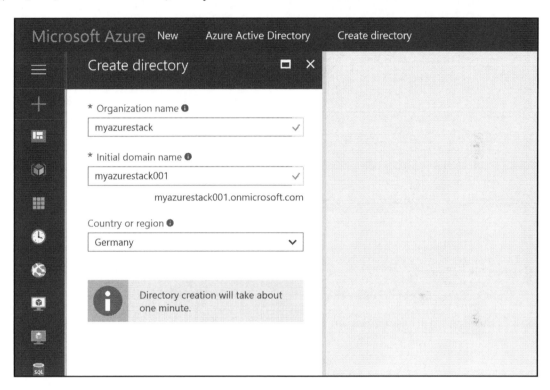

You will have to choose a unique internal Azure AD name called `xxx.onmicrosoft.com` and choose the corresponding country. It may take a moment to have the new directory up and running.

Optional – enabling premium Azure AD features

In case you need to enable Azure AD premium, this can be done as follows:

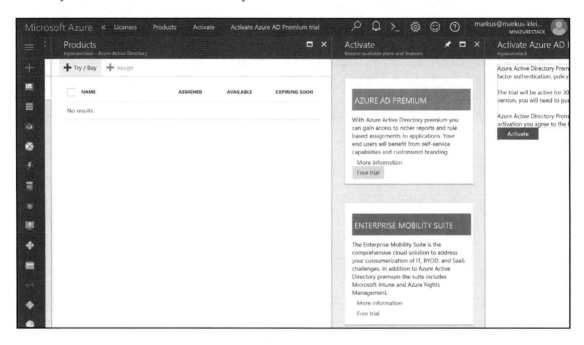

After you have enabled the premium features, they will be available, too.

Setting up a custom domain name

As you do not want your users to authenticate with @xxx.onmicrosoft.com, you should add a custom domain name. In general, this will be your primary company DNS domain name.

Adding a domain is done by clicking on +Add domain name. This can be done as follows:

After this, you will need to verify the domain as follows:

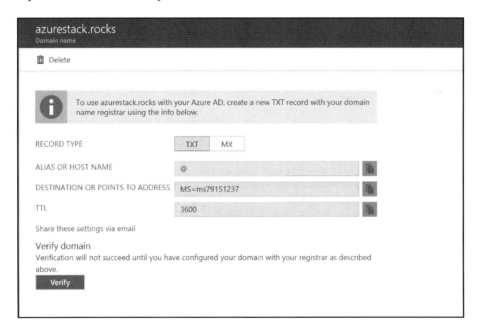

Bear in mind that DNS settings may take up to 48 hours to be synchronized through the internet!

Optional – multi-factor authentication

If you need to provide higher security for authentication, you should think about implementing Azure **Multi-Factor Authentication**. This provides a second factor (SMS, call, or authenticator app) for a successful authentication:

As you can see, today this feature is still available only with the Azure Classic portal and looks as follows:

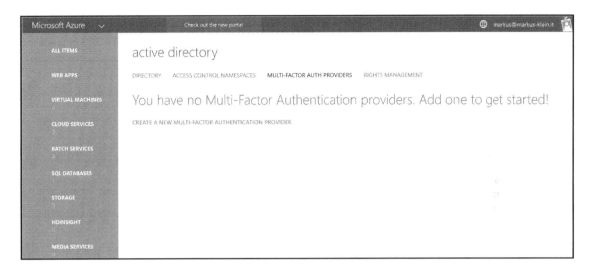

After you choose **CREATE A NEW MULTI-FACTOR AUTHENTICATION PROVIDER**, the GUI looks as follows:

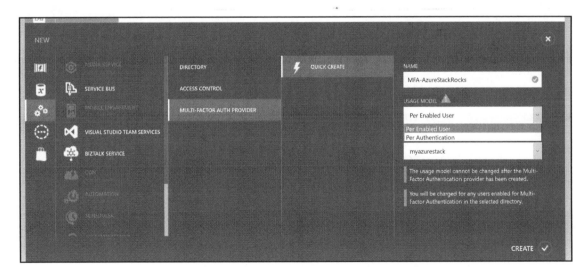

As you can see, you will have to pay for multi-factor authentication for **Per Authentication** or **Per User**:

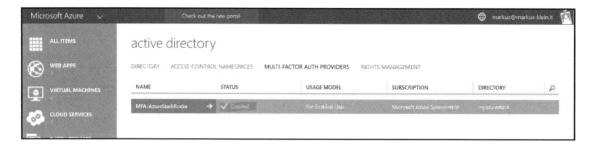

Now you can start managing multi-factor authentication **Per User** in the dedicated MFA portal:

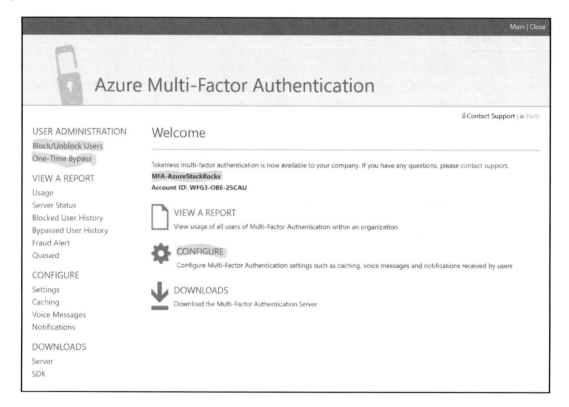

Keep in mind that MFA is not supported during the setup process of Azure Stack for the user part. You will need to enable a *bypass* during the installation. After the installation is finished, you should enable it again.

Docker/container services

In recent years, virtualization has ever been on the minds of IT administrators. Some companies have already embraced Linux Docker, its configuration, and design. With Windows Server 2016, Microsoft introduced this new virtualization solution that does not rely on the theory that each VM be using its dedicated resources, including the operating system:

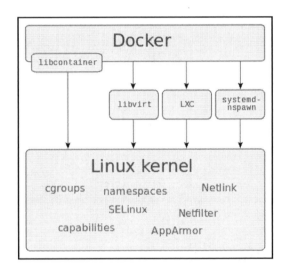

Source: https://upload.wikimedia.org/wikipedia/commons/thumb/0/09/Docker-linux-interfaces.svg/800px-Docker-linux-interfaces.svg.png

Especially during the development of an application, there are different stages during the staging process. This solution provides an easy setup of different environments, consuming fewer resources. Docker containers share one operating system with dedicated, closed environments:

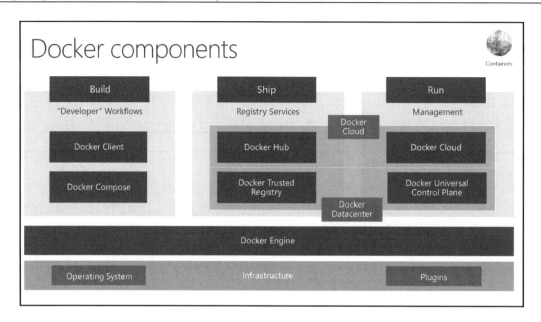

With Windows Server 2016, containers have been designed as follows. They are similar to Docker and are exchangeable:

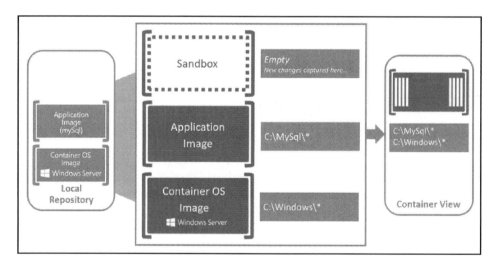

Source: https://docs.microsoft.com/en-us/virtualization/windowscontainers/about/media/containerfund.png

A common management solution for Docker, called **orchestrator**, can be Swarm, DC/OS, or Kubernetes, among others.

Azure Container Services

If you are willing to consume containers for Linux/Windows as a PaaS solution, **Azure Container Services (ACS)** could be a solution. The generic design of ACS is described here:

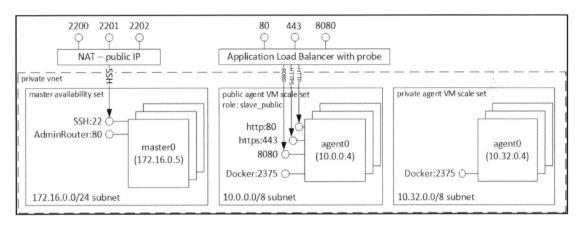

Source: https://docs.microsoft.com/de-de/azure/container-service/media/acs-intro/dcos.png

A good question is now how to design a container solution with Azure and Azure Stack in a hybrid way since—as of today—there is no PaaS solution with Azure Stack, but there are IaaS machines that support Windows containers or Linux Docker.

The answer is quite easy: as Azure and Azure Stack support site-to-site VPNs between each other, there is network connectivity enabled already.

So, we could set up containers in both solutions (with Azure- and Azure Stack-only IaaS based container images) and manage them with a dedicated orchestration solution such as Kubernetes. This means that you could just move workloads from Azure to Azure Stack and vice versa. As you can manage the location of a container/docker image with the orchestration solution, it is even possible to have a planned one for your containers.

If you are planning on running a PaaS solution, there is no need to design this solution from its technical perspective as the VM design for it is predefined and just needs to be deployed. As Azure Container Services is a PaaS one, there is adding containers/docker hosts to it is no different. In addition, the default orchestration solution for ACS is Kubernetes.

Setting up **Azure Container Services** is quite simple:

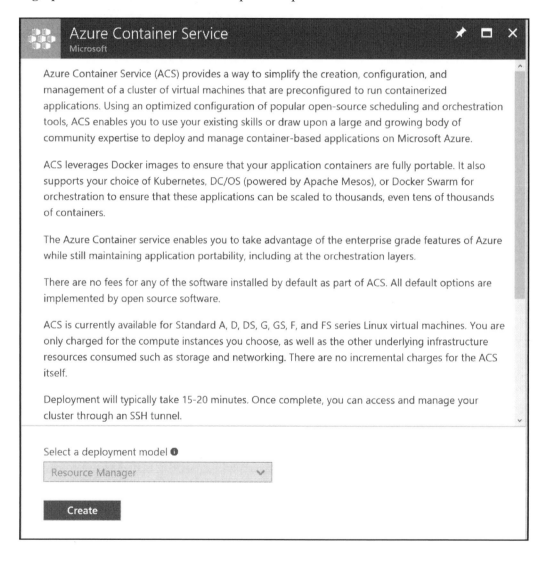

The next step is to hit the **Create** button to get to the details wizard (**Master configuration**):

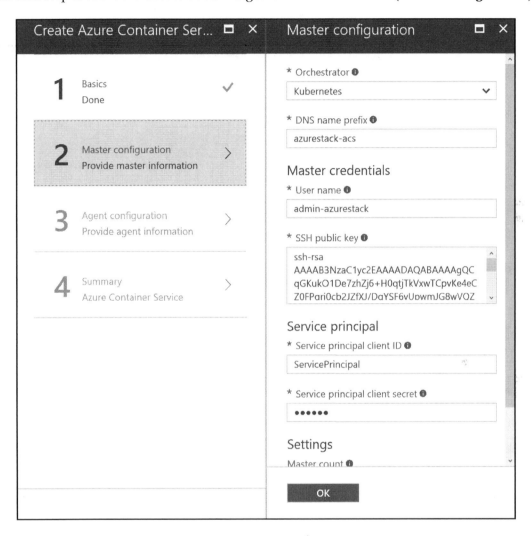

Setting the **Agent configuration** is the very final step before ordering ACS:

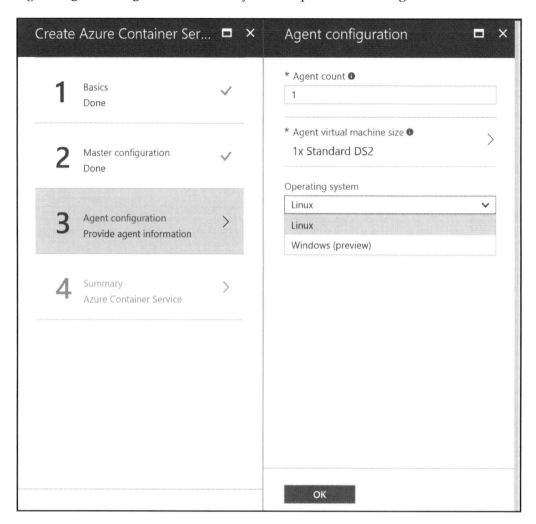

Within the next few minutes, your Azure Container Services will be set up and you can start using it and setting up containers used by your Azure Stack environment in a hybrid design.

Third-party Azure cloud services

As container solutions are becoming more and more interesting as an important step to move to a full-cloud solution sometime in the future, there is the need for an easy-to-manage, self-service-portal based solution for managing these containers. In today's container solution market, Cloud Foundry, and DC/OS, or Mesos are the most important ones, which we will have a look at and discuss in the next chapters.

Cloud Foundry

Cloud Foundry is a project that has been started as an open source solution for developing and deploying cloud-based software solutions. It provides automation, scale-out, and scale-down scenarios and manages cloud solutions:

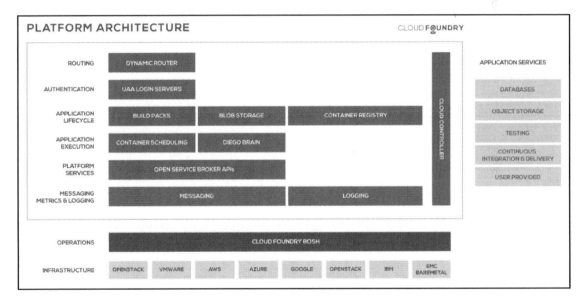

Source: https://www.cloudfoundry.org/wp-content/uploads/2017/01/cloudfoundry_platform_architecture-1200x575.png

As you can see from this diagram, it not only supports Azure, it supports several other cloud vendor solutions, too. The design goals of Cloud Foundry are as follows:

- Application lifecycle management
- Networking and configuration

- Logging and monitoring
- Platform solutions (service brokers)

 Cloud Foundry also hosts the BOSH, which is a dedicated CLI for its maintenance and management. In 2013, a new company called Pivotal (a joint venture with EMC and VMware) started developing a commercial release of Cloud Foundry.

As Cloud Foundry is supported with Azure and Azure Stack using the same ARM template, the setup is quite easy and has the same look and feel in both cloud environments (public and private). This is how the wizard will look:

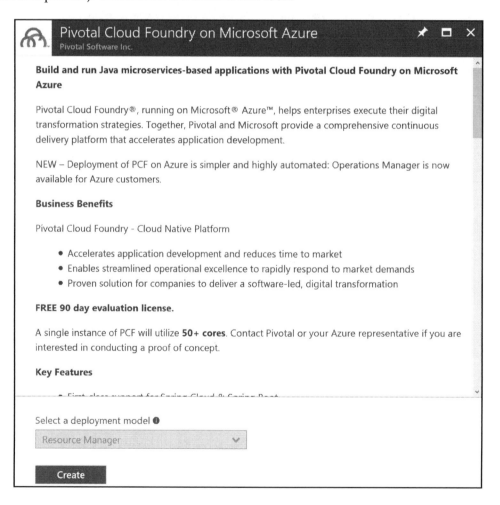

After hitting the **Create** button, the wizard will start collecting all the details for the deployment:

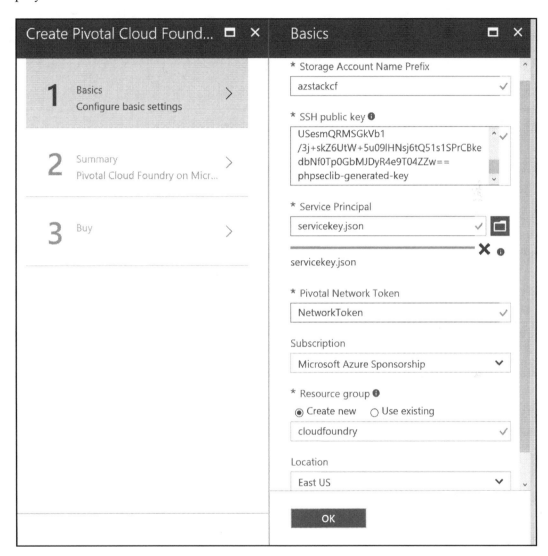

As you can see, we need another JSON file, which describes the **Service Principal** for Cloud Foundry. This might look like the following one:

```
servicekey.json    ⊓  X

Schema:  <No Schema Selected>
 5          "basics": [
 6              {
 7                  "name": "storageAccountNamePrefix",
 8                  "type": "Microsoft.Common.TextBox",
 9                  "label": "Storage Account Name Prefix",
10                  "defaultValue": "",
11                  "constraints": {
12                      "required": true,
13                      "regex": "^[a-z0-9]{1,10}$",
14                      "validationMessage": "Only lower-case letters and numbers are allowed, and the value must be 1-10 characters long."
15                  }
16              },
17              {
18                  "name": "sshKeyData",
19                  "type": "Microsoft.Compute.CredentialsCombo",
20                  "label": {
21                      "authenticationType": "Authentication type",
22                      "password": "Password",
23                      "confirmPassword": "Confirm password",
24                      "sshPublicKey": "SSH public key"
25                  },
26                  "toolTip": {
27                      "authenticationType": "",
28                      "password": "",
29                      "sshPublicKey": ""
30                  },
31                  "constraints": {
32                      "required": true
33                  },
34                  "options": {
35                      "hideConfirmation": true,
36                      "hidePassword": true
37                  },
38                  "osPlatform": "Linux"
39              },
40              {
41                  "name": "servicePrincipal",
42                  "type": "Microsoft.Common.FileUpload",
43                  "label": "Service Principal",
44                  "toolTip": "",
45                  "constraints": {
46                      "required": true,
47                      "accept": ".json"
48                  },
49                  "options": {
50                      "multiple": false,
51                      "uploadMode": "file",
52                      "openMode": "text",
53                      "encoding": "UTF-8"
54                  }
55              },
56              {
57                  "name": "pivnetAPIToken",
58                  "type": "Microsoft.Common.TextBox",
59                  "label": "Pivotal Network Token",
60                  "defaultValue": "",
61                  "constraints": {
62                      "required": true
63                  }
64              }
65          ],
66          "steps": [],
67          "outputs": {
68              "storageAccountNamePrefixString": "[basics('storageAccountNamePrefix')]",
69              "adminSSHKey": "[basics('sshKeyData').sshPublicKey]",
70              "tenantID": "[parse(basics('servicePrincipal')).tenantID]",
71              "clientID": "[parse(basics('servicePrincipal')).clientID]",
72              "clientSecret": "[parse(basics('servicePrincipal')).clientSecret]",
73              "pivnetAPIToken": "[basics('pivnetAPIToken')]",
74              "location": "[location()]"
75          }
76      }
77  }
78
```

After having everything collected, the wizard will show a **Summary** page and you can order it directly:

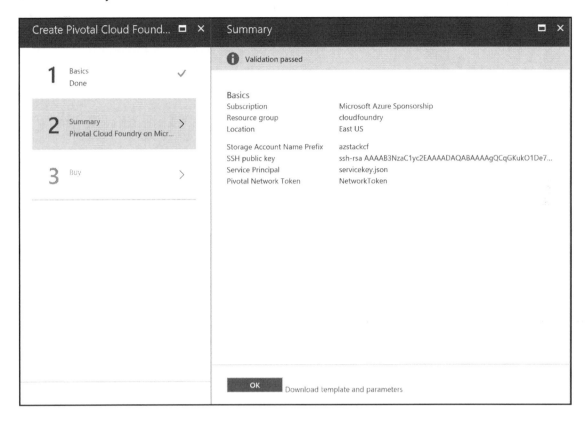

As Cloud Foundry is able to interact with other PaaS solutions using tools called **service brokers**, the only difference as of today is that there is no service broker support with Cloud Foundry on Azure Stack. The result is that only services that are available out of the box can be used. Cloud Foundry is based on different VMs for all services. If you need to split theses VMs between clouds (for what reason ever), you would have to set up the solution manually. Even this is possible.

After the setup has finished, you can start using Cloud Foundry with the UI, which you will already know if you have seen it before:

Source:
https://106c4.wpc.azureedge.net/80106C4/Gallery-Prod/cdn/2015-02-24/prod20161101-microsoft-windowsazure-gallery/pivotal.pivotal-cloud-foundryazure-pcf.1.0.8/Screenshots/Screenshot1.png

The Marketplace UI is illustrated as follows:

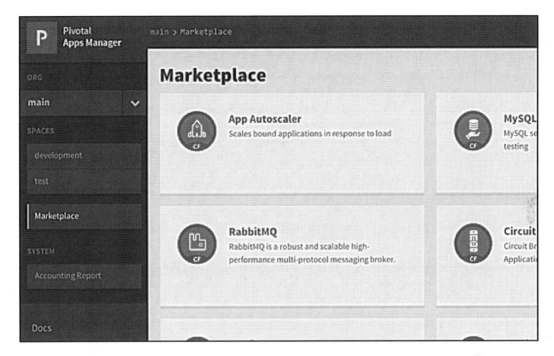

Source:
https://106c4.wpc.azureedge.net/80106C4/Gallery-Prod/cdn/2015-02-24/prod20161101-microsoft-windowsazure-gallery/pivotal.pivotal-cloud-foundryazure-pcf.1.0.8/Screenshots
/Screenshot3.png

DC/OS

DC/OS is a product from a company called **Mesosphere**. The product is being promoted as an operating system, cluster manager, and container platform, so basically as an all-in-one solution. From the container perspective, it supports two container solutions—Docker and Mesos—and provides *handlers* for services and jobs. One of its goals is support for handling advanced scenarios (such as setup, teardown, backup, restore, migration, synchronization, and rebalancing). It gives you as a developer the flexibility you need for your application, and as long as you follow the design architecture, you do not have to deal with the cloud readiness of your app: it is just there out of the box:

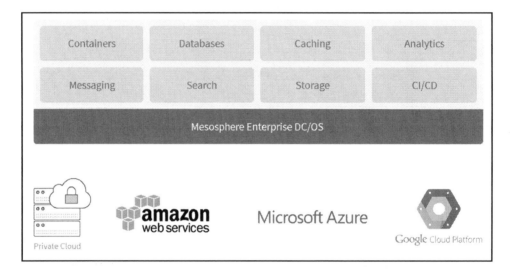

Source: https://mesosphere.com/

With this general solution overview, you will be able to serve the most important cloud services out of one solution:

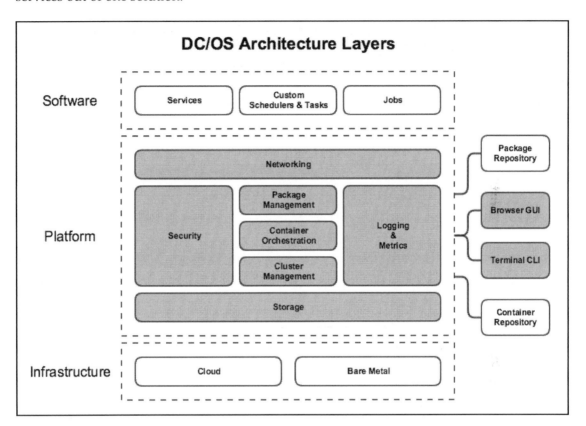

With this architecture, every developer should find all the services they really need for their cloud app. DC/OS is an overall solution framework and could not even be deployed with Azure, Azure Stack is supported, too.

As the ARM template for both solutions it the same, the look and feel compared to Azure is the same, too. If you deploy the template, you would just have to fill in some details, and the deployment will start:

After hitting the **Create** button, the wizard starts:

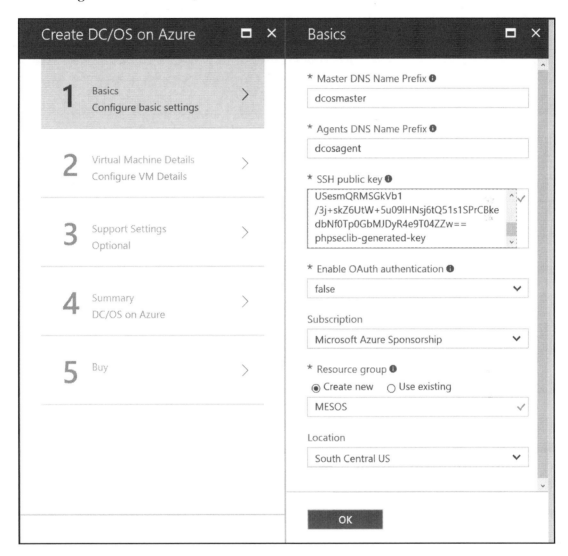

The next step is to define the VM details:

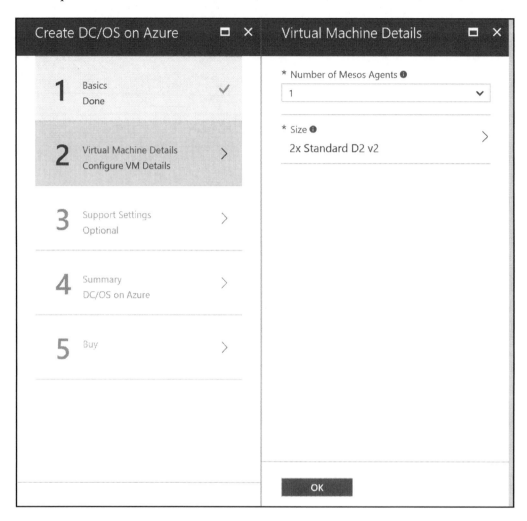

Finally, filling in the support details and ordering the services results in the deployment of DC/OS in your cloud environment:

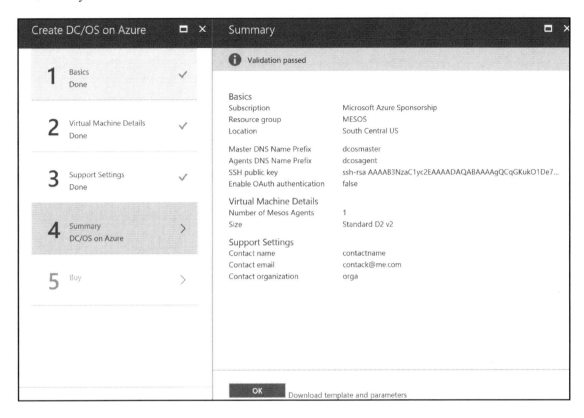

After you deploy the DC/OS environment, it is up and running and can be used:

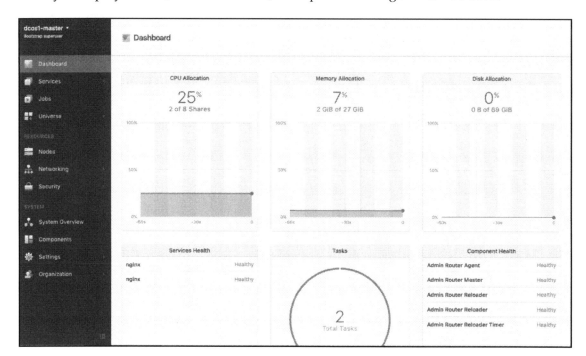

Source: https://docs.mesosphere.com/wp-content/uploads/2017/04/dashboard-ee-1-600x345@2x.gif

Choosing your container solution

As you have seen, there are a variety of container services available with Azure Stack and even Azure as a hybrid solution design. This means you will have a choice for every type of customer project.

Regarding the location of the containers, as of now the choice is between having them on premise on Azure Stack and running them as an IaaS solution, running them in public Azure, or even as a hybrid solution with parts of them on premise and the rest in the public cloud. From real-world experience, there is no chance of having a clear solution before you know the workload and the customer's requirements. Depending on this, the best way is to set up a decision tree and find the solution that fits best.

The five parameters of this decision tree are:

- Do we require a PaaS or an IaaS solution?
- Do we need a hybrid container setup?
- Which container solution fits best from the usage perspective?
- What about security, sovereignty, and latency with your customer's internet connectivity?
- Is a container solution already in place and do we need to migrate?

Summary

This chapter is one of the most important ones in the whole book as it talks about real-world scenarios, how to design the solution, and the possibilities you have today. The chapters before were all about features and how to configure them.

As you have seen, even with version 1 of Azure Stack, there is a lot of work that could be done from a hybrid perspective and to connect services directly from and with Azure public cloud. Azure Stack is not a dedicated solution—it is Azure in your datacenter, not more but mostly less. Why less is quite simple to explain: Azure is being designed on thousands of servers, and Azure Stack is being designed with a small number of services that from a **return on investment** (**ROI**) perspective are worth running in your or your service provider's datacenter and not being consumed from public Azure.

So, there is nearly no chance to just think about Azure Stack (unless you are a service provider yourself) and not even think about Azure and how to connect these two worlds into one solution for yourself or your customer. There are some services with Azure Stack that even rely on Azure technologies, such as Azure Active Directory. If you are in a connected scenario, you just need Azure AD to set up Azure Stack.

From a developer's perspective, Azure Stack with additional PaaS services from Azure or even Azure Stack is the basis for work on cloud-native applications that are stateful and do not fail if a service switches from one server to another or even from one cloud to another.

If we think more globally, it is even possible to connect Azure Stack to a cloud offering from a different vendor (such as Amazon Web Services or Google) and even set up hybrid solutions, especially using third-party solutions such as Cloud Foundry and DC/OS or just containers. As some enterprise customers rely on a two-vendor cloud strategy, Azure Stack could be the in-between place to connect each other with a simple but smart way of reusing Azure technologies.

In the next chapter, we will have a look at two scenarios of hybrid cloud solution design and discuss their setup and design and why to choose them.

11
Creating a Hybrid Cloud Solution

In the previous chapter, we talked about what technical features are available to set up hybrid clouds while integrating Azure and Azure Stack. In this chapter, we will discuss some scenarios from real-world projects and show how to prepare Azure Stack for a successful and growing path in the future in most companies. There are some major features that need to be addressed. As soon they are in place, Azure Stack becomes a self-runner in IT and later in general business.

The most important feature of Azure Stack is setting up the Marketplace. There are quite a few possibilities that are valid themselves. You just need to place them in the correct business case in order to succeed. We will talk about the following topics in detail:

- Setting up the Marketplace
- Setting up hybrid solutions
- Internal project marketing

As my experiences are from real-world projects, you will hopefully learn from my experiences that as soon as these three topics are set up properly, there is no further need to worry about Azure Stack anymore:

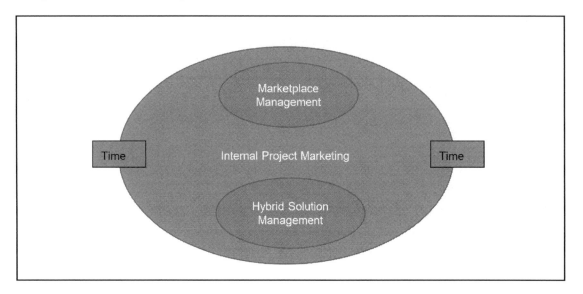

Marketplace management

The Azure Stack Marketplace is the overall summary of all cloud offerings from a single Azure Stack Stamp, which means one Azure Stack portal and one Azure Stack Resource Manager.

The most important basis for setting up hybrid cloud solutions the Azure Stack Marketplace. As it complies with the Azure one technology using **Azure Resource Manager** (**ARM**) templates, the technical basis is there. The next few pages will discuss the options to fill it properly.

Azure Marketplace syndication

As the past has shown us, the question is always about the process. If we prepare a golden image from a solution (if it was in **System Center Configuration Manager** (**SCCM**), **Virtual Machine Manager** (**VMM**), or any other VM management solution), there is the need to set up and live a process that will simply make sure that the image will be updated frequently. If that does not happen, the golden image will somehow become a **historical image** and everybody will start complaining that it takes too long to wait for a new environment because of all the updates that need to be installed if the virtual machine has been set up.

With Azure Stack, things could change and the process of rebuilding **golden images** would become quite simple. This solution is called **Azure Marketplace syndication** because if you somehow have internet connectivity for your Azure Stack environment, you could set up the syndication and implement a solution to set up a quick process to update the images: just re-download them to Azure Stack and you are fine. Microsoft will be your image updating team then. The question is this: how do you make a Microsoft image look like mine and fulfill all the modifications? Well, this is the simple answer: this is where PowerShell **Desired State Configuration** (**DSC**) will jump in and make sure that after deploying the default image from Microsoft Azure, it will modify the configuration of the solution to fulfill your requirements.

In the administrative portal, you will find the corresponding link:

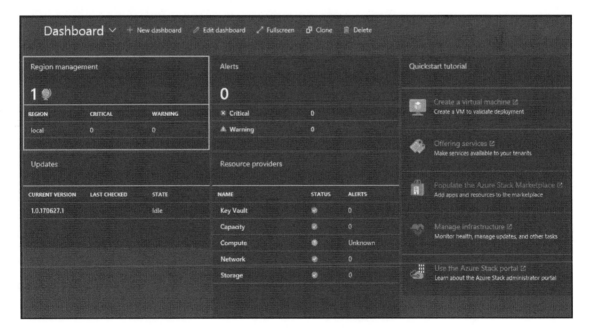

Azure Stack Marketplace syndication has the following requirements:

- A user account for an active Azure subscription with owner permissions on Azure AD
- Internet connectivity between Azure and Azure Stack
- Good internet connectivity (for quick downloads of some GBs of images)

 There is a PowerShell script available to register Azure Stack with an Azure subscription. The script called `RegisterWithAzure.ps1`, and it can be downloaded here `https://github.com/Azure/AzureStack-Tools/blob/master/Registration/RegisterWithAzure.ps1`.

Before running the script, we will need to collect the following parameters:

- Azure domain name (`xxxx.onmicrosoft.com`)
- Azure subscription ID:
    1. Log on to the Azure portal.
    2. Go to **Subscriptions**.
    3. Click on **Essentials** to get the ID.

Then, we can start with the registration process itself with the following steps:

1. Register the Azure Stack resource provider with Azure:

```
Login-AzureRmAccount -EnvironmentName "AzureCloud"
Register-AzureRmResourceProvider
-ProviderNamespace Microsoft.AzureStack -Force
```

2. Run the PowerShell script on an administrative PowerShell:

```
RegisterWithAzure.ps1 -azureSubscriptionId YourID
-azureDirectoryTenantName YourDirectory
-azureAccountId YourAccountName
```

3. The parameters need to be filled are as follows:
    - `YourAccountName`, is the owner of the Azure subscription
    - `YourID`, is the Azure subscription ID that you want to use to register Azure Stack
    - `YourDirectory`, is the name of your Azure Active Directory tenant that your Azure subscription is a part of

When running the script, you will get a pop-up window asking for the password of your Azure AD account, and you will have to hit *Enter* twice during the registration procedure.

After successful registration, you will see the following within your **Azure Stack - Administration** portal if you go to **Marketplace management** in the administrative part:

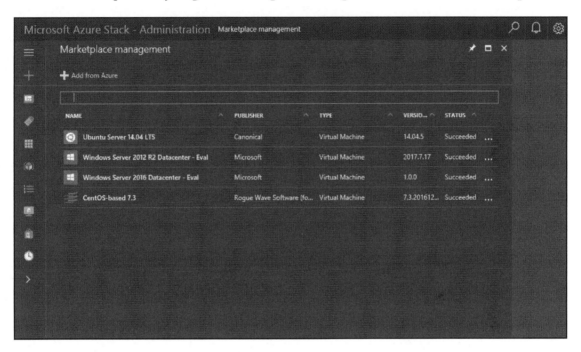

This screenshot shows a view with four items already added (Ubuntu Server, Windows Server 2012 R2, Windows Server 2016, and CentOS). After clicking on **Add from Azure**, Azure Stack will load all the available Azure Marketplace items tagged with Azure Stack and give you a chance to download them to Azure Stack:

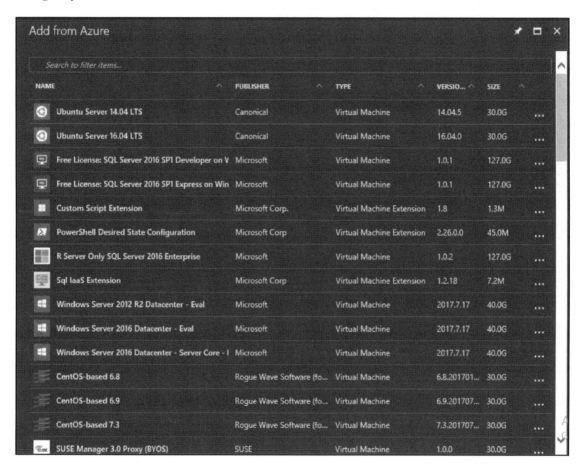

To download an item, click on the appropriate item on the right-hand side. You get three points to get the context menu of that item. Remember that downloading may take its time (refer to the column **SIZE** to get an idea about how long the download could take). From the licensing perspective, all non-Microsoft solutions are with a **bring your own license** (**BYOL**) in general, and you will need to make sure that you are licensing correctly.

As the Azure Marketplace is growing each day, the list of available Azure Stack compatible Marketplace items will grow consistently. For a complete list, this URL will help: `https://docs.microsoft.com/en-us/azure/azure-stack/azure-stack-m arketplace-azure-items`.

From the business point of view, this feature provides a great return on investment in comparison of the costs for maintaining the images yourself.

Adding Marketplace items with PowerShell

If you do not want to add VM images using the Marketplace syndication feature that comes with the product, there is still the option to manually add images to the Marketplace using PowerShell.

The process of adding new base images is described as follows:

1. Log on to a computer with Azure PowerShell and Azure Stack PowerShell tools installed. In addition, we need the PowerShell tools for Azure Stack too.
2. Download a Windows Server 2016 Evaluation version, for example, here: `https://www.microsoft.com/en-us/evalcenter/evaluate-windows-server-2016`.
3. Import the Azure Stack `Connect` and `ComputeAdmin` PowerShell module to your administrative PowerShell ISE, as follows:

   ```
   Import-Module .\Connect\AzureStack.Connect.psm1
   Import-Module .\ComputeAdmin\AzureStack.ComputeAdmin.psm1
   ```

4. Create the Azure Stack cloud administrator's AzureRM environment:

   ```
   Add-AzureRMEnvironment `
     -Name "AzureStackAdmin" `
     -ArmEndpoint https://adminmanagement.local.azurestack.external
   ```

5. Get the GUID from your Azure Stack tenant:
   - In connected scenarios, this is the code:

     ```
     $TenantID = Get-AzsDirectoryTenantId `
     -AADTenantName "<myDirectoryTenantName>.onmicrosoft.com" `
     -EnvironmentName AzureStackAdmin
     ```

- In disconnected scenarios, this is the code:

```
$TenantID = Get-AzsDirectoryTenantId `
-ADFS `
-EnvironmentName AzureStackAdmin
```

6. Log in to your Azure Stack environment using the follow PowerShell command:

```
Login-AzureRmAccount `
-EnvironmentName "AzureStackAdmin" `
-TenantId $TenantID
```

7. Upload the Windows Server 2016 image to Azure Stack:

```
$ISOPath = "<Fully_Qualified_Path_to_ISO>"
# Add a Windows Server 2016 Evaluation VM Image.
New-AzsServer2016VMImage `
-ISOPath $ISOPath
```

The following parameters are possible:

New-AzsServer2016VMImage **parameters**	Required	Description
ISOPath	Yes	The fully qualified path to the downloaded Windows Server 2016 ISO.
Net35	No	This parameter allows you to install the .NET 3.5 runtime on the Windows Server 2016 image. By default, this value is set to true. It is mandatory that the image contain the .NET 3.5 runtime to install the SQL and MySQL resource providers.
Version	No	This parameter allows you to choose whether to add Core or Full or both Windows Server 2016 images. By default, this value is set to **Full**.
VHDSizeInMB	No	Sets the size (in MB) of the VHD image to be added to your Azure Stack environment. By default, this value is set to 40,960 MB.

CreateGalleryItem	No	Specifies whether a Marketplace item should be created for the Windows Server 2016 image. By default, this value is set to `true`.
Location	No	Specifies the location to which the Windows Server 2016 image should be published.
IncludeLatestCU	No	Set this switch to apply the latest Windows Server 2016 cumulative update to the new VHD.
CUURI	No	Set this value to choose the Windows Server 2016 cumulative update from a specific URI.
CUPath	No	Set this value to choose the Windows Server 2016 cumulative update from a local path. This option is helpful if you have deployed the Azure Stack instance in a disconnected environment.

Publishing the image will take up to an hour, and from my experience, the `IncludeLatestCU` parameter will help be on the most recent patch level.

Adding existing VMs to Azure Stack

If you need to add existing VMs to Azure Stack. The process of adding new base images is described as follows and is quite similar to that of adding a new base OS:

1. Log on to a computer with Azure PowerShell and Azure Stack PowerShell tools installed. In addition, we need the PowerShell tools for Azure Stack too.
2. Import the Azure Stack `Connect` and `ComputeAdmin` PowerShell module to your administrative PowerShell ISE, as follows:

```
Import-Module  .\Connect\AzureStack.Connect.psm1
Import-Module  .\ComputeAdmin\AzureStack.ComputeAdmin.psm1
```

3. Create the Azure Stack cloud administrator's AzureRM environment:

```
Add-AzureRMEnvironment `
  -Name "AzureStackAdmin" `
  -ArmEndpoint https://adminmanagement.local.azurestack.external
```

4. Get the GUID from your Azure Stack tenant:
   - In connected scenarios, this is the code:
   - In disconnected scenarios, this is the code:

```
$TenantID = Get-AzsDirectoryTenantId `
  -ADFS -EnvironmentName AzureStackAdmin
```

5. Log in to your Azure Stack environment using the follow PowerShell command:

```
Login-AzureRmAccount `
  -EnvironmentName "AzureStackAdmin" `
  -TenantId $TenantID
```

6. Add the existing image to the environment using the following PowerShell:

```
Add-AzsVMImage `
  -publisher "Canonical" `
  -offer "UbuntuServer" `
  -sku "14.04.3-LTS" `
  -version "1.0.0" `
  -osType Linux `
  -osDiskLocalPath
  'C:\Users\AzureStackAdmin\Desktop\UbuntuServer.vhd'
```

The PowerShell command does the following steps:

1. Authenticates to the Azure Stack environment.
2. Uploads the local VHD to a newly created temporary storage account.
3. Adds the VM image to the VM image repository.
4. Creates a Marketplace item.

Parameter	Description
publisher	The publisher name segment of the VM image that user's use when deploying the image. An example is Microsoft. Do not include a *space* or other *special characters* in this field.

offer	The `offer` name segment of the VM image that user's use when deploying the VM image. An example is `WindowsServer`. Do not include a *space* or other *special characters* in this field.
sku	The `sku` name segment of the VM image that user's use when deploying the VM image. An example is `Datacenter2016`. Do not include a *space* or other *special characters* in this field.
version	The `version` of the VM image that user's use when deploying the VM image. This version is in the format `#.#.#`. An example is `1.0.0`. Do not include a *space* or other *special characters* in this field.
osType	The `osType` of the image must be either **Windows** or **Linux**.
osDiskLocalPath	The local path to the OS disk VHD that you are uploading as a VM image to Azure Stack.
dataDiskLocalPaths	An optional array of the local paths for data disks that can be uploaded as part of the VM image.
CreateGalleryItem	A Boolean flag that determines whether to create an item in Marketplace. By default, it is set to `true`.
title	The `title` name of Marketplace item. By default, it is set to the `publisher-offer-sku` of the VM image.
description	The `description` of the Marketplace item.
location	The `location` to which the VM image should be published. By default, this value is set to `local`.
osDiskBlobURI	Optionally, this script also accepts a Blob storage URI for `osDisk`.
dataDiskBlobURIs	Optionally, this script also accepts an array of Blob storage URIs in order to add data disks to the image.

To add other distributions to Azure Stack, follow this article for all the details:
`https://docs.microsoft.com/en-us/azure/azure-stack/azure-stack-l inux`.

To remove an existing VM from the Marketplace, the PowerShell will change to the following:

```
Remove-AzsVMImage `
  -publisher "Canonical" `
  -offer "UbuntuServer" `
  -sku "14.04.3-LTS" `
  -version "1.0.0"
```

Using the Marketplace publishing tool

The Marketplace publishing toolkit creates Azure Marketplace packages files based on an IaaS Azure Resource Manager template or existing VM extension. In addition, you can use it to publish `azpkg` files, either created with the tool or using manual steps.

The prerequisites for running the tool are as follows:

- You will have to run the tool from a machine with direct connectivity to Azure Stack
- You have already downloaded the Azure Stack quick start templates (https://github.com/Azure/AzureStack-QuickStart-Templates/archive/master.zip)
- You will have to download the Azure gallery packaging tool (http://aka.ms/azurestackmarketplaceitem)
- You will need icons and thumbnail files for your solution or use some sample ones (https://docs.microsoft.com/en-us/azure/azure-stack/azure-stack-marketplace-publisher#support-files)

The next step is to download and extract the Marketplace publishing tool available as part of the Azure Stack tools at https://docs.microsoft.com/en-us/azure/azure-stack/azure-stack-powershell-download.

Providing a new Marketplace item will look like this:

1. Start the Marketplace publishing tool:

   ```
   .\MarketplaceToolkit.ps1
   ```

2. In the **Create Solution Package** tab, you will have to add the values, as follows:

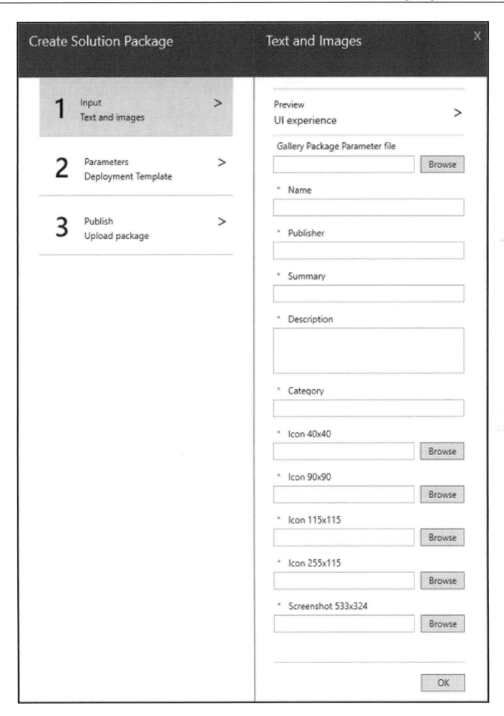

If you do not want to add them using a GUI, you can specify them in a parameters file.

3. After this, we will need to import the image and create the package as second step in the wizard:

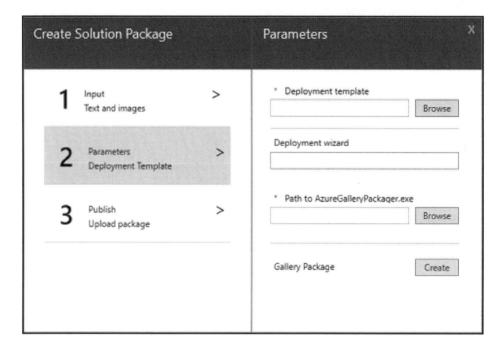

4. Finally, we will need to create the Marketplace items:

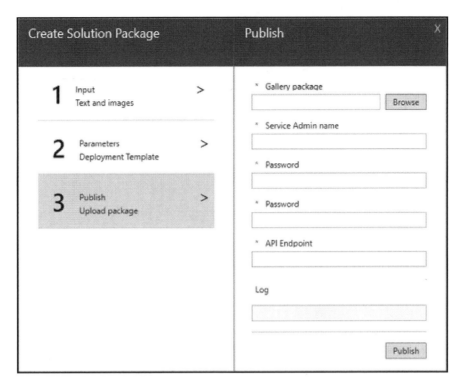

The required parameters are as follows:

Field	Description
Service Admin name	Service administrator account. Example: `ServiceAdmin@mydomain.onmicrosoft.com`.
Password	Password for service administrator account.
API Endpoint	Azure Stack Azure Resource Manager endpoint. Example: `management.local.azurestack.external`.

Regardless of which solution you used to populate new images, you will now see them in the Azure Stack Marketplace, and your tenant will be able to deploy them. Keep in mind that as of today, there is no tenant-based Marketplace available; each offering in the Marketplace will be available to every tenant. From real-world experiences, it is best to have some great Marketplace items in place with the **GOLIVE-Azure** and enhance them on a regular basis.

Setting up hybrid cloud solutions

As the Azure Marketplace is filled, we now have to talk about scenarios where hybrid cloud solution designs make sense. In general, it is quite easy to define where we need hybrid solution designs:

- Data sovereignty
- Sensitive data
- Regulations
- Customizations
- Legacy support

Hybrid cloud solution, therefore, can be defined as a business- and law-driven cloud solution as nobody really needs it but there are reasons defined by the business and the law that may lead to it.

Data sovereignty

Especially with high sensitive data, there is often the requirement in some business areas where data needs to be in the building, the county, or the country, and there is no change to save it somewhere else as if this intellectual property is lost, the company could close because they may lose their patents and business trademarks.

Sensitive data

For companies working with personal data (for example, health care and doctors), there are countries around the world where this data does not have to be saved somewhere in the cloud or even in different countries than where the company is themselves.

Regulations

Based on government requirements, data needs to be saved onsite, in the county, or the country. If this is the case, we need a hybrid solution.

Customizations

If you as a company are running a Microsoft-technology-based networking infrastructure and you have to modify an offering, you may have to modify the default offering and add additional features (such as specific backups) to a solution, Azure Stack may fit. In addition, as if you are, for example, running SAP or any other third party at a hosting provider, it may be better to have your solutions next to SAP and not somewhere else. Yes, you could run SAP in Azure too, but if you rely on contracts, it may take time to move everything to Azure and you will need a workaround for the next year, for example.

Legacy support

Especially high technology, industries rely on cost-sensitive solutions (for example, in a production environment) where replacing existing solutions may be very expensive. Based on the number of controlling and ROI calculations, the solution must be online the next year, although it relies on old server technology, for example. This is where a hybrid cloud solution will help.

With that in mind, you can have hybrid solutions, as follows, Wand set them up using hybrid technologies of Azure Stack and Azure to be agile and solve the DevOps issues in your company without the need to learn different technologies.

A solution that may fit most of your customer environments may look like this:

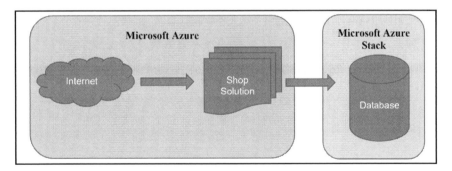

 A sample solution, as described earlier, will is available on `http://www.azurestack.rocks/hybridsample`. It is a web frontend (shop solution) that saves new entries to a storage queue and then transfers this queue to an Azure Stack-based MySQL server database.

Internal project marketing

Regardless of the best solution for a company's business case or workload that needs to be planned, built, and run in an Azure Stack based hybrid cloud solution, what's more important is the internal project marketing. What does that mean? In one sentence: *Let's talk about good things we did from IT.*

As today's IT world needs to be agile in its development as well as operations, we will need to set up a solution to support these. We need to align development, operations, and security to set up a solution design that will work as planned. In general, we would need to rebuild the subject called **DevOps** and rename it to **DevSecOps**. This would lead to a successful and agile cloud environment that will support the public and the private world using hybrid cloud solutions.

If we set things up properly, the next stage would be to make sure that it is not just a great new solution. You will need to align it with the communication processes in the company and make sure that you choose use cases and workloads everybody understands-from the upper to the lower level in the organizational structure. It this solution succeeds and everybody in the company talks about it, then your entrepreneurship will have value in succeeding completely throughout the whole company.

You should plan the project in three steps:

- Make sure you are ready to go.
- Make sure the company is steady.
- Make sure the project will start to go.

Finally, do not forget to make today's **IT Infrastructure Library (ITIL)**-based processes agile. If you succeed with agile ITIL processes, your hybrid world will prepare for cloud technologies using hybrid cloud solutions.

Summary

As Azure Stack is designed to be a hybrid cloud solution there is in general the need to have services that will be integrated from public Azure, like the Marketplace syndication feature. As this is, more or less, one of the most important feature to have less TCO than with another solution, for that you would have to create your own templates. It's more or less a reuse-option that will save time and money.

With the next chapter we will talk about function apps or so called **Code as a Service** and discuss some ideas that may come in future updates of Azure Stack as they are on *UserVoice* and already have a high rating because a lot of customer really looking for it.

12
Infrastructure as Code – Azure Functions and Other Future Scenarios

In the previous chapters of this book, we talked about virtual machines and PaaS solutions; nevertheless, it was all about how many resources we need for a specific service and how we host these services (single tenant or multi-tenant). In regard to the cloud technology, we could go one step forward: we do not talk about resources; we just talk about code that is being run somewhere in the cloud and we do not care about the services on which it is running and how many resources it consumes. We just care about the results we are getting from it. This is the concept of **Infrastructure as Code** (**IAC**), or serverless cloud computing.

Microsoft Azure supports these service too, and so does Microsoft Azure Stack. In this chapter, we will talk about the following:

- A simple hello world Azure Stack Function
- Common scenarios for Azure Functions
- Possible Azure Stack future features

 The technical requirement for being able to use Azure Functions with Azure Stack is that the Azure App Service resource provider be installed. This is something we described in Chapter 8, *Creating PaaS Services in Microsoft Azure Stack*.

Azure Functions itself could, by the way, be a hybrid cloud solution too. As it is available with Azure and Azure Stack, there are different scenarios possible, where we could have parts of this service running in Azure and some others in Azure Stack in one solution design, for example, running a web shop with automatic Azure Functions to automate shop updates and in the same solution Azure Stack Functions that are responsible for the invoicing process and the internal automation for communicating with CRM services or even SAP.

A simple hello world Azure Stack Function

To provide a smart overview how Azure Stack Functions work and how to use them, a simple hello world function is described here.

To start, you just have to deploy the corresponding **Function App**:

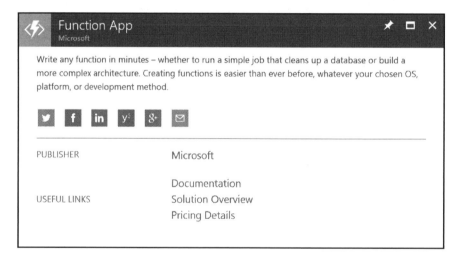

For being deployed, you will have to set a unique name and a storage account. After it has been deployed, you can set your function type:

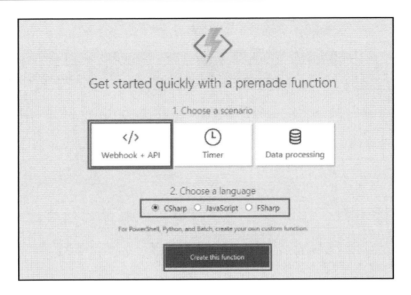

And now you can start writing your code:

```
run.CSX        Save          ▶ Run                          </> Get function URL

 1  using System.Net;
 2
 3  public static async Task<HttpResponseMessage> Run(HttpRequestMessage req, TraceWriter log
 4  {
 5      log.Info("C# HTTP trigger function processed a request.");
 6
 7      // parse query parameter
 8      string name = req.GetQueryNameValuePairs()
 9          .FirstOrDefault(q => string.Compare(q.Key, "name", true) == 0)
10          .Value;
11
12      // Get request body
13      dynamic data = await req.Content.ReadAsAsync<object>();
14
15      // Set name to query string or body data
16      name = name ?? data?.name;
17
18      return name == null
19          ? req.CreateResponse(HttpStatusCode.BadRequest, "Please pass a name on the query
20          : req.CreateResponse(HttpStatusCode.OK, "Hello " + name);
21  }
22
```

In the function detail, you will find the following view:

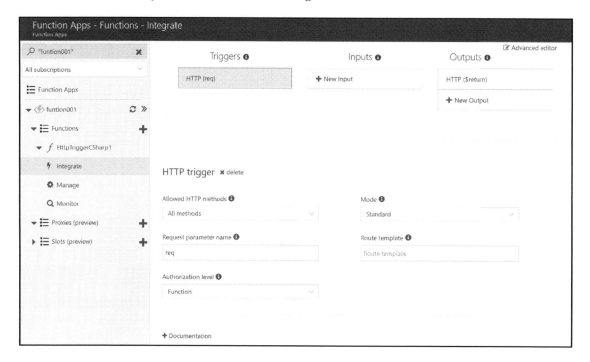

As you can see, you can define the **Triggers**, the **Inputs**, and the **Outputs**:

You can write the code for your function in a language of your choice and save the code and configuration files in the same folder. The JSON configuration data is being named `function.json`. It defines the `bindings` and other configuration settings. The function uses this file to determine how to send data into and return it from function execution.

This is a sample JSON file:

```json
{
    "disabled":false,
    "bindings":[
        // ... bindings here
        {
            "type": "bindingType",
            "direction": "in",
            "name": "myParamName",
            // ... more depending on binding
        }
    ]
}
```

The code for the functions in a defined Function App has to be saved in a `root` folder that contains a host configuration file and some subfolders, and in each of them, a separate function can live:

```
wwwroot
 | - host.json
 | - mynodefunction
 | | - function.json
 | | - index.js
 | | - node_modules
 | | | - ... packages ...
 | | - package.json
 | - mycsharpfunction
 | | - function.json
 | | - run.csx
```

The `host.json` file is the file for runtime-specific configuration and it is saved in the `root` folder of the Function App. Each function has a folder that contains the code files and `function.json` contains the configuration and other dependencies.

Common scenarios for Azure (Stack) Functions

Common scenarios for functions are as follows:

- Timer-based scenarios (for example, cron-jobs on databases for cleaning up)
- Event procession based on Webhooks (for example, export newly discovered data in a BLOB storage to a SQL database)
- SaaS event processing (for example, email in Outlook exports attachment to OneDrive)
- Serverless web application architectures (for example, transfer web page inputs to an automation script)
- Serverless mobile backends (for example, after a picture is taken, a thumbnail needs to be created)
- Real-time stream processing (for example, transform data of thousands of devices and save the important data to a database)

As you can see in this list, there is a wide variety of solution scenarios where Azure Functions really make sense.

> For more details on Azure Functions, the following GitHub URL could help visit https://github.com/Azure/Azure-Functions/wiki.

Possible Azure Stack future features

As Azure Stack has been designed from Microsoft as an agile product with monthly or bi-monthly updates, we will see updates to Azure Stack itself on a regular basis. These updates will be pushed as notifications to your Azure Stack environment and shown in the portal, as shown in the following screenshot:

If an update is available, you will see it on the **Updates**-pane, and your choice is to install it or not. This is one of the most important differences to Azure public as you do not have any choice to decide for an update there:

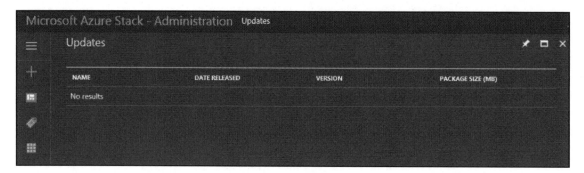

Regarding support, the question is how often can I skip an update in order to still be supported: the answer is quite simple and it is **two**. If you skip three update cycles, you will be out of support and need to updated to be in again.

With the Azure Stack update cycle, not only will patches arrive, but more or less all feature updates will be in there as well.

As the update will be done using offline patching, there is no risk to be in an unstable state. The system powers on a copy of the existing VHD, patches that, and if patching is successful, it switches to that VM and powers off the running one. If errors occur later, the old VM is still available and can be set online again for rollback tasks.

 The Azure Stack Development Toolkit will never have updates and you always will have to reinstall it completely.

Life cycle management host

If we take a look at all the different hardware OEMs (such as HPE, Dell-EMC, Lenovo, Cisco, or Huawei, the hardware components for the 4/8/12 node clusters are nearly a 100% the same. The big difference for all of them is a fifth host called **life cycle management host**. It is placed *outside* of Azure Stack and is responsible for a number of tasks:

- Deployment of Azure Stack; here, it all starts with a multi-node environment
- Switching configuration for BGP

- Responsibility for firmware, BIOS, and other updates as it will run the hardware management solution of the hardware vendor
- The target for the backup of Azure Stack as all VMs are backed up using the Microsoft InMage solution; this host has connectivity to this storage, and even you can install it if you're the backup agent of your vendor's choice on it

As you already could have imagined with the Azure Stack Development Toolkit, this one is not available too.

Integrating Azure Pack

The former product for hybrid clouds from Microsoft's Windows Azure Pack. It is not the former version of Azure Stack; it is just a completely different product as it does not rely on the same technology as Azure. Azure Pack relies on the System Center Suite and provides a self-service portal that has a similar look and feel than the *old* Azure portal (code named **red dog frontend**):

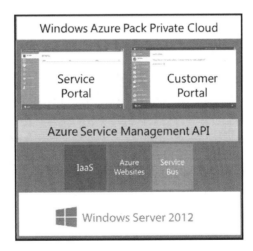

The Microsoft System Center Suite contains the following products:

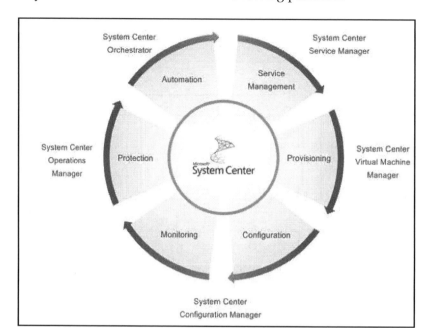

Azure Pack has been using the following System Center Suite products:

- **System Center Virtual Machine Manager (SCVMM)**
- **System Center Service Provider Foundation (SCSPF)**
- **System Center Operations Manager (SCOM)**

If a customer has deployed this solution in his data center, the challenge is how to integrate Azure Pack and Azure Stack. Therefore, Microsoft created a tool called **Windows Azure Pack (WAP)** connector.

WP connector for Azure Stack provides the following functionalities for IaaS machine clouds in Azure Pack in your Azure Stack portal:

- Browse resources
- Examining configuration values
- Stopping or starting a virtual machine
- Connecting to a virtual machine through **Remote Desktop Protocol (RDP)**
- Creating and managing checkpoints
- Deleting virtual machines and virtual networks

As these are the most important things when running a VM cloud, the features are available within the Azure portal:

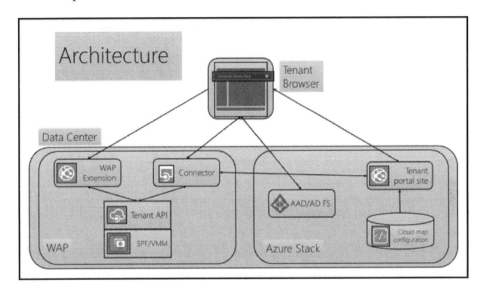

Source: https://docs.microsoft.com/en-us/azure/azure-stack/media/azure-stack-manage-wap/image1.png

As soon as your authentication provider is ADFS, you will have a pass-through authentication from one hybrid cloud solution to the other:

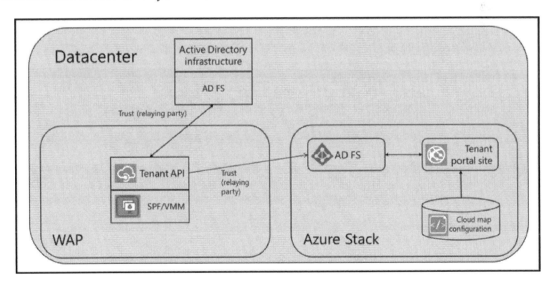

Source: https://docs.microsoft.com/de-de/azure/azure-stack/media/azure-stack-manage-wap/image2.png

You can download the WAP connector at `https://aka.ms/wapconnectorazurestackdlc`.

The technical requirements to make it work are as follows:

- Access to each other without any port blockings on firewalls in between.
- Azure Stack must trust the certificates of Azure Pack (and vice versa).
- `AzS-WASP01` virtual machine on Azure Stack must be able to connect to the Windows Azure Pack tenant portal computer.
- Windows Azure Pack tenant portal computer must have the URL Rewrite IIS extension installed. This can be downloaded from `https://www.iis.net/downloads/microsoft/url-rewrite`.

The following PowerShell scripts do the basic configuration tasks to make the connector work properly:

```
# Install Connector components
cd C:\temp\WAPConnector\Setup\Scripts
.\Install-Connector.ps1

# Configure Certificates for the new Connector services
.\Configure-Certificates.ps1

# Configure the Connector services
.\Configure-WapConnector.ps1 -TenantPortalFQDN "wapcomputer1.contoso.com" `
    -TenantAPIFQDN "wapsrv1.azurestack.rocks" `
    -AzureStackPortalFQDN "portal.local.azurestack.external"

# Install the updated TenantAPI
.\Update-TenantAPI.ps1

# Establish trust with the Azure Stack AD FS
.\Configure-TrustAzureStack.ps1 -SqlServer "wapsrv1" `
    -DataFile "C:\temp\wapconnector\AzurePack-07-30-15-50.txt"
```

 For further details on troubleshooting or to enable the WAP connector with a specific Azure Pack designs, you should review the details provided by this URL:
`https://docs.microsoft.com/de-de/azure/azure-stack/azure-stack-manage-windows-azure-pack`

After a successful installation, the Azure Stack portal should be enhanced with the following UI addition:

Migrating to Azure Stack

As of today, Microsoft does not provide any migration tool to directly move resources from Azure Pack to Azure Stack. This means that from a customer perspective, you will need to manually migrate resources from the old hybrid cloud solution to the new.

The easiest way to migrate your resources, depending on what solutions you are running, can be as follows:

- **IaaS**: You can simply establish a VPN connection between an Azure Pack cloud and an Azure Stack one, create a new VM, and move the solution manually from one VM to another. If you need to move the VM directly to Azure Stack, you would have to export the machine from Azure Pack and prepare it to run with Azure. As Azure and Azure Stack use the same format, there is an easy way to import it to Azure Stack.
- **PaaS SQL**: Export the database on Azure Pack SQL/MySQL and import it to Azure Stack SQL/MySQL
- **PaaS web apps**: Re-create the web app using the Azure App services feature of Azure Stack and update the public DNS to migrate the accessibility.
- **Service bus**: As the service bus feature is unavailable with Azure Stack, you will need to migrate to the public Azure service bus or run a mini Azure Pack for it.

To summarize everything is a manual step; there might be third-party solutions that will solve this. This means a smooth migration, and within the next weeks and months, there will not be any services with Azure Pack anymore and you could completely tear down this infrastructure.

Azure Stack Site Recovery

If we talk about migrating to Azure, Azure Site Recovery is the best solution to migrate. It has the following technical design, and the good thing is that it is free for about 30 days.

Site Recovery replicates workloads it is running on, which means that although the servers are running, ASR is replicating all data to another cloud service:

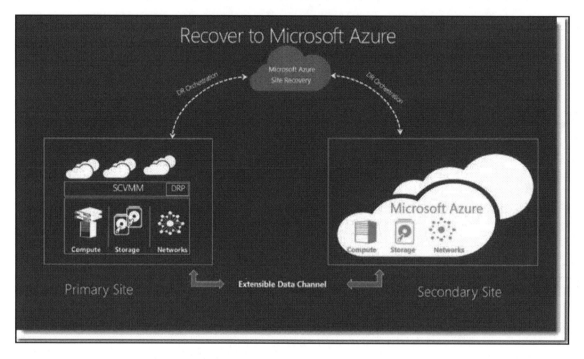

Source: https://msdnshared.blob.core.windows.net/media/TNBlogsFS/prod.evol.blogs.technet.com/CommunityServer.Blogs.Components.WeblogFiles/00/00/00/59/30/metablogapi/Fig1RecoverToMicrosoftAzureSlide1_thumb_6AA21F53.jpg

If you could imagine that the new target for any VMs that need to migrated to any cloud solution could be Azure Stack, this is one of the easiest migration options from somewhere to Azure Stack itself.

Azure Stack IoT Hub

Azure Stack IoT Hub could provide a service for IoT devices-for example, Raspberry Pi or something else-to communicate to any cloud-based backend services, as shown in the following diagram:

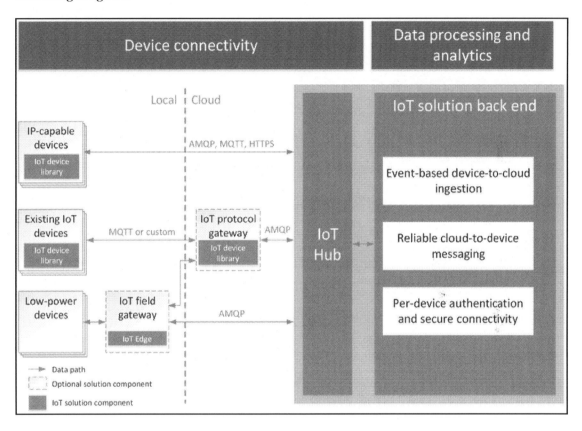

Source: https://docs.microsoft.com/en-us/azure/iot-hub/media/iot-hub-what-is-iot-hub/hubarchitecture.png

If this service would be available with Azure Stack soon, it would be a perfect way to collect IoT data somehow, transfer it to Azure Stack, and provide a basis for further data analysis. As this would be another resource provider for Azure Stack, and it would mean that you run 1-2 VMs in addition to providing the underlying technology.

Azure Stack ExpressRoute

Azure ExpressRoute is the MPLS network from Microsoft Azure and provides a QoS-based high-speed intra connectivity to the data centers worldwide:

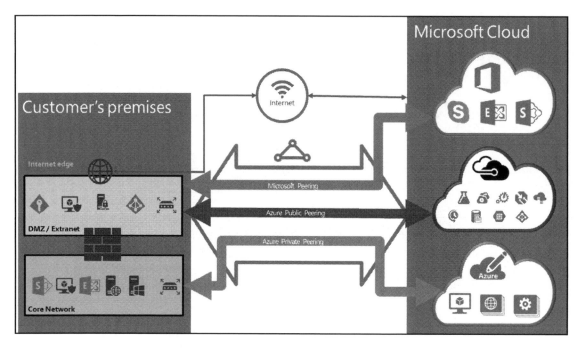

Source: https://docs.microsoft.com/de-de/azure/expressroute/media/expressroute-circuit-peerings/expressroute-peerings.png

Therefore, Azure ExpressRoute has different columns to fit Azure Stack. The first is a connectivity layer for hybrid clouds. If you are providing hybrid cloud solutions with portions of Azure Stack and Azure, the service provider is responsible for the line quality. ExpressRoute would be the perfect solution and would provide the best connectivity.

If we talk about general **Quality of Service (QoS)** connectivity to Azure Stack from a customer perspective using Azure Stack services, ExpressRoute could mean connecting a customer to its Azure Stack-based services with a QoS featured line. Today, this needs to be solved with a network service provider of your choice.

Summary

As you saw in this book, Azure Stack is the optimal basis for running Azure workloads on your own or your service providers' private cloud solution, mostly connected to the Azure public. As of today, Microsoft is the only cloud vendor that provides a hybrid cloud solution with *1:1*, which the same technology that is running on Azure today.

In regard to TCO and RoI, there is a great option to order not just Azure Stack as a software and be responsible for setting it up by yourself and making it run properly. This could mean weeks and months for the deployment. Azure Stack comes with the hardware solution as an integrated solution. You would only have to set it up by connecting it to the internet, power it on, and provide cooling and rack space. So, it may take only a few days to have Azure Stack up and running and in place.

The more interesting point, then, is to design your services in a way you would really need them. This solution design is not a technical deep dive; it is more a technical service design. Finally, these solutions will need to result in Azure Resource Manager templates using PaaS or IaaS solutions. They could be private or public only; additionally, they could he hybrid, and based on the workloads, they will mostly be hybrid. If something happens in a service that runs after the completely deployment, PowerShell DSC is your friend.

From the administration point of view, there is a wide variety of tools, starting with the ARM portal and leading to CLI, PowerShell modules, or even Visual Studio. The same administrative tools as Azure means that the administrators do not have to learn different technologies--everything is the same. This reduces training costs enormously; it even means that your IT staff would be able to run these technologies because otherwise, a different cloud service means a different cloud technology. The only thing you would need to be responsible for is the administrative part (maintaining the hardware, and so on).

Finally, there are a lot of technologies that would need to make the IT world more comparable and would lead to an industrial IT revolution. This is already in the middle of taking place, and you and your IT needs to deal with it. Azure Stack is the product of the future, which will give you all the technology to go with the cloud and go with it on a hybrid layer.

Index

Made in the USA
San Bernardino, CA
31 July 2019